Mad Jack Percival

LIBRARY OF NAVAL BIOGRAPHY

Mad Jack Percival

Legend of the Old Navy

James H. Ellis

Naval Institute Press
Annapolis, Maryland

Naval Institute Press
291 Wood Road
Annapolis, MD 21402

Library of Congress Cataloging-in-Publication Data
Ellis, James H., 1932–
        Mad Jack Percival : legend of the old Navy / James H. Ellis.
            p.   cm.—(Library of naval biography)
        Includes bibliographical references and index.
        ISBN 1-55750-204-8 (alk. paper)
            1. Percival, John, 1779–1862. 2. United States. Navy—Officers—Biography.
        I. Title. II. Series.
        V63.P4 E43 2002
        359'.0092--DC21
        [B]   2001059615

Printed in the United States of America on acid-free paper ∞
09 08 07 06 05 04 03 02   9 8 7 6 5 4 3 2
First printing

Frontispiece courtesy of U.S. Naval Academy Museum

To my wife, Ruthie

❧ Contents ❧

⤙ *Foreword* ⤚

John Percival was one of the most colorful and controversial officers of the Old Navy. Like many eighteenth-century mariners he went to sea as a cabin boy while barely in his teens. In less than five years he became second mate on a merchantman. Caught by a British press gang in Lisbon while still a teenager, the young man served against his will in the Royal Navy for two months before managing to escape. The Quasi-War with France attracted Percival to the new U.S. Navy, and after almost a year as a master's mate he was warranted a midshipman. This marked the beginning of an off-and-on career that would span six decades, ending when Percival was placed on the reserve list in 1855. Discharged at the end of the Quasi-War, Percival did not abandon the sea but reentered the merchant service, in which he traveled much of the North Atlantic and built a reputation that gained him the nicknames "Mad Jack," "Crazy Jack," and "Roaring Jack," all of which he relished and at times used to refer to himself.

Percival reentered the navy, this time as a sailing master, following the *Chesapeake-Leopard* affair and was assigned to the Norfolk Navy Yard near where the incident had taken place. Britain's violations of American maritime rights enraged the mercurial Percival. They ultimately led to the War of 1812, during which Percival received his first naval command, a gunboat stationed at New York City. It was a small vessel, but Percival led it aggressively to save two merchant vessels under attack by boats from a British ship of the line. Transferred to Boston after the war, Percival was commissioned a lieutenant and formed a lifelong friendship with Isaac Hull. The two were diametric opposites in temperament; Hull was as calm as Percival was unpredictable, but both were superb seamen and taut disciplinarians.

Over the next forty years Percival made both enemies and friends as he pursued mutineers in the South Pacific, fought with missionaries in Hawaii, commanded Old Ironsides on a round-the-world voyage, and intervened in Vietnam. It was a time "when the eagle screamed"—when a self-confident United States took its first steps toward a maritime empire. Percival was there, serving in the vanguard of American expansion. Virtually everywhere he went, controversy accompanied him. Percival had one of the longest careers in U.S. Navy history—he was not placed on the inactive list until he was seventy-six—but command of a squadron, the goal of every naval officer, eluded him. With such a command came the right to be called "Commodore" for the rest of one's life. Seniority ensured continued service in the antebellum navy, but it did not guarantee high command, and his failure to become a commodore rankled Percival. He became convinced that his enemies had conspired to deny it to him. Percival never saw that he was his own worst enemy. It was as much the way he did things as the things he did that alienated people.

Though well known to the public in his own day, Percival is not as widely remembered today as such contemporaries as Stephen Decatur, David Porter, John Rodgers, Charles Wilkes, and Matthew Calbraith Perry. He has not been totally neglected. He has been the subject of a book-length biography before, but not one as insightful and balanced as this one by James H. Ellis. Drawing on new materials and using keen insight, Ellis captures the character of both Percival and the navy in which he served. His is a sympathetic portrait, and an entertaining one. At long last, after more than a century, "Mad Jack" receives his due.

The Library of Naval Biography provides accurate, informative, and interpretive biographies of influential naval figures—men and women who shaped or reflected the naval affairs of their time. Each volume explains the forces that acted on its subjects as well as the significance of that person in history. Some volumes explore the lives of individuals who have not previously been the subjects of modern, full-scale biographies; others reexamine the lives of better-known individuals, adding new information, a differing perspective, or a fresh interpretation. The series is international in scope and includes individuals from several centuries. All the volumes are based on solid research and are written for general readers as well as specialists.

With these goals in mind, the length of each volume has been limited. The notes are placed at the end of the text and restricted primarily to direct quotations, and a brief essay on "Further Reading" is provided to assess previous biographies of the subject and to direct the reader to the most important studies of the era and events in which the person lived and participated. It is the intention that this combination of clear writing, fresh interpretations, and solid historical context will result in volumes that restore the all-important human dimension to naval history and are enjoyable to read.

James C. Bradford
Series Editor

~❧ Preface ❦~

I think that, as life is action and passion, it is required of a man that he should share the passion and action of his time at peril of being judged not to have lived.

Justice Oliver Wendell Holmes Jr.
Memorial Day Address, 1884

Men such as Carlyle and Emerson thought there is no history per se, only a vast body of biography. If this premise is valid, the history of the infant U.S. Navy is the history of the men who made measurable and meaningful contributions to the service and its traditions during its first fifty years. Some men—Preble and Hull come to mind—are considered in the first rank of early naval leaders. Biographical material on these men is plentiful. The men in what might fairly be called the second tier are less well known, even though many of them played important roles in the development of the navy. John Percival is in the second group. A review of his life demonstrates that he met Holmes's test. He participated fully in the events of his day; in a word, Percival lived.

Percival was controversial, irritable, short-tempered, and contentious. He was also courageous, decisive, warmhearted, and highly skilled in seamanship. As much as anything, he was plainspoken and open. There was no artifice about him. To say that Percival was unique is not an overstatement. He served in three navies, two unwillingly, and in four wars. His first and last ship assignments suggest his status. He was introduced to naval service as an impressed seaman on HMS *Victory* just after the great Battle of Cape St. Vincent in 1797. In his last assignment, he captained the USS *Constitution* on her memorable 1844–46 cruise around the world. The *Victory*, though now high and dry in Portsmouth, England, serves as the flagship of the Second Sea Lord of Britain and is considered the oldest commissioned warship in the world. The *Constitution*, berthed in Boston, is regarded as the oldest commissioned warship afloat in the world. Both ships are national shrines.

John Percival was born in 1779 on Cape Cod, Massachusetts, the nursery of an inordinate number of outstanding deepwater masters during the age of sail. He stands out in this select fraternity because he was the only one who gained fame for his service in the navy. The others followed one of the two goals of the initial settlers of the Cape, "to worship God and make money," and sailed in New England's great merchant fleet.[1] Capt. William Sturgis, a good friend of Percival's and a fellow townsman, is an example; he made a fortune during this period. The Sturgis and John Bryant partnership operating out of Boston reputedly controlled one-half of America's China-Pacific trade.

Although he began his career sailing in merchantmen, when the Quasi-War with France developed in 1799, Percival left the merchant service and volunteered for the navy. He entered as a master's mate, but before long he received a midshipman's warrant and seemed to be on course for a typical naval career. The war ended within a year, however, and Percival was released from the service in the general demobilization that followed. If the navy had kept Percival, he almost certainly would have played a more prominent role in the War of 1812—and he just might have risen to the first rank of early naval officers.

When he returned to the navy just before the second war with Great Britain, he returned as a thirty-year-old sailing master with the reputation of a superb mariner. This was not the normal route for advancement. Eleven former midshipmen from the Quasi-War took this step. Only one— John Percival—progressed to lieutenant.

His relationships with other officers during the course of his career tell a lot about the development of the officer corps. After the War of 1812, the navy again had a surplus of officers, leading to intense competition for promotions and posts. Sectionalism and politics influenced officers' conduct; bickering and quarreling prevailed. Courts of inquiry and nuisance courts-martial were common, and even dueling was an option. Percival was right in the middle of the controversies. He made lasting friendships and lasting enemies. Most of his close friends were fellow New Englanders. John Downes and Joseph Smith, like Percival, came from southeastern Massachusetts; Isaac Hull was a native of nearby Connecticut. His enemies, such as William Bainbridge, Jesse Elliott, and James Renshaw, came from the Middle Atlantic states.

Percival's direct, outwardly rough nature generated intense feelings on the part of others, but he achieved a positive rapport with almost all of his officers and crews. His men admired him because he was courageous, competent, and caring. He set high standards in these critical categories and strived to live up to them.

Military leadership involves a number of virtues, but none carries greater weight than courage. There is little doubt that Percival possessed superb physical courage. It appeared first in 1797 when he led the escape of a band of impressed seamen and was evident throughout his career. At sixty-six years of age and in failing health, he did not hesitate to force himself single-handed, pistol at the ready, onto the deck of an unfriendly Cochin Chinese man-of-war. A few months later, on the way to the Philippines from China in the *Constitution*, he found his ship becalmed alone with six European warships bearing down on him. The times were uncertain and he did not know if peace or war prevailed. An irresolute man might simply have waited for developments and hoped for the best. Percival beat to quarters, cast loose the guns, and prepared to fight against overwhelming odds. Fortunately, the unknown squadron was a peaceful British force.

One school of thought advances the proposition that leadership involves three components: interpersonal skills, conceptual skills, and technical competence. Few leaders reach the upper grade in all three categories. In fact, many who rise to leadership positions fail to achieve anything approaching perfection in even one. With this in mind, it is noteworthy that men from navy secretaries through commodores and midshipmen to ordinary seamen agreed that Percival was in all respects an expert in the techniques of his craft.

His skill is credited with saving two frigates. When the *Macedonian* was imperiled in an 1818 hurricane, his quick thinking and action saved the day. In 1843, when the *Constitution*, the nation's most beloved ship, was unfit for sea and in danger of being scrapped because there were insufficient funds to pay for the necessary repairs, Percival stepped forward and supervised the repairs at one-seventh of the official cost estimate. He was the first American officer to sail into a number of locations in the Pacific and Indian Oceans. His success in tracking down the survivors of the whale ship *Globe* mutiny in the uncharted reaches of the Pacific in 1825 displayed seamanship at its best. Even in his last years of active service he could be found in the rigging when the occasion demanded. His men admired him because he would never order them to do something he could not or would not do.

More important, Percival cared for his men. In the Pacific in 1825, for example, shortly after suffering a double hernia, he risked his neck to rescue a nonswimming crewman from raging surf. On more than one occasion he turned his cabin over to sick seamen, and he diligently administered a trust established for several injured sailors.

Perhaps because of his nickname, there is a misconception that Percival was a ruthless martinet. The facts show otherwise. He was a strict but fair disciplinarian, and he took a paternalistic interest in his midshipmen. His advocacy of shipboard education for young officers is an important part of his legacy.

Mad Jack Percival may be best remembered for two controversies. Ironically, both involved missionaries. In the first instance he was criticized for not doing enough, and in the second he was viewed with disfavor for doing too much. This is forever the lot of anyone acting in a police capacity, one of the responsibilities of U.S. Navy captains sailing in foreign waters at that time. When he arrived in Hawaii in 1826, most Americans and Hawaiians welcomed him, and likewise regretted his departure after several months. But the American missionaries, threatened by his superior authority, accused him of being soft on licentiousness and pilloried him as a result.

The French were grateful for his strong attempt in 1845 to gain the release of one of their missionaries imprisoned in Cochin China (now Vietnam), but the U.S. government feared the impact it might have on American trade. Revisionist historians label Percival's action the first Western military adventure in the region and a precursor of the modern Vietnam War. This is an exaggeration, but Percival attracts exaggeration.

Most of the tales told about Percival are untrue, but they do make one wonder why he was the subject of so much gallant invention. Even his early life has received the fictional treatment. His traditional departure for the sea at a young age is explained as impulsiveness. His impressment is glorified by the fabrication that he was in the *Victory*'s foretop with Nelson at Trafalgar. Even today he is the subject of this kind of attention. The current folk trio Schooner Fare spins a lively ballad about his capture of HMS *Eagle* on the Fourth of July in 1813. The answer seems to be that his indisputably colorful character supplied ample fodder. His rollicking encounter with Neptune at the equator in 1844 is a case in point. Interestingly, there is no evidence that Percival himself ever told or promoted any of the tales.

One thing Percival did try to promote was his own advancement. He succeeded in that he rose to the rank of captain, the highest grade in the navy in his day. However, his command of Old Ironsides on her only circumnavigation of the globe was his only independent command. The explanation for his shortage of command experience is twofold. First, he came out of the War of 1812 as a junior lieutenant instead of a captain like some of his peers who were retained after the peace of 1801. The intense competition for billets worked against him. Second, after his 1825 injury his health was often tenuous. He had to be relieved on the *Erie* and the *Cyane* because of chronic illness. He was so debilitated while with the *Constitution* that he had the ship's carpenter fashion a coffin for him. He did not need the long box while on the voyage, but its existence added to his legend.

This brings to mind a final Percival trait worth mentioning. He set a high standard for economy and frugality. Percival would be the darling of a modern budget officer. He completed the repair of the *Constitution* at such a low cost that his critics thought she must be unseaworthy. To prove that they were wrong, he took the venerable old ship on her longest cruise. Along the way, with the full cooperation and concurrence of the crew, he demonstrated that the navy was paying too much for rations. His illness cut short a similar experiment on the *Cyane*.

In 1844, Percival's reputation for frugality prompted Secretary of the Navy John Y. Mason to solicit his views on promoting efficiency and economy in the service. Percival responded that too much money was being spent on outmoded methods and gimcracks. He targeted contract abuses and cautioned against the excesses of master constructors at the navy yards. And he urged recognition for honest economy. Yet he had a sense of balance. He criticized congressmen who compared naval costs on foreign stations with the lesser expense of provisions in Ohio and Kentucky. We do not cruise in Ohio and Kentucky, he noted.

Writers and historians today tend to treat Percival poorly or not at all. Some of this treatment is due to misconceptions, and some is traceable to the habit of assessing two-hundred-year-old actions by today's standards. And some is due to a lack of information about this plain and straightforward man. What follows is an attempt to fill this void.

❧ *Acknowledgments* ❧

Years of research went into this book. A host of people assisted. The list is long, and I hope that gratitude personally extended will suffice. However, two people deserve particular mention and special thanks. At every turn, from researching to proofreading, my wife, Ruthie, pitched in. Her help was immeasurable. Mindy Conner, the copy editor, also made an invaluable contribution. She added the polish.

A number of institutions and organizations also merit special gratitude. The Massachusetts Historical Society, Boston; the National Archives, Washington, D.C.; the U.S. Naval Academy Museum, Annapolis, Maryland; and the USS *Constitution* Museum, Charlestown, Massachusetts, provided extensive assistance and material.

I am also indebted to the Boston Athenaeum Library; the Boston Public Library; the Connecticut State Library, Hartford; the Hartford Public Library; the Library of Congress, Washington, D.C.; the Massachusetts State Library, Boston: the Sturgis Library of Barnstable, Massachusetts; the U.S. Coast Guard Academy Library, New London, Connecticut; the U.S. Navy Department Library, Washington, D.C.; and the Whelden Memorial Library of West Barnstable, Massachusetts.

I am grateful for comparable help provided by the Admiralty in London, England; the Connecticut Historical Society, Hartford; the New England Historic Genealogical Society in Boston; the Peabody Essex Museum of Salem, Massachusetts; the Public Records Office in London, England; the U.S. Court of Appeals for the Second Circuit in New York; the U.S. Naval Institute; and the U.S. Department of the Navy.

~❦ Chronology ❦~

3 Apr. 1779	Born on Cape Cod to John and Mary (Snow) Percival
1793	Ships as cabin boy and cook on Boston coaster
1797	Second mate in merchant service
24 Feb. 1797	Impressed in Portugal for Royal Navy and assigned to HMS *Victory*
Mar. 1797	Transferred to eighteen-gun British brig
Apr. 1797	Escapes from British navy while serving on a prize crew
July 1799	Signs on the *Delaware* as master's mate
13 May 1800	Receives a midshipman's warrant
July 1801	Discharged in general demobilization following the end of the war; returns to merchant service
1805	Jailed for several months at Santa Cruz, Tenerife, his ship confiscated
6 Mar. 1809	Returns to navy as sailing master; assigned to Norfolk Navy Yard
16 Aug. 1809	Ordered to the *Syren*
27 Sept. 1809	Marries Maria Pinkerton in Norfolk County, Virginia
15 Dec. 1809	Furloughed; returns to merchant service
13 Aug. 1812	Reports back for duty; assigned to New York Navy Yard
4 July 1813	Captures British tender *Eagle* off New York in borrowed smack *Yankee*
23 Aug. 1813	Placed in charge of U.S. gunboat *No. 6*

3 Nov. 1813	Saves the grounded schooner *Sparrow* in fight with the *Plantagenet*'s boats at Long Branch, New Jersey
4 Mar. 1814	Transferred to the sloop *Peacock*
29 Apr. 1814	Sailing master in the *Peacock*'s defeat of the *Epervier*
9 Dec. 1814	Commissioned lieutenant
15 Mar. 1816	Detached from the *Peacock*; assigned to Boston Navy Yard
23 Apr. 1816	Reports for duty on the *Macedonian*
13 May 1819	Acting first lieutenant of the *Macedonian*
9 Jan. 1820	Detached in Panama and ordered to Norfolk
16 June 1821	Appointed executive officer at Boston
17 Sept. 1823	Transferred to the *United States* on Pacific station
30 Apr. 1824	Given command of the *Dolphin*
1 Sept. 1826	Named executive officer on the *United States*
5 Nov. 1827	Acquitted of extortion charge made by a merchant captain encountered in Hawaii
8 Nov. 1828	Convicted in civil court of assaulting captain in Hawaii
20 Jan. 1829	Secretary accepts court of inquiry findings and absolves Percival of wrongdoing but censures him for lack of restraint
19 Oct. 1830	Sails the *Porpoise* to the West Indies
11 Feb. 1832	Placed on leave due to poor health
27 Apr. 1832	Notified of promotion to master commandant effective 3 March 1831
5 May 1834	Assigned to command of the *Erie*
11 Aug. 1835	Relieved of command of the *Erie*; placed on leave
1 July 1836	Appointed executive officer at Boston
14 Apr. 1838	Assigned to the *Cyane* command in Mediterranean
24 Jan. 1840	Arrives in New York after giving up the *Cyane* due to health reasons and is placed on leave
8 Sept. 1841	Promoted to captain
July 1843	Assigned command of the *Franklin* to supervise repairs of ship

13 Oct. 1843	Assigned to the *Constitution* to supervise repairs at Norfolk
29 May 1844	Leaves New York with the *Constitution* on her only round-the-world cruise
28 Sept. 1846	Ship returns to Boston
1 Oct. 1846	Detached from command of the *Constitution* and placed on leave, awaiting orders
13 Sept. 1855	Placed on reserved list
17 Sept. 1862	Dies, Dorchester, Massachusetts

Mad Jack Percival

❧ I ❧

AN EARLY TRIUMPH

*T*he inhabitants of New York City had been troubled for weeks. Citizens up and down the entire Atlantic coast felt the same distress. The Second War of Independence, the War of 1812, was more than a year old, and the British navy apparently had swept the infant American navy from the seas along with its merchant marine.

Fresh from trouncing the Danish, Dutch, French, and Spanish navies, the British had eighty-five sail in American waters. The United States had but six frigates and ten lesser men-of-war. A blockading British squadron had the port of New York shut down. American naval forces in the area, under Commo. Jacob Lewis, were essentially captives of the Royal Navy. The *New York Columbian* found some consolation in the fact that during the winter of 1812–13 the authorities had raised "a valuable and powerful body of volunteers . . . composed of sailors and boatmen" for the port's protection.[1]

The Americans had enjoyed a few successes against the British. In August 1812, for example, the *Constitution* under Isaac Hull shattered HMS *Guerrière*. Five months later the *Constitution* under William Bainbridge whipped HMS *Java*. David Porter in the *Essex* and Stephen Decatur Jr. in the *United States* scored victories as well. On 1 June 1813 HMS *Shannon* under P. B. V. Broke took the ill-fated *Chesapeake* under James

Lawrence in a fifteen-minute battle off Boston. The *Shannon*'s success disheartened and shocked the American public. The action turned out to be one of Britain's few outstanding naval triumphs of the war. Lawrence, who was mortally wounded during the fight, became a national hero when he issued the unforgettable order: "Don't give up the ship!"

John Percival, a little-known U.S. Navy sailing master assigned to the New York Navy Yard, felt that enough was enough. British ships might outnumber American vessels, but Percival, like many Americans, believed that American seamen, man for man, were vastly superior to their British counterparts. The British did not completely agree with this oft-expressed claim, suggesting that superior American seamanship could be traced to the many Englishmen in the American navy—and they were not necessarily the best Englishmen, either. They merely fought "more *desperately* than those we have," asserted a Briton, "because the rascals know that if they are taken they will be hanged."[2]

The coasters and fishermen around Sandy Hook considered the king's sloop *Eagle* particularly obnoxious and troublesome. The *Eagle* was a tender to the British ship of the line *Poictiers,* the flagship of Commo. J. B. Beresford. The *Poictiers* herself was unpopular in the United States as well, of course. Earlier she had come upon the crippled U.S. sloop *Wasp* and captured her, thus spoiling the *Wasp*'s victory over HMS *Frolic.* The *Eagle,* however, was the immediate target. By July 1813 the Americans were "determined to capture her at any cost."[3]

Commodore Lewis picked the energetic John Percival for the task, an ideal selection. By his very nature, Percival abhorred passiveness. And he was anxious to get into a scrap. After developing a scheme of "singularly daring nature," Percival went in search of the right vessel to carry it out.[4] At the Fly Market on the East River he found an acceptable fishing smack, appropriately named the *Yankee,* whose owner agreed to let Percival take her out against the British. Before leaving the market, Percival also obtained a calf, a sheep, and a goose. Then he returned to the naval facility at Mosquito Cove. At the yard he selected thirty-six volunteers, all well armed with muskets. He concealed thirty-four of them in the cabin and forepeak of the *Yankee.* The livestock—the bait—were left on deck in full view. Percival and two others donned fishermen's costumes consisting of sheepskin jackets, baggy calfskin pants, yellow cowhide boots, and tarred canvas hats. Though seasonably warm, the weather had been overcast. The skies cleared by noon on Saturday, 3 July. Percival was ready. Early the next morning the *Yankee* "stood out to sea as if going on a fishing voyage to the banks."[5]

The watchful *Eagle* spotted the *Yankee* as she cleared the Hook and promptly gave chase. The British tender rapidly closed on the fishing boat and soon came alongside. The *Eagle's* commander, Master's Mate H. Morris, noticed the animals secured on the *Yankee's* deck. After an almost endless diet of salt rations, the Englishman jumped at the prospect of fresh food—just as Percival expected him to do. Fresh meat would be a treat for Commodore Beresford and his flagship officers, too. Morris ordered Percival to take his livestock down to the *Poictiers*, about five miles off.

Percival answered, "Aye, aye, sir!" and put up the helm, evidently for that purpose, bringing the *Yankee* closer to the *Eagle*. When she was not more than three yards away, honoring the slain captain of the *Chesapeake*, Percival shouted: "Lawrence!"

Hearing the watchword, his armed men rushed on deck and poured into the *Eagle* "a volley of musketry, which struck her crew, with dismay, and drove them all down so precipitately into the hold of the vessel, that they had not time to strike their colors." Just as important, the attack was so sudden that the *Eagle's* crew had no time to discharge the ship's loaded 32-pound howitzer.[6]

As soon as Percival saw the last of the *Eagle's* thirteen astounded men scamper below, he ordered his men to hold their fire. Then, as he expected, "one of the Englishmen came out of the hold and hauled down the colors." The "stratagem" had "succeeded to a charm."[7]

John Percival promptly went over to the badly injured Morris and gently assured him that they would soon reach the shore and medical aid. Morris raised himself on one elbow and replied, "We have had enough of you!" He fell back and expired.[8] Percival attached a line to the *Eagle* and began towing her back to New York.

That afternoon, he landed his prisoners at Whitehall "amidst the shouts and plaudits of thousands of spectators assembled on the Battery, celebrating the Fourth of July."[9] "Although the day seemed well provided with entertainments and amusements suited to all," one observer noted, Percival's success "gave more widefelt and hearty joy and amusement than could have been anticipated."[10] Years later, the New England folklorist Alton Blackington maintained that Percival "knew how to celebrate July 4th without listening to a band concert."[11]

Commodore Lewis's report to Secretary of the Navy William Jones on the engagement praised Percival effusively. Lewis reported that Percival "performed in a most gallant and officer-like manner" and stressed that the Americans had suffered no injuries because of Percival's outstanding management.[12] Three members of the British crew died in the action.

This was an escapade not easily forgotten, but it was only the first of many. By the time he ended his active naval service thirty-three years later, Capt. John Percival would be a legend. In the Old Navy, no name came up more often in wardroom mess talk than that of Mad Jack Percival.

Once when he was visiting London, John Percival traced his ancestry back to the period of William the Conqueror and "had the good luck not to run against a single fellow who met his end on the gallows." He decided to stop further inquiry at that point, "lest I might come across some scoundrel." He concluded that his family "seemed to be a pretty respectable lot."[13]

Percival's research was sound. Modern genealogists have tracked the family back to Brittany and Normandy. James Percival, the first of the line in the United States, arrived in Virginia about 1668. Two years later he moved to Sandwich on Cape Cod and immediately got into trouble. For refusing to leave Plymouth Colony "according to order and for his making an escape from one with whome he was sent, in reference to his goeing to Verginnia to cleare himself of suspicion of having a hand in running away with a boate, etc.," the Plymouth court fined him five pounds.[14]

James Percival married Mary R. Bassett and spent much time in Falmouth, Massachusetts, before his death in 1691. One of his sons, John, settled in nearby Barnstable after marrying Mary Bourne in 1703. On John's passing in 1738, his homestead went to his son James. By this time the Percival holdings in the "Westward plains," or Scorton Hill, vicinity of Barnstable and Sandwich were sizable. The Percivals owned some of the best farmland on the Cape, not to mention many acres of woodland and some valuable meadowland. The woodland was located around Snake, Hog, and Tryangle Ponds. The meadow property, part of the Great Marshes, was at the northern base of Scorton Hill. Under salt water only during the periodic flood tides, the marshland provided vast quantities of salt hay useful as straw. This valuable resource so dominated the local scene that for many years the village of West Barnstable was generally known as "The Great Marshes."

The second James, the future naval officer's grandfather, married Ann Thomas, and they had a son, John, in 1740. John married Mary Snow in 1765. John and Mary Percival had one daughter and three sons. Their second son, John, who would later be known as "Mad Jack," was born at their West Barnstable home on Scorton Hill on 3 April 1779. New owners moved the house down to the nearby county road years afterward, and it has long since been demolished.

John Percival Sr. was active in town affairs during this period. In 1773 his was the lowest bid to fill the job of constable, and the town voted to make him "Constable accordingly for the year . . . and that he collect the Town, County and State taxes."[15] Tax collecting was a profitable as well as responsible job. The system allowed him to keep 5 percent of the money he collected.

John Percival seemed to enjoy the esteem of his fellow townsmen. In 1787 the town meeting chose him and four others to prepare instructions for their legislator. He was also assigned to a committee to look into repairs for a bridge and the old county road. A year later, he was chosen along with Simon Jones as a caretaker of Sandy Neck, the six-mile barrier beach protecting the Great Marshes from the onslaughts of northern storms. He was not allowed to relax the following year, either. The March meeting picked him to be one of nine hog reeves.

Subsistence farming kept food on the family's table, but the elder Percival's principal interest was the sea. In the years leading up to the American Revolution, he commanded a galley listed as a Massachusetts privateer. He continued in the merchant service off and on until he died in 1802.

Seafaring was a central part of the makeup of both the Percival family and the community as a whole. The senior Percival's father-in-law, Capt. Joseph Snow, was a skilled navigator of the "apple-tree" class. John and Mary's oldest child, Abigail, married a sailing captain, John Crocker Jr. of Barnstable. And in addition to John Jr., one of his other two sons, Isaac, spent a lifetime at sea, rising to master.

Public-minded, self-sufficient, seafaring elders and neighbors molded young John Percival's character, personality, and skills. Most of the important decisions he made and actions he took as an adult reflect some aspect of his upbringing. By today's standards, formal schooling played a minor role in molding his character, even though the town was progressive about education. As early as 1735 Barnstable employed a grammar-school master at both ends of town. Barnstable erected its first public school building in 1771. Despite the privations of the Revolutionary War and its aftermath, the town appropriated money for schooling even when it could not pay state taxes.

The Percivals were able to permit John Jr. to attend school for a total of nine months. At that time, only a few West Barnstable youngsters received more schooling. Rev. Oakes Shaw's son Lemuel, a lifelong friend of Percival's, was one of them. His family expected young Shaw to progress through college and into the ministry; instead, he became a great jurist. For his part, Percival had to rely on home instruction. Since seafaring was a large part of the family's background, maritime training became the central feature of his upbringing. Future events would attest to the thoroughness of this instruction.

The legend of "Mad Jack" begins in 1793, when redheaded young John Percival, thirteen years of age, left the Cape for Boston and the sea beyond. Legend has it that he left home in a fit of temper. Displeased with home life, especially the steady diet of hasty pudding, he walked down the hill to the shoreline of the marsh below and climbed upon a favorite boulder. He proceeded to spin himself dizzy and fell to the ground. When he picked himself up, he decided to run away in the direction he faced. Fortunately, he was facing the northwest and Boston.

The yarn is amusing but unlikely to be true. There was nothing unusual about a Cape Cod boy going to sea. It was the logical career choice for the men of the Cape. And in his book about Hyannis sea captains, C. E. Harris notes that a large percentage of his subjects started their sailing careers before their teens. The choice of a career on land would have been more noteworthy. The historian Frederick Freeman observes that "a large proportion of the male inhabitants of the Cape are . . . early addicted to the seas. . . . Perhaps no portion of the globe, of similar extent, has furnished so many able commanders of ships."[16] John G. Palfrey may have said it best when he declared in 1839 at Barnstable's second centennial celebration: "The duck does not take to the water with a surer instinct than the Barnstable boy," who "can hand, reef, and steer, by the time he flies a kite."[17]

Like many before him, then, young Percival made his way to the seaport of Boston. If he did not have a job awaiting him, that did not matter. Right away he found work as a cabin boy and cook on a coaster.

Coasting sloops, schooners, and brigs were the basic means of transportation along the eastern seaboard during this era.

Percival was a second mate in the merchant service by the time he was seventeen. A year later he got out of coasting and sailed under Capt. Daniel Crocker aboard the *Thetis* out of Boston. The captain appears to have been a member of the extensive Crocker family of Barnstable, and he would have been quite familiar with the Percivals and young John. The *Thetis* went to Europe, stopped at Dunkirk, and moved south to Lisbon. At this Portuguese port, Percival's naval education began.

February 1797 was an inopportune time for an American seaman to be in European waters. The British under Adm. Sir John Jervis had just won a decisive Saint Valentine's Day victory over the Spanish fleet off Portugal's Cape Saint Vincent. Before the battle, Jervis, aboard his flagship, HMS *Victory* (100 guns, Capt. Robert Calder), declared: "A victory is very essential to England at this moment."[18] After the violent battle, Jervis decided that replacements for battle casualties were very essential to England. Captain Calder willingly accepted the unwilling John Percival aboard the *Victory* in that capacity.

On 24 February, Percival fell into the hands of a Portuguese press gang supplying seamen to the British. The details of his seizure are not recorded, but when a gang put its hands on a prospect, things generally turned ugly, particularly if the subject resisted. Percival would have been acting completely out of character if he had submitted quietly. Onboard the *Victory*, an officer examined Percival according to regulations to see if he had any ailments or diseases. Regardless of the energy expended by the press gangs and the bruises they inflicted on the impressed, the navy rejected few men. The officer readily deemed Percival, a young experienced seaman, fit for service at sea.

The origin of British impressment has never been precisely determined, but it dates at least to the Saxon kings. The term itself indicates that the practice had an early beginning. *Impressment* does not, as is often believed, stem from the English word *pressed,* meaning "to urge with force." It derives from the obsolete French term *prest,* meaning "ready." This recruiting method was initially known as "presting." The king's men would offer a potential servant "imprest," or "ready money." Once the man accepted the king's shilling, he was "ready" to serve his majesty. Over the years, the royal agents learned that most candidates declined the opportunity to serve even when offered a fee. Therefore, the gangs ceased to rely on money and added to their inventory of clubs and cutlasses. Once they began their service, however, impressed seamen were paid. The 1797 salary was twenty-four shillings a month.

Percival found it useless to protest that he was an American and thus could not be forced to serve in the Royal Navy. In theory, foreigners were exempt, but any Englishman could readily obtain counterfeit papers attesting to American citizenship. If the navy had honored all documents attesting that their bearers were citizens of another country, it would have seriously reduced its manpower sources. The Admiralty further rationalized that since its mission was to save the rest of the world, the rest ought to be of some help in that endeavor. Ironically, British officers frequently ruled Americans to be Englishmen because they "spoke English very well."[19] In truth, a few British naval officers had developed a certain dislike for Americans during the War of Independence. This group gleefully accepted impressed Americans after summarily rejecting their "fraudulent" claims of U.S. citizenship.

Objectionable as impressment was to the men so recruited, the officers that they were captured to serve were not unanimously in favor of the practice either. Lord Nelson displayed extra satisfaction at being elevated to admiral's rank because it meant he would no longer have to be directly involved in forceful conscription. One captain seemed to reflect the view of most of his counterparts when he declared that impressment gave him "more trouble and uneasiness than all the rest of my duty."[20]

Naval ships periodically had to send out their own press gangs or stop passing vessels to grab the pick of their crews, but more often they relied on professionals to supply their need for men. By the late eighteenth century, press gangs were omnipresent in and around Great Britain. A seaman had to have some luck to evade their grasp. The gangs operated afloat as well as on shore. Mariners entering British harbors had to run a gauntlet of them. When victims became scarce along the waterfront, the gangs would move inland, sometimes at considerable peril to themselves. This was not the preferred hunting ground, however. A man taken fresh from the sea was worth six from shore. All too often, the men from land turned out to be nothing more than rascals, villains, or beggars.

The British abandoned the practice of pressing in the early 1800s because of the demoralizing effect it had on the navy, not to mention the international antagonism it created. The wholesale mutinies at Spithead and Nore in 1797 were the opening round in the fight to abolish impressments, but Lt. John Percival, U.S. Navy, would exact some revenge of his own before the contest closed. In fact, he would be on hand when the last shots were fired off Java in June 1815.

Percival's British service had at least one bright spot. While he waited in Lisbon for an assignment, he met an unusual Bostonian: Capt. Isaac Coffin of the Royal Navy, later Admiral of the Blue Sir Isaac Coffin. At the time, the thirty-eight-year-old Coffin was the commissioner of the navy in Lisbon. Coffin was born in Boston of Nantucket parents and had been an officer in the British navy since his late teens. In 1790 he badly ruptured himself while rescuing a man overboard. He aggravated the injury in 1794 and became unfit for active or sea service.

Captain Coffin led a lonely life in Lisbon, and he retained a good deal of affection for his native land. His interest in America culminated in 1826 when he founded the Coffin School on Nantucket to give children a sound English education. Coffin was also an early proponent of an American naval academy. The initial exchange between the two sons of Massachusetts boosted the morale of both men, and a lengthy friendship developed.

A large number of seamen joined the *Victory* in March, Percival among them. Once aboard, he had no idea when he would set foot on land again. Any ill-prepared attempt to escape from Jervis would be foolhardy. A firm and fair disciplinarian, the admiral nevertheless had earned his nickname of "Hanging" Jervis. He made it a practice to hang deserters promptly from a yardarm.

Captain Calder designated the young and agile Percival a foretop man. Percival's name does not appear on the *Victory*'s biweekly muster books prepared during the short time he was on the ship. However, he might have given a false name and birthplace when he was impressed; many men did.[21] In any case, an impressed seaman would almost certainly have served as a rating, and "apart from the muster books," a source at the Admiralty notes, "no records of ratings of that period were kept."[22]

Percival's duties were among the most dangerous on the man-of-war; a slip while working the sails high above the tossing deck could be fatal. The work was also important. By tradition, the smartness of a ship was judged by the skill and speed of her top men as they scrambled through their chores. The flagship, of course, was expected to be the smartest in the fleet.

Even when he was busy aloft, Percival had an opportunity to observe and learn the methods of the mightiest naval power of the era. His language in later years indicated that he listened well to the British officers he encountered at this time. Profanity was a common tool of command, and most officers were addicted to blunt and rough speech. Seamen receiving orders were never in doubt regarding the nature of their character and destiny. The habit of profanity became a problem when there were ladies visiting on deck; many officers were forced to restrict their usual fluency. A few adapted well to the situation, like the quick-witted lieutenant, surrounded by women guests, who bellowed: "Main-topgallant there! God bless you! God bless you! *You know what I mean!!*"[23]

After a short tour on the *Victory* that apparently lasted just a few weeks, Percival's luck began to change. The navy transferred him to an eighteen-gun brig that went on patrol in search of Spanish merchantmen. Not long after leaving the safety of the main British fleet, the brig closed on what appeared to be a merchant convoy. After a closer look, the British identified nine Spanish sail of the line. Consternation and apprehension replaced anticipation. The brig turned and ran. To lighten the vessel and increase her speed, the crew tossed all weighty expendables overboard, including sixteen of her guns. The ship made good her escape among the Canary Islands. As the flight ended, the British brig captured a Spanish vessel loaded with wheat.

The British captain designated Percival a member of the prize crew under the command of the ship's doctor, a Doctor Miller, who was ordered to take the vessel north to Madeira. This proved to be the opportunity the redhead from Barnstable had been anticipating. Percival knew that the relatively casual discipline on the prize would not be repeated when he returned to a regular navy vessel.

Once in Madeira, he learned that a Captain White of the American merchantman *Washington* was having difficulty filling his crew. Percival was able to contact White and present him with a straightforward plan to his liking. The scheme called for the *Washington* to stand out to sea, thereby allaying suspicion. White would wait well outside the harbor for a given time. Percival, the epitome of confidence, assured White that he and several compatriots would be on their way soon after dark.

After Doctor Miller finished his supper, he retired to his cabin and fell into a deep sleep induced by overindulgence at the table. Percival gathered his comrades together and led them topside, where he nonchalantly approached the officer of the deck. When he came within reach of the unsuspecting Briton, Percival grabbed him by the throat "with no gentle touch" and pressed a pistol to his heart. "Silence or Death!" he growled.[24] His companions hastily bound and gagged the frightened officer. With the way now clear, the escaping men appropriated one of the vessel's boats and set out for their rendezvous with White. After rowing twenty-one miles, Percival and his mates reached the safety of the *Washington*.

His voyage home was just beginning. Percival probably would have found it easier and faster to row all the way from Madeira to Massachusetts. Before he saw Boston again, he went to Rio de Janeiro, stopped at Goa, and was impressed a second time. While the *Washington* was at Batavia on the northwest coast of Java, the Dutch laid their hands on Percival and put him on the Dutch navy frigate *Samarang*. Benefiting from experience, he quickly escaped by a coup de main similar to the first. He made his way to England on the East India Company's ship *Rose,* got a job on the American merchantman *Hector,* and worked his way back to the United States.

In July 1798 the long-strained relations between France and the United States developed into an undeclared war, now known as the Quasi-War with France. The two nations had been at odds for a number of years. As a seafaring neutral, the United States found it impossible to carry on free trade without antagonizing at least one of the contending European powers, Great Britain and France. And in order to keep American goods out of the hands of one another, both nations seized U.S. vessels. Though Americans were just as angry with the British, the two nations avoided a break because the British usually paid reasonable compensation for seized goods. The French, on the other hand, did not make it a practice to pay for property seized from foreign merchantmen.

France and the United States moved even further apart after Congress ratified the pro-British Jay Treaty in 1795. France refused to recognize a newly appointed U.S. minister to Paris; in fact, the French ordered the ambassador to leave the country. President John Adams asserted that France's treatment of America was tantamount to considering the United States less than a sovereign state. Adams tried to resolve the dispute by sending three envoys to Paris in 1797. The trio concluded that France's primary interest was not a real discussion of the issues, but rather money. The mission failed, and Americans rallied behind the fighting slogan: "Millions for defense, but not one cent for tribute!"

President Adams and Congress moved to meet the developing threat. On 30 April 1798 Congress established the Department of the Navy. Important authorizations followed, all directed toward building a strong navy and developing the means to annihilate the offending French privateers. On 7 July the United States abrogated its remaining treaty with France, the 1778 Treaty of Alliance. Two days later the government authorized American naval vessels to seize any armed French ships within the territorial waters of the United States or anywhere on the high seas. Although there was never a formal declaration, a state of war existed between the two countries.

Congress at that time limited the period of navy enlistments to one year in the belief that good men would not enlist for a longer period. In the summer of 1799, those vessels out to sea since the beginning of hostilities returned to the United States for replacement crews. Capt. Stephen Decatur Sr. returned to Philadelphia in the *Delaware* in June, and Capt. Thomas Baker took command of the ship and began picking a new crew. Lt. Thomas Wilkey did much of the recruiting. The secretary of the navy directed Baker and Wilkey to secure "none but sound and healthy persons, and suffer no indirect means to be used."[25] John Percival saw this as a tolerable system, especially since recruits were given the customary advance of two months' pay, and in July he signed on the *Delaware* as a master's mate.

By the end of the month, Captain Baker had the *Delaware* ready for a second war cruise. He took her down the Delaware River past New Castle and out to sea. His orders were to escort a convoy including a navy supply ship to the Guadeloupe station in the Lesser Antilles. The Navy Department directed Baker, once on station, to fall in under Capt. Thomas Tingey. "Do all in your power," Baker was told by the secretary, "to Capture the French Privateers & to protect our Commerce from their depradations."[26] When the *Delaware* arrived in the West Indies, Tingey ordered her to guard the area from the island of Saint Bartholomew to the windward of Nevis and to the lee of Barbuda. Baker's crew got into its first action early in October when the *Delaware* helped her smaller companion, the *Pickering*, recapture the brig *Henrich* and capture the *Atalanta*.

On 29 October, Percival and the rest of the 180-man crew of the *Delaware* had the opportunity to earn some prize money on their own when they fell in with the French privateer brig *Ocean*. After a seven-hour pursuit in which Baker got the most out of the slow *Delaware*, he overtook and captured the Frenchman. During the spirited chase the ten-gun *Ocean* tried in vain to gain greater speed by throwing overboard eight of her guns and other heavy items, including her boat. A group of American captives contemplating imprisonment in Guadeloupe were among the seventy men on board.

In November, Baker headed to the southwest and Curaçao in the Netherlands Antilles. But misfortune overhauled the *Delaware* before the year was out. A considerable and persistent sickness spread throughout the ship, forcing her into port and inactivity. In May the Navy Department, anticipating the expiration of *Delaware* enlistments, ordered the ship to leave Curaçao and put in at New Castle.

Before the ship left the West Indies, Percival received a promotion that prolonged this period of his naval career for another year. On 13 May 1800 he received a midshipman's warrant. Two months later Baker returned to the United States and paid off most of his crew—but not experienced and ranking men like Percival—and then turned the *Delaware* over to Capt. J. A. Spotswood. Percival stayed on for a fairly uneventful year under the new skipper.

At the outset of fighting, France and the United States renewed their negotiations. On 30 September 1800, at the so-called Convention of Peace, Commerce and Navigation, the parties drew up a compromise agreement; and on 31 July 1801 final ratifications were exchanged. Although the settlement was not entirely satisfactory to the United States, it put a formal end to the hostilities.

In April 1801 the navy dispatched the *Herald* to the West Indies, where most of the fighting took place, to recall the American warships there. This ended the undeclared war. The previous January the administration had begun making plans to reduce the new navy for reasons of economy. To this end, on 3 March 1801 Congress passed "An Act providing for a naval peace establishment, and for other purposes."

The economy measure reduced the number of officers by three-fifths. At the end of the Quasi-War there were 499 officers, including 354 midshipmen, in the navy. The act eliminated nine captains and thirty-six lieutenants, and directed the president to retain only 150 midshipmen. Twenty ships were released and their crews discharged; fourteen ships and their crews were retained. The act specified the retention of the

United States, Constitution, President, Chesapeake, Philadelphia, Constellation, Congress, New York, Boston, Essex, Adams, John Adams, and *General Greene.* As an afterthought, the legislation also saved the *Enterprise,* a national favorite.

Except for five revenue cutters that were returned to the Treasury Department and the *George Washington,* the remaining vessels were sold in 1801. In general, the Navy Department dropped ships too small or built for the short term. The government rated Percival's ship, the *Delaware,* a slow ship, sold her in Baltimore, and released her crew. With this reduction, the United States set a dangerous precedent. Swift demobilization would become an American practice.

The navy did not have a system at that time to assess its men. In view of the fact that only limited personnel information existed, the retention method adopted—keeping those men whose ships were retained—seems as good as any that might have been used. Naval historian Charles Peterson believes that the process led to the release of "numerous efficient officers" as well as "many who were never worthy of belonging."[27] Some of those retained became outstanding officers, but other holdovers had lackluster careers. If Percival had been assigned to one of the ships retained, his opportunity to stay in the navy would have been virtually assured. In any event, the navy discharged Midn. John Percival in July 1801, leaving historians to speculate how he would have developed if the navy had retained him and thrown him in with "Preble's boys." Percival collected the bonus of four months' pay over and above what may be due that Congress granted to all commissioned and warrant officers being discharged and returned to the merchant service.

He spent the next eight years in the merchant marine, much of it in the West Indian and European trades, and acquired a reputation as an outstanding stick-and-string sailor that remained with him throughout his life. His many adventures during this period fed a steadily developing legend. One of the traditional Percival tales is traceable to this time. Legend has it that soon after he sailed in a schooner from the Leeward Islands, yellow fever broke out on board. He alone survived the disease. In woeful condition, he summoned enough strength to lash the helm. With only a pet dog for companionship and resigned to his fate, the young Barnstable skipper drifted southward for six weeks until a passing vessel rescued him off Pernambuco. The local authorities suspected him of piracy and threw him in jail.

Another voyage ended in personal tragedy. In 1802 Percival brought a cargo into Bordeaux, where he was dumbfounded by the sight of a familiar face. His father was wandering about the docks of the French port. The senior Percival had been in London attempting to recover damages from the English government for his vessel and its cargo seized earlier by the British and became discouraged when the authorities in London refused to consider his claim. Footsore and penniless, the sixty-two-year-old Percival made his way across the English Channel to Bordeaux, where he chanced to meet his son. An emotional young Percival wept as he embraced his forlorn and sick father, whom he carried to his ship. Tragically, the elder Percival died on the way home. On 10 August 1802 John Percival Jr. buried John Percival Sr. at sea. A family stone in the West Barnstable cemetery commemorates the lamentable event.

In 1805 young Percival again found himself in jail, this time in Santa Cruz, Tenerife, in the Canary Islands. When he returned to this port in command of the *Constitution* in 1844, he brought his young clerk, Benjamin F. Stevens, to see the city prison where he had been detained for several months after being deprived of his ship. A British merchant captain helped him to escape and took him to London, whence he made his way home.

A persistent legend placing Percival in command of HMS *Victory*'s foretop under Lord Nelson during the 1805 Battle of Trafalgar is thus disproved. The origin of this myth is unclear. Percival never made such a claim. When he described his Santa Cruz imprisonment to Stevens, he said that it took place during the period of Nelson's wars, around 1805. He could not have been in both places at the same time. Further, though muster books have limitations, the *Victory*'s book does not support the story. Officers checked the crew four days before the famous battle. Twenty-two Americans were among the many foreigners listed, but Percival was not one of them.

In the early 1800s America was caught up in the lengthy European struggle generally known as the Napoleonic Wars. England and France were the principal antagonists. Once again, both countries, but especially Britain, seized U.S. shipping. The British blockaded America and impressed U.S. seamen into service in their navy. In June 1807 the American public became aroused when HMS *Leopard* forcefully took four supposed British deserters off the USS *Chesapeake*. The *Chesapeake* affair could not be overlooked. She was a U.S. Navy ship. Moreover, this insult to national pride came at a time when the country's commerce was being hurt by British restrictions on U.S. trade.

President Jefferson reacted by ordering all British vessels out of American waters. When the British and French placed additional restrictions on American traders, the president sought remedial legislation. Late in December, Congress granted him the authority to place an embargo on American shipping to foreign ports. By refusing to traffic with England, Jefferson hoped to coerce the British into rescinding their harmful trade policies. The embargo also would protect American seamen from impressment and American vessels from seizure.

The following months were difficult for men like John Percival, who found themselves torn by competing loyalties. Jefferson's embargo had the unintended consequence of ruining the U.S. merchant service. In New England, vessels rotted at their berths and men were out of work. No part of the region was affected more than Percival's native Cape Cod, where gangs of surly mariners passed their idle days berating Jefferson. Only a few were fortunate enough to be employed by Boston merchants who "hurried away their property as they lawfully might in order to escape the vengeance of their own Government."[28]

Its economy threatened, New England became a hotbed of dissent and unrest. An exasperated Jefferson complained of the lack of support. London, meanwhile, considered a brief war in order to chastise the insolent Americans. With this threat looming, Congress authorized the president to increase the size of the navy.

As war drew near, a sharp division of opinion developed along the coast, especially around Cape Cod. While the majority in the region opposed hostilities, there were pockets of the populace anxious to fight the British. Significantly, Barnstable was such a place. When the time came, the town's congressman broke with the New England delegation and voted for war.

The split became more apparent after the fighting started. A number of Cape area towns consorted with the blockading British fleet, and some towns paid the Royal Navy ransom to avoid bombardment. Nantucket effectively seceded from the United States. The island town entered into a neutrality agreement with the British naval force and withheld its national taxes. But not Barnstable. Percival's hometown drew a line, acquired four cannons from the state, and dared the British to show up.

Once again, Percival's roots influenced his behavior. This is not to say that he did not have a personal stake in things. He knew firsthand about impressments, and he attributed his father's death to British highhandedness. As well, it was uncharacteristic of him to overlook an insult to the American flag and the degradation of a U.S. Navy ship. Whatever the reason, John Percival's course was clear. In February he contacted his old commander, Capt. Thomas Baker, seeking a letter of recommendation for naval service. Baker wrote to the secretary of the navy saying that while on the *Delaware,* Percival had performed as a faithful and persevering officer who exhibited zeal and sobriety. On 6 March 1809 the former midshipman from West Barnstable returned to the U.S. Navy. He received an appointment as a sailing master and an assignment to the Norfolk Navy Yard in Virginia. Eleven others discharged as midshipmen in 1801 took the same step at this time and returned as masters. Only one—John Percival—would gain promotion to lieutenant.

After participating in the mobilization at Norfolk, Percival was detached from shore duty on 16 August 1809 and ordered to the USS *Syren.* He served uneventfully on the brig, a sister ship to the better-known *Argus,* until 12 November.

On 27 September 1809, while he was still serving on the *Syren,* John Percival married Maria Pinkerton in Norfolk County, Virginia, in what is now the city of Chesapeake. His bride was the daughter of Dr. David Smith and Mary Fitzrandolph Pinkerton of Trenton, New Jersey. James Smith, surety, made oath that Maria was of lawful age. Percival was thirty, and she had turned sixteen the month before.

After James Madison succeeded Jefferson early in 1809, both men prevailed upon Congress to repeal the unpopular embargo. The crisis subsided, and on 15 December 1809 the navy furloughed Percival and he returned to the recovering merchant service. Initially conditions improved under Madison. The government suspended the nonintercourse policy and Napoleon offered to revoke his decrees unfavorable to the United States if Britain did likewise with its orders. Madison pressured the British for revocation. He failed, and early in 1811 the United States again terminated trade with Great Britain. British squadrons returned to blockade the American coast. Although war was at hand, the country was displaying an alarming degree of disunity. New England, the stronghold of the opposition Federalist Party and the area most afflicted by government measures, led the outcry over Madison's embargo policy. The administration tried to gain popular support by stressing the evil of impressments. The Federalists, out of power for a decade, tried to weaken Madison's position by downplaying the extent and harm of the practice. The controversy raged. There were widely varying estimates of the number of impressed Americans serving in the Royal Navy. Massachusetts merchants could recall only 123 cases. The government claimed to know of 6,000. The Committee on Foreign Relations felt the nation had been soiled. Madison decried the enormity of the insult.

In mid-June, under strong internal pressure, England revoked its antagonistic trade policies and lifted its blockade of America. Peaceful coercion through economic sanctions appeared to have succeeded. Ironically, on 18 June, unaware of Britain's submission, Congress, led by western "War Hawks" interested in throwing Great Britain out of the Great Lakes region of Canada, voted seventy-nine to forty-nine for war.

Wars are hard to fight without slogans. The War of 1812 would be known as the war for "Free Trade and Sailors' Rights." Along the coast, the motto was generally rejected as a hypocritical distortion of the truth advanced by westerners unfamiliar with the sea. A Boston newspaper quoted a seaman who thought sailors could look out for themselves. When left alone, he said, he did very well. Since the war, however, "I've scarcely made shift to earn my biscuit." While asserting his loyalty, he wished the country would "let my rights alone."[29]

Percival found himself among a host of New England seamen who did more than voice their willingness to fight. On 13 August 1812 he reported back to the navy. Two days later he was on his way to the New York Navy Yard. This time he was in the navy to stay.

⚜ 2 ⚜

THE WAR OF 1812

fter his stirring capture of the British tender *Eagle* on the Fourth of July in 1813, Percival received his first command. On 23 August the navy placed him in charge of U.S. gunboat *No. 6*, one of a new flotilla of small boats designed for harbor defense. The earliest of the group, like *No. 6*, were flat bottomed, about forty-five feet long, and commonly armed with a 32- or 24-pound medium gun in the bow and a smaller stern gun. The boats were not an offensive threat, and they handled poorly. A typical crew consisted of thirty-five men.

On 9 September, along with gunboat *No. 47*, Percival got into a skirmish off Sandy Hook, New Jersey. He pestered the enemy frigate *Acasta*, Capt. Robert Kerr commanding; and the sloop-of-war *Atalante*, under Frederick Hickey. *No. 6* fired her stern gun and the frigate returned two broadsides that fell short. Then the British chased the Americans back to shore.

Percival settled down to a routine of patrol and escort work along with the other New York gunboats. On 5 October, while going downriver opposite White Hall, a sudden squall hit *No. 6* and carried away the mast. The gunboat had to be towed into port for repairs, but by 25 October the navy yard had her ready for action once again. With the British at Sandy Point,

Percival took up a position four miles east of Rikers Island. A quiet week passed, but on 3 November a lively action commenced.

The eighty-three-ton schooner *Sparrow*, a Baltimore privateer under the command of Ezekiel Hall, attempted to get inside Sandy Hook. The *Sparrow* had already been captured once by the enemy and then recaptured by the Americans. En route to New York from New Orleans with a load of sugar and lead, she ran into trouble again. Hall had his ship running before winds of forty miles per hour in heavy seas. Off Long Branch, HMS *Plantagenet*, Capt. R. Lloyd commanding, spotted the straining schooner and gave chase. The *Plantagenet* had the upper hand in the strong winds because she could carry much more canvas without risk. Hall had to be prudent in laying on sail. Too much canvas would crack the *Sparrow*'s masts or drive her under. The English ship steadily gained and began to fire her bow chaser. Percival saw the chase off the point of the highlands and heard heavy firing, but he was too far away to be of immediate help.

Knowing he could not outdistance the *Plantagenet,* but hoping at least to save his cargo, Hall headed for the shore. The *Sparrow* grounded at Long Branch and her crew scrambled over the beach to safety. Hall shouted to them to help him and the mate to take away some of the load, but to no avail. As four barges from the *Plantagenet* approached, the captain and his mate went over the side and into the fields beyond.

Percival, at the head of several American gunboats, quickly covered the six miles that separated him from the action and went ashore just above the scene, then marched his men down the shoreline until they were inside musket range. He found the British climbing about the *Sparrow* and ordered his men to open fire. They poured in a heavy barrage, and the British responded in kind. "After a very spirited resistance on both sides," Percival reported in his log, "we succeeded in driving them off."[1]

Once his returning men were safely out of his line of fire, Captain Lloyd sent broadside after broadside into and around the *Sparrow,* mixing grape with round shot. With the British barges also peppering away, Percival knew he could not remain on the schooner. The Americans retired to the beach, and Percival sent men to nearby houses to borrow shovels so he could entrench within musket shot range of the *Sparrow.* To the shame of the neighborhood, the residents refused to help. Worse, they refused with such language that Percival was provoked to arrest one of them, although he released the man after a leading citizen pleaded for mercy.

Unable to dig in, the Americans lay down on the beach to limit their exposure to the British guns. As soon as the British barges approached, Percival's men jumped to their feet and beat them off. Finally, realizing he had more to lose than to gain, Lloyd withdrew and left the wrecked privateer to Percival. Commodore Lewis reported to the navy secretary that while a number of the British fell, the Americans suffered but one fatality. Over the next few days Percival and his men salvaged everything possible of the *Sparrow*'s cargo, sails, and rigging, leaving only a battered hull to the inconsiderate locals, who had denied them the loan of a shovel even to dig a grave for their fallen comrade.

By the end of the month the *Plantagenet* was back at her game, and on 29 November 1813 she chased another schooner on shore. This time it was the *John and Mary* out of New Orleans with a load of cotton, sugar, and lead for Cox and Montaudavert in New York. The Englishman ran her aground five miles below Long Branch. Once again, Percival saw the chase and raced to get on the scene, but several British barges beat him to the grounded schooner. He deployed his one hundred men ashore and opened fire with small arms. After a lively but ineffectual fire from the *Plantagenet* and its four armed barges, the Americans succeeded in driving the enemy away.

Once the British commander sent a flag of truce ashore, Percival dispatched Sailing Master Rogers to accept the flag. The British claimed the *John and Mary* as their prize, but offered to ransom her for one thousand dollars. If Percival did not accept the demand, they would destroy not only the schooner but all the houses of Long Branch. The threat to the dwellings probably did not concern Percival in light of the conduct of the local citizens earlier in the month. In any event, as one might expect, he rejected the offer.

The log of gunboat *No. 6* reports: "The [British] boats soon returned on board and the Truce ended when the Enemy's Ship commenced a heavy fire on us but without effect. The barges also did their best."[2] The heavy fire from the *Plantagenet* continued until dark as the British threw nearly seven hundred shots onshore. In his report, Lewis said that only one American was injured, wounded by a splinter. The houses went unscathed and the schooner suffered only minor damage. Percival saved the schooner along with its cargo.

Percival and the New York gunboat flotilla continued to patrol the area throughout the winter. They helped boats in distress, and boarded and inspected others. When stormy weather kept them in port, the navy gave the men liberty or sent them to work on board the sloop-of-war *John Adams*. On 4 March, Percival's New York tour of duty ended when the navy transferred him to the sloop *Peacock*. During his service under Lewis, Percival routinely commanded more than one vessel.

The U.S. strategy in the first year of the War of 1812 emphasized defense, but not very successfully. British naval forces were able to apply heavy pressure at will along the eastern seaboard. From time to time, the Americans struck back and enjoyed some success, but such was not the norm. Realizing that offensive measures would be necessary if hostilities were to be carried to a satisfactory conclusion, the U.S. Navy changed its strategy in 1813 and began to look toward the enemy's commerce. The American frigates were not designed to run down British merchantmen. Might smaller, faster ships do better?

Perhaps the success of the smaller and faster American privateers, which preyed on commercial ships for profit, influenced government policy at this stage. In any case, the navy shifted to warships of lesser size and greater speed than the frigates and constructed a group of "cruizers" for the purpose of carrying the war to the British trade routes and home waters. Prominent among these early raiders were the *Argus*, *Essex, Frolic, Wasp,* and *Peacock*.

Adam and Noah Brown built the ship sloop *Peacock* at the Corleears Hook yard in New York late in 1813. It took them seventy-two working days, and the navy considered the result a fine piece of workmanship. The Navy Department gave command of the ship to Lewis Warrington, an unassuming captain from Virginia. Although not well known at the time, he had fine credentials. The navy had retained Warrington in the service after the 1801 demobilization and placed him under Preble in the war against the Barbary States. Able and respected, he was a good judge of men, and he proved it when selecting his crew.

Warrington chose many of the men from the crew of the *Hornet*, which the British had kept bottled up in New London since June 1813, along with the *United States* and the *Macedonian*. To handle the crew the Virginian picked John B. Nicholson, first lieutenant; Samuel Henley, second lieutenant; and Philip F. Voorhees, third lieutenant. To handle the *Peacock* Warrington selected John Percival, already well known for his seamanship, as sailing master. The two men had begun a warm, lasting friendship when both were assigned to the Norfolk yard in 1809. By all accounts, Warrington put together an outstanding team. William James, the British naval historian, points out that Warrington's hand-picked crew did not have "a boy among them."[3]

Percival joined Warrington on 9 March 1814. Three days later he was at the helm as the swift *Peacock* eluded the British blockade outside New York harbor and stood to the south. The *Peacock* had planned to rendezvous with the U.S. frigate *President,* but the larger ship failed to escape from New York. Consequently, Warrington headed alone for Saint Marys, on the southern coast of Georgia, where he landed a quantity of war munitions. During the passage, British frigates and ships of the line chased the *Peacock* several times, but she easily outsailed her pursuers.

Warrington continued on a southerly course, hoping to intercept British merchantmen traveling out of Cuba or Jamaica. His cruise took him as far south as Great Isaacs in the Bahamas, then to Maranilla Reef, and back north along the Florida coast. From 18 April to 24 April he reported spotting only three ships. One was a neutral; two were privateers. He chased the latter but did not overhaul them, although one was run among the shoals of Cape Canaveral into four fathoms of water.

Warrington learned that British merchant ships fearful of American patrols were forming a convoy in Jamaica that was scheduled to sail sometime during the first ten days of May. When the convoy moved eastward through the "Gulph" it would be under the protection of a seventy-four-gun ship of the line, two frigates, and two sloops. Warrington wisely had Percival stand to the north in search of easier game.

About twelve miles off Cape Canaveral, Florida, at 5:00 on the morning of 29 April, a lookout spotted a sail. The day began with clear weather and a light wind out of the east. At 5:30 a second sail came into sight, and by 7:00 two more had appeared. All four vessels hauled their wind and scurried to the east-northeast with the *Peacock* in hot pursuit.

When Warrington got closer, he identified a British hermaphrodite brig, a Russian commercial ship, and a Spanish merchantman, all escorted by a Royal Navy brig. The hermaphrodite was the first English merchant ship the *Peacock* had seen since leaving Georgia. The Russian and the Spaniard had little to fear from an American armed vessel, but the British merchantman was a juicy target at last. The convoy was heading to Bermuda from Jamaica.

The man-of-war turned out to be HMS *Epervier* out of Halifax, Comdr. Richard Wales commanding, built two years earlier in Rochester, England. Of the *Bacchus* class, she mounted eighteen 32-pound carronades and carried a crew of 128. By comparison, the *Peacock's* armament consisted of twenty 32-pounders and a pair of long guns, and she shipped 166 men. The metal each threw in a broadside would have been about the same, with the American firing about twenty pounds more.

After an hour passed and he realized that he was being overhauled, Commander Wales took up a position between the onrushing *Peacock* and his charges. As the three merchantmen continued their flight, the British commander ran up a private signal. Warrington answered by hoisting the American colors. At this point, Warrington had the advantage of a heavier ship. Wales had the advantage of being to windward.

The *Peacock's* log describes the events that followed. As the two antagonists approached one another, the *Epervier*, now "with English collors flying, took in royals and flying jib, beat to quarters & cleared ship for action. . . . At 5 before 11 AM commenced the action."[4] The *Epervier* fired her starboard guns. Now within pistol shot, the *Peacock* matched the Briton with her own starboard broadside. The *Epervier's* first and most successful round went high. Two 32-pound round shot struck the U.S. vessel's foreyard, depriving Percival of his fore and foretop sails. Thus impaired, the sailing master had to keep the ship large throughout the rest of the fight.

The *Epervier* eased off, came around on a parallel course, and found herself in serious trouble. Her carronades were proving defective. During her first broadside, three guns became unshipped when their fighting-bolts gave way, a defect traced to an absence of cotters. Her guns continued to upset with each new round. Heavy fire from the American ship put three of the *Epervier's* guns out of action in quick succession.

Wales found his position untenable. In close fighting, star shot from the *Peacock* ripped away at his rigging and spars. Heavier shot pounded his larboard hull. If the faulty fighting-bolts were not a sufficient impediment, the breeching-bolts began to draw out of the side of his ship. Unable to maneuver and almost devoid of firepower, Wales called in desperation for boarders. But his crew "declined a measure so fraught with danger," replying: "She is too heavy for us."[5] There was but one alternative: surrender.

Mahan, Roosevelt, and other historians have pointed out that accounts of the naval engagements in this war are meager and sometimes conflicting. So it is with the duration of this scrap. Some reports have the *Epervier* giving up after forty-two minutes of actual fighting. The *Peacock's* log says: "At 4 Past 11 she struck her colors"; that is, nine minutes into the fight.[6]

Warrington believed the Briton's fate would have been determined quicker if Percival had had the use of all his headsails and had not been compelled to keep slightly off the wind. *Niles' Weekly Register* reported, "There are many little things belonging to this glorious event that ought not to be forgotten."[7] Significantly, early in the engagement the *Epervier's* colors came down. Warrington eased up and hailed the British to determine if they had struck. They had not. The Englishman's colors had been shot away, and the battle resumed.

In a letter to the secretary of the navy dated 29 April, the skipper of the *Peacock* reported that when the *Epervier* struck her colors she had five feet of water in her hold; the main topmast was over the side; the main boom was gone; the foremast was tottering; the fore rigging and stays were shot away; and there were forty-five shot holes in the hull, twenty within a foot of the water line. He described her as dreadfully mauled.

Lieutenant Nicholson, reporting independently to the department on 1 May 1814, said the British brig was battered while the *Peacock* sustained relatively little injury. As well as the noted foreyard damage, the American lost a few topgallant backstays and there were some holes in her sails. Not a single round shot hit her hull! Within forty-five minutes of the battle's end, Percival had his injured foreyard sent down and braced, the foresail back in place, and the *Peacock* in good order.

Reports of British casualties range from three to twenty killed, and eight to fifteen wounded. Warrington initially said that eight British sailors were killed and thirteen wounded. Later, after Nicholson made a closer examination, Warrington raised the totals to eleven dead and fifteen wounded. It is well established that the *Peacock* had but two wounded. Among the *Epervier's* dead were three impressed Americans named Johnson, Peters, and Roberts. "This is horrible," *Niles' Weekly Register* mourned, "and must not be."[8]

Otherwise the American press expressed elation and exultation. The *Boston Weekly Messenger* discussed "another splendid victory," and the

Connecticut Courant suggested the *Peacock* had "adorned with another most brilliant laurel, the naval history of our country."[9] One report noted that Great Britain considered the *Epervier* one of its "'*bragging vessels*'; for it is said that when she left London bets were three to one that she would take an American sloop of war or small frigate."[10]

Although the American press exaggerated the overall importance of the fight, the British were slow to forget the humiliating defeat. The Royal Navy later convicted the *Epervier*'s boatswain, Joseph Deane, and seven seamen of deserting their battle stations. The court acquitted the other officers and crewmen of the same charge. Clearly, Wales demonstrated poor management. He had been at sea for a year and a half and had not gained control of his crew. As well, Wales neglected gun drills. Still bitter after seventy-two years, British historian William James suggested that "even one or two discharges" in gunnery practice "would have shown the insufficiency of the fighting-bolts," although he doubted whether any amount of training "could have amended the Epervier's crew." After all, two were seventy years old, and there were "some blacks, several other foreigners, lots of disaffected, and few even of ordinary stature . . . a disgrace to the deck of a British man-of-war." James concluded: "For any damage that such a vessel as the Epervier could have done to her, the Peacock might almost as well have fought with the unarmed Russian."[11]

Without the immediate emotions of war to influence them, later American writers agreed with James's evaluation of the *Epervier* and her crew. James Soley, for instance, claimed that her "slovenly" conduct was "far behind what one would expect in a British sloop-of-war."[12] In reality, the *Peacock-Epervier* engagement illustrated an important factor in the War of 1812: American seamanship and gunnery generally were superior to British. Ralph Paine felt that in "this instance the behavior of the American vessel and her crew was supremely excellent and not a flaw could be found."[13] Unfortunately the *Peacock*'s efficiency was diminished by the *Epervier*'s incompetence.

The American crew received warm praise for their victory nevertheless. On 5 May, Warrington cited his men in a special communication to the Navy Department. He recommended a lieutenancy for Percival because of his professional knowledge and steadfast attention to duty. During the fight, Warrington said, Percival "handled the ship, as if he had been working her into a roadstead."[14]

Later in the year, Congress resolved that the president should award a gold medal to Warrington, silver medals to his officers, and a sword to each midshipman and the sailing master in testimony of the gallantry and good conduct of the men of the *Peacock* in the fight with the *Epervier*. Percival's sword, made of fine steel, was inscribed on one side: "John Percival, Sailing Master, Epervier Capture, April 1814"; and on the other side: "Altius Ibunt Qui Ad Summa Nituntur" (They will rise higher who aim at the greatest things). A medallion on the sword bore the inscription: "Presented by the Congress of the United States of America to John Percival for the Capture by the Peacock of the English Frigate Epervier, April 29, 1814."[15]

By sunset on 29 April a repair crew had the *Epervier* ready to sail. The Americans exerted themselves to keep their prize afloat. And the prize included more than the ship itself. The victors found private specie in the amount of $118,000 aboard. Warrington assigned sixteen men to Nicholson and placed the senior lieutenant in charge of the captured brig. The *Peacock* and the *Epervier* sailed north toward Savannah.

During the evening of 30 April, off Amelia Island, Florida, trouble appeared. The Americans observed two British frigates to the north. Warrington ordered Nicholson to race for the safety of Saint Marys while directing Percival to make a run for it to the south. When the weather frigate indicated interest in the *Peacock,* Warrington thought Nicholson would be safe from the other frigate, which was well to leeward of the *Epervier*. As it turned out, both Americans were in for a chase.

The *Peacock* lost sight of her pursuer at 9:00 P.M., but Percival continued to press southward through the darkness in an effort to get clear of the Englishman. When daylight came, Warrington had his sailing master shorten sail and resume the northerly course. Before long, the *Peacock* made out the British frigate ahead. A second southward chase lasted until early in the afternoon. In the evening, Warrington turned again to the north. The *Peacock* sailed all that night without incident, but when the sun appeared, a crewman spotted the persistent frigate giving chase. The American sloop again ran her out of sight. The veteran John Percival and the swift *Peacock* were becoming a fine combination.

Meanwhile, Nicholson ran into trouble. The second frigate caught up with the *Epervier* and drove her into shoal water. Unable to get his own ship close to the captured prize, the captain sent several boats after the

Americans. When the boats got close, Nicholson picked up his trumpet and loudly ordered his helmsman to yaw. He continued the subterfuge by issuing preparatory orders for a broadside. This ruse intimidated the British and they withdrew, unaware they could have retaken the under-manned *Epervier* with little if any loss to themselves. Soon thereafter Nicholson got away and made port at Savannah on 1 May 1814. Three days later Warrington cleared Tybee Light and moved up to an anchor-age in the Savannah River alongside the *Epervier*.

After a one-month layover, Warrington had the *Peacock* ready for a more venturesome cruise—a voyage to the British home waters. On 4 June Percival took her out into the familiar Gulf Stream. Once past the British blockaders, Warrington allowed the current to carry him north-east past Cape Cod and out to the Grand Banks, where the *Peacock* made her first capture of the cruise. The 187-ton brig *Sea Flower* of Bermuda was en route from Saint Johns to Barbados with a cargo of cod-fish. Her master, George R. Hinson, had only a nine-man crew and two guns, so he surrendered without a fight on 17 June. The Americans burned the brig.

Afterward, the *Peacock* moved eastward to the Azores. While off the western island of Flores on 5 July 1814, she intercepted the Greenock brig *Stranger*. The 180-ton ship was carrying a load of hides and tallow from Buenos Aires. Her skipper, James Lawdon, realized that his thir-teen men and four guns were no match for the American man-of-war. The *Stranger* submitted and was likewise burned.

Percival next turned for the Irish coast. Before the month ran out, the *Peacock* took three more prizes. The 88-ton Liverpool sloop *Fortitude,* James Waters commanding; the 165-ton Irvine brig *Venus,* David Kennedy commanding; and the 140-ton Liverpool brig *Adonia,* K. I. Halwell com-manding, all submitted. Warrington sank the first two, although not before saving the shipment of brandy the *Venus* was carrying, and used the *Adonia* as a cartel for the thirty-eight prisoners he had collected.

The American raider got off to a good start in August. On the first, she took and sank the 116-ton Campbelltown sloop *Leith Packet,* carrying a load of Tenerife wine. On the following day the *Peacock* sank the 64-ton Rathsey sloop *William and Ann.* And on 3 August she sent the 97-ton Cumbria sloop *Peggy and Jane* to the bottom.

As Warrington continued his cruise up the west coast of Ireland and on to the Shetland and Faroe Islands, his unprecedented destruction began to excite British merchants. True, American privateers were also active in the Irish Channel and were taking a toll on British shipping. From the businessmen's point of view, however, they presented a lesser problem. Privateers went out for commercial profit, not military destruction. They usually did not sink prizes; therefore, the seized vessels became liable to recapture while being sent in for sale. But naval raiders like the *Peacock* burned and destroyed. The raids had caused insurance rates on vessels plying the waters between England and Ireland to increase from the usual premium of below one pound sterling to a high of five guineas, and the British merchant community overwhelmed the Admiralty with letters of complaint.

Yet the American captain considered his cruise to be "not so great" a success. He had planned to continue up to the coast of Norway, but this leg of the venture "was omitted in consequence of that whole coast being under a strict blockade by a combined squadron of English and Swedish ships."[16] Hence, Warrington retraced his path back down the west coast of the British Isles.

On 14 August the *Peacock* fell in with the 207-ton Bristol barque *William*, M. Whitney commanding, and burned her. The day after, Warrington decided to make a cartel out of the 307-ton ship *Sir Edward Pellew*. Though she had twelve guns, her master, George Kelly, had only a thirteen-man crew, an insufficient number to fight off the American vessel. Warrington put fifty prisoners on the *Pellew* and stood for the Bay of Biscay, leaving the enemy's home waters.

John Percival was unusually busy handling the *Peacock* during this phase of the cruise. The ship was subjected to continuous southwest and northwest gales from the moment she struck the Irish Channel until after leaving the Shetland Islands. Percival was forced costantly to beat off a lee shore. In addition, as Warrington later observed, the "uncommon severe weather . . . had the double effect of keeping in all their trade."[17]

By this time the ship owners and underwriters of Glasgow had decided to go over the heads of the Admiralty with their complaints. On 7 September, unaware the *Peacock* had left the area, they presented a memorial directly to the prince regent. The audacity of American men-of-war, they insisted, was not only injurious to their business but also humbling to their pride and a discredit to the Royal Navy. The commercial interests prayed that measures would be taken to stop the insulting depredations.

The Irish newspapers increased the alarm by reporting that the *Peacock* had destroyed "at least *one hundred* British vessels on the coasts of Great Britain!"[18] *Niles' Weekly Register* gleefully informed its readers of the destruction the *Peacock* was dealing "to the enemy in his own waters . . . even in Dublin bay." The account added that "several sloops of war went after her," including the *Pelican*. Using the American minister in France and Irish and London papers as sources, the newspaper confidently reported that the *Peacock* "also has sent a sloop of war 'down cellar,' as the sailors say."[19] The victim was believed to be the *Columbine,* sunk with "every soul perishing" after "a very short action."[20] When the *Peacock* eventually returned to the United States, a disappointed *Niles'* had to retract. "It appears she did not sink a sloop of war, as was so variously reported as to obtain entire belief."[21]

Nonetheless, Warrington's cruise up and down the west coast of Great Britain had a marked psychological effect in Britain and in the United States. The legendary power of the Royal Navy—"not a sail but by permission spreads"—was becoming a myth. The *Naval Chronicle* admitted that insurance rates were three times higher than when England was "at war with all Europe!"[22] And Americans gained satisfaction from learning that the British people disliked experiencing the wrath of enemy men-of-war just as much as they did.

Percival sailed the *Peacock* into well-known waters as he crossed Biscay and turned down the Portuguese coast. On 21 August, off Cape Ortegal, Spain, Warrington's ship fell in with the 258-ton Jersey brig *Bellona,* H. Langlois commanding. The Americans, now short of water, did not leave much of the cargo of brandy and wine on board when they sank her. The *Peacock* cruised between Ortegal and the Rock of Lisbon for seven days and saw only twelve sail. Nine were spoken, but only one turned out to be British. The Teignmouth brig *Triton* submitted. The Americans sank the 111-ton brig off Cape Finisterre on 23 August.

After crossing the mouth of the Mediterranean, the *Peacock* ran close to the Madeiras, hoping to fall in with the British West India and Tenerife trade. Luckless there, she made the Canary Islands on 1 September and attempted to procure a supply of water at Fentaventura and Lanzarote. Unable to find water, Warrington lessened his need for it by unloading some of his prisoners at Lanzarote. On 2 September he added to his captives by taking ten men off the 174-ton London brig *Duck* before sinking her. Warrington then elected to run for the Cape Verde Islands. He landed at Saint Vincent and, after a week of digging and clearing wells, the *Peacock*'s crew finally obtained sufficient water.

With the embarrassed Admiralty zealously hunting him, Warrington proceeded slowly to the west. He had Percival alternate between southwest and northwest courses, prolonging the *Peacock*'s stay between the longitudes of 20 and 40 degrees west, the principal track of Britain's East India, Africa, and South America trade. On 6 October the American cruiser made the mouth of the Maroni River on the coast of Guiana after failing to sight a single vessel since leaving the Verdes. From South America, the *Peacock* ran for Barbados, arriving on the ninth. Warrington remained to windward of Barbuda for several days. On 12 October the Americans intercepted their final prize of the cruise, the 270-ton ship *Mary* belonging to Guadeloupe and bound for Halifax with a load of sugar, coffee, rum, and molasses. The *Peacock* sent her down cellar off Barbuda.

Percival steered for the United States, arriving off Cape Henlopen, Delaware, early on 28 October. The next day the *Peacock* sailed impudently past the British blockade and into New York harbor. Warrington and his crew completed 147 days at sea. While they were out, they took or destroyed fourteen enemy merchantmen amounting to 2,364 tons and worth an estimated $610,000. By any measure, this cruise was an American highlight of the War of 1812.

The men of the *Peacock* returned home to a nation in peril. As a consequence, England was able to unleash its full fury on America. The British burned Washington. Percival learned that, closer to his home, the enemy was raining destruction on assailable property all along the northeast coast.

While Warrington refitted the *Peacock* in New York, the Navy Department promoted Percival to acting lieutenant as of 18 November 1814. His great wish to be a permanent member of the navy became final on the following 9 December when President Madison, with the Senate's approval, signed the standard lieutenant's commission for Percival. The commission indicated the president's "Trust and Confidence in the Patriotism, Valour, Fidelity and Abilities of John Percival." The warrant would "continue in Force during the pleasure of the President of the United States for the Time being."[23]

January 1815 found the *Peacock* and several other American men-of-war waiting for an opportunity to slip out past the New York blockade and cruise against enemy shipping. On 14 January, during a northwest storm, the *President* and the *Macedonian* broke out. The *President* should have remained in the harbor, where she had passed the previous year. Two days after she left New York, the British captured her through the combined efforts of HMS *Endymion, Pomone, Tenedos,* and *Majestic.*

Waiting in the lower bay for their chance, the *Peacock,* the *Hornet,* and the store-schooner *Tom Bowline* all evaded the British on 22 January in broad daylight. The trio set out for a rendezvous with the *President* at the South Atlantic island of Tristan da Cunha, unaware that she had been taken by the British. The swift *Peacock* got to the island first. Blown out to sea by a storm, she returned on 24 March, only to learn that the day before, Capt. James Biddle in the *Hornet* had made a "perfect wreck" of the British sloop-of-war *Penguin,* Capt. James Dickinson commanding. Percival and his crewmates saw the remains of the British sloop before Biddle scuttled his victim. The *Hornet-Penguin* duel is most noteworthy because it came one month and one week after the war ended. Unaware that on 17 February 1815 the president, with the advice and consent of the senate, had ratified the Treaty of Ghent, Biddle took the *Penguin* in twenty-two minutes.

In a letter of 10 April written at Tristan da Cunha and printed in *Niles',* an anonymous *Peacock* officer described the *Hornet's* victory. He closed by saying: "We are off tomorrow to the eastward and you will probably not hear from us again till the *cruise* is either knocked up and we in Bombay, or accomplished, and the Peacock in her native port."[24]

Still unaware of the *President's* fate, Warrington and Biddle waited for three weeks at Tristan before giving up on the frigate. The two American officers decided to send away the *Tom Bowline* as a cartel with the prisoners from the *Penguin.* Prowling together on 27 April, the *Peacock* and the *Hornet* spotted what appeared to be an East Indiaman and closed for a fight. The stranger turned out to be the HMS *Cornwallis.* Always a fast ship, the *Peacock* turned tail and got out of danger. The British ship almost overhauled the *Hornet.* After a long chase, she escaped largely because the *Cornwallis* dropped back to save a royal marine who had fallen overboard. Biddle jettisoned all but the skin of his ship in order to decrease his weight and thereby increase his speed.

Alone, Warrington's ship continued to stand to the east. In May she reached the islands of Saint Paul and Amsterdam in the Indian Ocean, a predetermined rendezvous site. Warrington found a letter left there by the *Macedonian* advising him of the *President's* probable capture. Warrington planned to wait at the meeting place for the *Hornet,* but he got carried to leeward chasing a strange sail, and strong gales made a return difficult. Owing to the winds, the *Peacock* bore up and on 8 June made Java.

Although he was not altogether new to this part of the world, Percival found himself engrossed in the peculiarities of the Pacific. The equatorial heat in the Sunda Strait, for instance, seemed more oppressive than the West Indian climate he knew so well. The ship's crew, outfitted for the cooler weather of Tristan da Cunha, found the temperature and humidity oppressive. An opportunity to address the need for lighter clothing presented itself shortly after the *Peacock* entered the strait, when she pounced on the British merchant ship *Union* plowing for Malaya. Before burning the Englishman, the Americans divested her of her cargo of pepper and several bales of lightweight piece goods. The captain distributed the timely supply of tropical clothing to his needy crew.

In quick succession the *Peacock* seized the ships *Venus* and *Brio.* Warrington turned the *Venus* into a cartel and sent her into Batavia with 150 prisoners. He burned the *Brio.* From these three captures the Americans took about twenty thousand dollars in specie and gold. Captain Warrington divided five thousand of it among his officers and men. The ordinary Jack Tar probably spent his share as soon as he reached port, but Percival turned at least some of his silver into mementoes such as cups, epaulets, and the like.

The *Peacock's* next action, her last, turned out to be the final engagement between the belligerents of the War of 1812. James Fenimore Cooper's *History of the Navy of the United States of America* calls it an "unfortunate mistake."[25] Others have called the incident everything from reasonable to criminal. Warrington called it a "rencontre."[26]

The facts are fairly well established. As he passed up the Sunda Strait on 30 June 1815, Warrington sailed under the British flag. In the afternoon, the *Peacock* encountered the English East India Company's brig

Nautilus, Lt. Charles Boyce commanding. The confrontation took place off Anjier. The chief British civil officer of that place, Master Attendant MacGregor, and an army officer came across to Warrington from the *Nautilus.* A British account originating in the *Calcutta Times* claims that Warrington affected to disbelieve the master attendant when he informed the American of the peace settlement. When he arrived back in the States, Warrington wrote a report giving his version of the incident and sent it to Secretary of the Navy Benjamin W. Crowninshield, knowing that the secretary would hear conflicting reports. The *Peacock*'s commander said that since he expected to be fired into at any moment, he passed the attendant, the officer, and their entourage below, having "concluded that they had been misled by the British colors." Warrington added: "No questions in consequence were put to them, and they very improperly omitted mentioning that peace existed."[27]

The *Peacock* then ran up the Stars and Stripes and ranged alongside the *Nautilus.* Lieutenant Boyce hailed and inquired if the Americans knew of the peace. Captain Warrington said he "replied in the negative—directing him at the same time to haul his colours down, if it were the case, in token of it—adding that if he did not, I should fire into him."[28] The Briton refused to comply with the demand, and one of the *Peacock*'s forward guns fired into her. The *Nautilus* immediately retaliated with a broadside that in turn brought forth a countering broadside from the *Peacock.* The Calcutta newspaper account describes a valiant scrap lasting some fifteen minutes. The facts seem to bear out Warrington, however, who said the *Nautilus* struck after receiving the *Peacock*'s first broadside.

Six *Nautilus* crewmen, all lascars, were killed, and seven or eight more including Boyce and his first lieutenant, Mr. Mayston, were wounded. Mayston died of his wounds five months later. The action left the brig battered in her hull. Whether because of the *Peacock*'s continued good fortune or the Royal Navy's continued poor shooting, the crew of the American sloop went unscathed.

In justifying his action, Warrington wrote: "I considered his assertion, coupled with his arrangements for action, a finesse on his part to amuse us, till he could place himself under the protection of the fort."[29] On the following day, the American officers viewed the peace intelligence the British had on hand, all of it unofficial, and skeptically decided to give up the *Nautilus*. Although Warrington's men labored to stop up her shot holes and put her rigging in order, the British had to send the *Nautilus* into Samarang for repairs.

Warrington explained to Crowninshield his fear that he might be criticized for ceasing hostilities without better evidence of peace and his hope that a consideration of his distance from home and insufficient communications would lead to the decision that he should "not be thought to have decided prematurely."[30] To put the incident in perspective, recall that Captain Barron received a five-year suspension for striking the *Chesapeake*'s colors to HMS *Leopard*. Such punishment did not promote restraint in the naval service. Thereafter, no American captain, unless he wished to risk mutiny by his crew, would permit an English or unknown man-of-war to come within range without taking necessary precautions if not preparing for battle. With this action the unwanted War of 1812 reached its end.

Touching at the island of Réunion in the Mascarene group, then at Saint Helena, the *Peacock* made her way back to the United States, bearing home the honor of having fired the last shot in the war. She arrived in New York on 30 October 1815. Well commanded, well officered, and well built, the *Peacock* earned one of the best records of the war. Twenty-two U.S. Navy men-of-war made it to sea during the hostilities. They took a total of 165 prizes. The *Peacock* alone accounted for 19 prizes, or 12 percent. When the war ended, only four other ships—the *Constitution*, *Hornet*, *Wasp*, and *Tom Bowline*—remained out.

John Percival considered the war more than a four-year conflict. From his perspective, it began eighteen years earlier with his impressment on the *Victory*. The death of his father in 1802 aggravated matters. Yet his satisfaction went much deeper than the glory of being an officer on the American cruiser that emerged victorious from the last fight of the war. Percival had established himself in the U.S. Navy. This satisfaction was unique in itself; most mariners favored the lucrative merchant service. Of the more than eight hundred Barnstable shipmasters of the nineteenth century, only five men other than Percival were masters of navy ships. What kind of man forsakes the common goal of fortune in favor of his country's service?

The men of 1812 were an exceptional group—at least Percival's hometown judged him to be extraordinary. At the 15 October 1816 town meeting, they voted to proffer the thanks of the town for "his daring and intrepid behavior" during the war as well as his "good conduct and Nautical skill." Percival promptly acknowledged the "very flattering testimony." He assured his townsmen: "It has and will ever be my highest ambition to merit and receive the approbation of my Countrymen."[31]

~3~

BICKERING AT BOSTON

The Navy Department detached Percival from the *Peacock* on 15 March 1816 and transferred him from New York to the Boston Navy Yard. On 23 April he reported for duty on the frigate *Macedonian*. Built at the Royal Woolwich Dock Yards on the Thames River, she slid down the ways in June 1810. Her British career lasted a little more than two years. In a brilliant action on 25 October 1812, the dynamic Capt. Stephen Decatur in the frigate *United States* defeated and captured the *Macedonian* under Capt. John Carden. When Percival arrived on board the only British frigate taken during the war, she was employed as a training ship. With Percival as one of the officers, the ship went briefly to the Caribbean during the summer of 1816. She returned to Boston in August and went into ordinary, or became inactive. A complete overhaul followed.

During this period Percival developed a warm friendship with the station commander, the glorious Capt. Isaac Hull, that lasted until Hull's death in 1843. Both men came from common backgrounds in small New England towns—Percival from Cape Cod and Hull from Derby, Connecticut—but a greater force drew the two together. Each had an exceedingly high regard for the other's professional ability. Many years later, Percival, "expressing himself forcibly and to the point," told Benjamin

Stevens, "Hull knew as much more than I did, as Christ knew more than one of the apostles!"[1]

Another anecdote related by Stevens best illustrates Hull's esteem for Percival. The incident took place in 1839 when Commodore Hull commanded the Mediterranean squadron and had the swift *Ohio* as his flagship. Percival commanded the notoriously slow *Cyane* under Hull. One day Hull ordered his small force to proceed to a certain harbor. The normal procedure, dictated by custom and prudence, called for subordinate commanders to slacken sail if necessary to permit the flagship to precede the flotilla. On this occasion, however, when the *Ohio* arrived at the destination, Hull found the *Cyane* already at anchor. After the *Ohio* came to rest, Percival went on board "to pay his respects." Immediately taking Percival to task for his breach of etiquette, Hull demanded to know why he had forged ahead.

"Give me the 'Ohio' when we go back, and you take the 'Cyane,'" replied Percival, "and I'll get there first!"

Mellowing, Hull conceded: "I have no doubt you would, for Jack, you are the best sailor I ever saw!"[2]

In 1817, Captain Hull gave Percival an unusual assignment that would later become an issue. James Baker, the carpenter at the navy yard, had invented a mechanism known as an elliptical pump. Hull placed the device in the *Macedonian* to try it out and was pleased with the results. Thinking that profits from its sales would supplement his relatively meager navy pay, Hull bought shares in the invention. Navy agent Amos Binney and the acting clerk at the yard, Benjamin Hichborn Fosdick, were the other principals in the venture. In January, Hull gave Baker permission to travel to Washington to obtain a patent and promote the pump with the naval authorities. On 17 April he detached Percival from duty and sent him to London to sell the right to manufacture the pumps in England.

Percival remained on paid leave of absence in England promoting the Baker pump until the following January. He got back to the United States in March 1818 and returned to the *Macedonian*. While this kind of behavior is illegal and somewhat shocking by today's standards, in the nineteenth century the government deemed the practice completely acceptable. The worst offense historians and biographers can commit is to look at the past through the lens of the present.

Capt. John Downes commanded the *Macedonian*. Like Hull from a similar background, he too became a lifelong friend of Percival's. When his son was a young midshipman in 1838, he made sure his boy broke in under the vigilant tutelage of Percival. Many considered Downes, born in Canton, Massachusetts, something of a diamond in the rough. Nathaniel Hawthorne thought he had "rather more of the ocean than the drawing-room about him."[3] Certainly his speech could be coarse and profane, but that was not unusual in a man who had spent his life at sea.

Early in September 1818 the secretary instructed Downes to take the *Macedonian* to the west coast of South America to give aid and protection to U.S. citizens and their property in the region, which was beset by civil unrest. Blockades, seizures, and impressments plagued American merchant and whaling vessels. The navy told Downes to spend time in Buenos Aires and take note of the state of affairs and the activities of European operatives there. His instructions included the admonition to pursue "a strictly neutral course toward all nations and flags."[4] On 21 September the *Macedonian* got under way from the Boston Navy Yard at 2:00 P.M.[5] By 9:00 that evening, Lt. Charles Gauntt recorded in his journal, "Cape Cod light bore, by compass, South, distant 5 leagues."[6]

One week later the *Macedonian* encountered serious trouble off Bermuda: the "most tremendous hurricane ever known to the oldest seaman on board, which lasted about 15 hours and left their gallant ship a miserable wreck."[7] Newspapers all along the coast covered the story. *Niles' Weekly Register* said the storm was "represented to have been undescribably awful."[8] The ship's log depicts the storm in less emotional terms. In rain and strong gales, it notes, at "7 PM lost William Wilkins (Seaman) overboard by a flap of the Mizen Storm Staysail Sheet."[9] Between 8:00 and midnight, the wind increased with a tremendous sea running. The main storm staysail stay parted and the mizzen storm staysail split. For more than three hours, Downes laid to under the fore storm staysail. At 1:30 A.M. the mainmast sprung between the spar and main decks. A half-hour later, the fore storm staysail parted. At 4:00 A.M. the mizzen mast sprung in two places. The crew cut the mizzen rigging when the mast went by the board carrying away the stern and larboard quarter boats. Men knocked the damaged starboard quarter boat to pieces. At daylight the fore mast sprung in three or four places. A team cut away the foretop, which carried with it the spritsail yard. The main topmast went over the side, bringing down the main yard, which carried away the starboard yardarm. About 8:00 A.M. a sea knocked in the starboard waist nettings. What remained of the lower sections of the fore and main masts pounded away at the keel. The heavy load of provisions added to the danger. In the midst of the peril, an anxious Lt. Josiah Tattnall came to Percival and told him that the carpenter had begun to cut away the mainmast. Percival's years at sea told him that the mast would be essential to the ship's survival in the following hours. The carpenter had struck five or six blows with an ax before Percival charged forward and shouted above the howling storm: "Avast there, or we shall all be in eternity in five minutes!"[10] The carpenter dropped his ax, allowing the mast to remain. As a result of Percival's quick action, "the credit of saving both ship and crew was awarded to him."[11] Percival's official service record takes note of this act.[12]

Lieutenant Gauntt's journal indicates that from 8:00 A.M. to noon all hands were employed in clearing "the general wreck to which we were now reduced." Strong braces were applied to what remained of the masts, and the crew worked the reduced sails as the wind abated to moderate breezes with heavy swells. Downes, of course, postponed his mission and headed for the Gosport Navy Yard at Norfolk. "Upon a review of the whole," Gauntt noted in his journal, "it was acknowledged by all on board that our situation was at one time extremely doubtful."[13]

As the *Macedonian* approached the coast, the once proud frigate spoke the Guernsey brig *Eliza*. The captain was not impressed with the battered American. In fact, he was "very insolent," obliging Downes to "direct a gun to be pointed" at him, "which had the desired effect of compelling" the Guernsey man "to heave to."[14]

So damaged was the *Macedonian* that no one recognized her when she reached Norfolk on 11 October until she had come to anchor. Among other things, she required a complete new set of masts, spars, sails, and boats. Downes completed the refitting in eighteen days. Percival and his fellow officers lost all of their personal possessions in the storm, and the department compensated them for the misfortune. On 10 November, a throng cheered the frigate as she sailed from Norfolk and continued on her voyage.

In addition to expecting the *Macedonian* to show the "striped bunting" in foreign ports, the navy had designed the cruise to train young officers as well as the crew. By and large, the men who served under Downes liked him. He had a sense of humor and demonstrated interest in the welfare of his men. On Christmas Day he provided special theatrical entertainment. The carpenter's yeoman had authored two plays: "Weather Cock" and an afterpiece entitled "Sailor's Fortune." The plays were performed in the evening by some of the crew, and everyone, including officers, had a merry time.

But the inevitable storms, sickness, and short rations got the best of some of the 385 souls onboard. Early in the trip, the captain's clerk, Charles J. Deblois, described his disgust with seafaring life. He declared in his journal, "I am determined should God spare my life & allow me once more to return safe to the land of *Liberty, U.S. America,* never to step foot on board of another Vessel & go to sea while my name is Charles Jarvis Deblois."[15]

By January 1819 Downes had taken his ship around the Horn and was sailing along the Pacific coast of South America. Before leaving Norfolk, Downes had received directions to establish a permanent American presence in this remote corner of the world. After an eight-year campaign, Chile was about to gain independence from Spain, and the United States wanted to set up a consulate to oversee U.S. interests there. Much of the fighting took place in and around the Chilean seaport of Valparaiso and the Peruvian port and royal stronghold at Callao, ports widely used by U.S. mariners. On 28 January, seventy-nine days out of Virginia, the *Macedonian* anchored at Valparaiso.

Downes saw first to the ship's immediate needs, taking on provisions and water and attending to various maintenance chores. The Chileans hosted the officers ashore soon after they arrived. Downes returned the compliment with a Washington's Birthday ball on the ship on 22 February. Gauntt observed that due to much eating and drinking, "many 'Chilanos' found it difficult to preserve equiliborium [*sic*]," and the officers "too carried a heavy press of sail."[16]

Not to be outdone by Downes, the *Macedonian* officers organized their own gala. On 27 February, Deblois was "much engaged with Lt. Percival writing Invitations to Lady Cockrane & a great no. of Ladies & Gentlemen to a ball . . . on board Macedonian." The clerk expected a "first rate Ball."[17] But after writing 150 invitations, he tired of the whole thing and wished the ship were back at sea.

The entertainments introduced Downes and his officers to the influential people of Valparaiso, including Lady Katherine Cochrane, the wife of Adm. Lord Thomas Cochrane, the head of the Chilean navy. The powerful admiral was away at sea and did not attend. Nonetheless, Downes was familiar with the man. The Scottish-born Cochrane had an out-standing reputation as a daring and skillful Royal Navy officer. When he was tossed out of the service in 1814 after being implicated in a private financial scheme, Chile invited him to head its navy. He had arrived there only a few weeks ahead of Downes. Notwithstanding the consider-able interaction between the two men, they did not meet face-to-face until July 1820, six months after Percival had left the ship.

Less than a month after the round of parties, the atmosphere began to change. Percival found himself at the center of a hair-raising experience when, on 12 March, he went horseback riding in the country with several gentlemen. Without provocation, a soldier blocked Percival's way along the route and ran a bayonet into his horse, killing the animal immediately. Although he did not record the incident in the ship's journal he main-tained, Percival did not take the incident calmly. Downes was outraged when he learned of it. He dispatched a letter to the governor of Valparaiso demanding that the offender be punished. He asserted that the attack on one of his officers and the insults directed to other officers of his ship were unprovoked and unreasonable in the extreme. Deblois was not con-fident that satisfaction would be received. "There are no laws here," he noted in his journal. "These Cut throats . . . are the Scrapings of *Hell, Bedlam* & *New Gate* & every other *infernal hole.*"[18]

Downes spent some time surveying harbors and took the ship on a brief cruise to Peru. By the first part of April, when the *Macedonian* returned to Valparaiso, conditions appeared to have improved. Deblois observed, "We do not hear of quite so many murders & robberies . . . as before we sailed." He thought that Downes's protest had "put a stop to their villanies." Percival learned that the soldier who had killed his horse was on trial. Clerk Deblois thought it likely that the trial was "only a sham," but later in the month, the authorities reported that the culprit had "been tried & condemned to be shot & sent to the City for that pur-pose."[19] Deblois remained skeptical: "Whether his sentence will be car-ried into execution, God only knows."[20]

On 3 April, marine Henry Plue absented himself from the ship with-out leave by swimming the half-mile to shore. Downes sent Percival to pursue him. When Percival received intelligence indicating that the fort had given the deserter sanctuary, he hastened there and demanded the return of Plue. The sergeant denied that he was there. Percival threatened to go to the governor. In short order, the locals gave up Plue, and Percival had him back on the ship before evening.

Two weeks later Percival went out on another manhunt. First Lt. John Maury learned from the ship's carpenter, Holbrook, that the Chilean privateer *Andes* was sheltering a *Macedonian* deserter named Foster. A well-armed Lieutenant Percival and several midshipman went after him. Following protocol, they went first to the governor to get permission to search the vessel. With the permission granted, Percival went on board to look for Foster, leaving a boat at the *Andes*'s bow, boats on each side, and two at her stern to prevent his escape.

When Percival climbed on board and demanded Foster, the lieutenant of the *Andes* denied having him or any deserter on his ship. The other Chilean officers told the same story, but Percival did not take their word for it, insisting that he would get his man. Deblois thought the Chileans "a d—d pack of privateersmen." Percival, Deblois added, called them "every thing he could and went into the hold." He searched every nook and cranny for some time, "driving his sword in every part, under cables, water casks, & etc." Finally, he found the "rascal" concealed in the lower hold. The Chileans had nailed down the boards concealing him in a fashion to allow enough space for breathing. Percival shoved his sword through a gap in the boards and "fortunately stuck him in the Leg," prompting Foster "to sing . . . lustily."[21]

After getting his prisoner into one of the boats, Percival demonstrated his fluency in Spanish in a "Tete a Tete with the 1st Lt. & others of the [Chilean] Ship. He d—d them most high & said every thing he could to them & they dare not nor could not say a word." Deblois considered the Chileans consummate villains. "We have been at great trouble in catching this fellow for 4 or 5 days & nights we had midshipmen ashore after him. We have him now hard & fast, buggered in a clink."[22]

Up to this point Deblois seems to have held a high opinion of Percival. When he had trouble with a midshipman, he looked to "my friend Lt. Percival," who was "very friendly & kind," for advice and assistance. Deblois noted in his journal that Percival "is considered one of the best officers in the Ship, he is a great favorite of our Gallant Young Captain."[23]

On 13 May, Percival became acting first lieutenant when John Maury fell ill, and Deblois's opinion suddenly changed. "Lt. P. carries a taught hand, is very tyrannical to the Sailors!" he wrote. "He goes by the name of *Mad Jack*."[24] This is the earliest recorded use of the nickname that would stick with Percival for the rest of his life.

The practice of nicknaming officers may seem odd today, but it was routine at the time. Seamen referred to Hull as "Uncle Isaac." They called Matthew C. Perry "Old Bruin." Many other examples exist. The custom reached its height during the Civil War. Almost every general officer had an additional descriptive name. There was Winfield "Old Fuss and Feathers" Scott, George "Little Mac" McClellan, and "Uncle Robert" E. Lee. Gen. Thomas J. Jackson of the Confederacy remains almost unknown, but "Stonewall" Jackson is a national legend.

Deblois claimed that all hands considered Percival "a first rate Seaman, but a complete Horse." The clerk longed for the return of Maury. Percival, he said, "rows the Reefers in style & flogs the men continually. As long as I have known him, he had been very severe with the Sailors."[25]

At the end of May, the captain's clerk reported that Percival and Lieutenant Tattnall (who eventually rose to the rank of captain in the U.S. Navy) were at odds. Over the course of their careers, the two men would become quite close. Tattnall resigned his commission in 1861 and obtained a captaincy in the Confederate navy, which charged him with the naval defense of Georgia and South Carolina. But in 1819 Percival outranked Tattnall by twenty-eight months, and this matter of seniority was at the root of their continuing conflict on the *Macedonian*.

On 29 May, Downes suspended Mad Jack and ordered him to go below and confine himself to his room after the two men had a hard talk on the deck. Deblois noted: "The principal part of the Midm & all the men is very glad he is suspended. . . . [A]lmost everyone in the Ship hates him & hopes he will remain below." That wish went unfulfilled. Downes and Percival "had a long confab in the Cabin" that night and the lieutenant returned to duty the next morning.[26] Peace seemed to reign by the afternoon, when all the officers went hunting and fishing onshore, but Percival was not satisfied.

Shortly after the disagreement with Tattnall, Percival confided to Deblois his intention to leave the ship. He would never consent to obey the orders of a junior officer, he said, but Downes had ruled that senior officers must follow the orders of a duty officer even if the latter was the junior. Deblois, who seems to have recovered his good opinion of Percival, thought this was "d—d hard and unjust." He "never heard & I doubt there is an Officer on board that ever heard" of an older, veteran officer ordered around by a young junior officer. He thought the situation "Cruel & shameful in the extreme." When Percival leaves, he noted, the ship "will loose a fine officer, a complete seaman & navigator."[27]

Downes took the *Macedonian* up the coast to Mexico but was back at Valparaiso by October, remaining clear of the volatile and suspicious Admiral Cochrane. Both the Spaniards and the rebels resented the neutrality of the United States, which did business with both sides. But Downes thought that the insurgent Cochrane favored British traders while harassing American merchantmen. It was ridiculous, Downes thought, for the head of the rebel Chilean navy to think that he could blockade the greater part of the coast with his small fleet of seven warships.

In November, Downes tested Cochrane's resolve. According to Gauntt, the Chilean admiral had threatened to sink the *Macedonian* if she attempted to enter Callao, the port for Lima, Peru. A gentleman on board the ship later wrote a letter describing the confrontation that appeared in *Niles' Weekly Register*. Captain Downes was reluctant to make a foolhardy move because Cochrane's flagship, the *O'Higgins*, rated a 50, outweighed him. Yet the American skipper was not overawed by Chile's navy. He welcomed a Chilean boarding party to let them "see that we apprehended no danger from his threat." The gentleman correspondent wrote: "The officers and crew were all at quarters, matches lighted and every thing ready for action." He described Downes as determined "to have fought his way, provided his ship would float."[28] Lieutenant Gauntt reported that the decks were sanded and the guns trained, indicating that the *Macedonian* was prepared to fight.

The boarding officers reported back to Cochrane, who was impressed by the Americans' readiness for battle. He made some complimentary remarks about Downes's short passage from the United States and wished the *Macedonian* an agreeable cruise to anchorage in the besieged harbor. The two commanders exchanged correspondence outlining their differing views on international law relative to blockades.

Downes's stance must have intimidated Cochrane. In a few days, the *Macedonian* signaled her intent to pass through the blockade escorting five American and three British merchantmen. Downes cleared the decks and prepared for action as he moved toward the open sea. Tension was high. The blockading Chilean vessels seemed oblivious to the approaching convoy. Then, as the *Macedonian* passed, an *O'Higgins* top man leaned out and doffed his cap in sailor fashion. Cochrane ignored the challenge and avoided hostilities. A few days later Cochrane raised his blockade altogether and moved on, plundering along the coast.

Downes sailed to Panama, arriving there on Christmas Day. On 9 January 1820 he detached Mad Jack from the ship for health reasons and detailed him to bring a number of ailing sailors home. Percival crossed overland to the Chagres River and found passage to Havana. He arrived at Norfolk, Virginia, on 1 March. On 28 March the navy ordered him to duty back at the Boston yard.

Percival arrived in Massachusetts early in April. The time at sea and in the tropics had taken a toll on his health. During his first few weeks at his home base, he suffered from a malarial fever and a liver condition. His health returned, and on 16 June 1821 he showed up to begin the duties of executive officer at Boston, the second-ranking post at the installation. He served in that position for some fourteen months.

John Percival possessed a deep sense of loyalty. Faithfulness to his country would be expected of a navy man, but he exhibited a pronounced degree of faithfulness to his friends as well. And despite occasional differences, he displayed steadfastness to superiors such as Hull and Downes. An early example of this trait occurred shortly after his return to Boston.

As mentioned above, nineteenth-century naval officers found ways to earn money that would be considered wholly unacceptable today. When Decatur captured the *Macedonian* in 1812, for instance, he sold his prize to the U.S. Navy for $100,000. Decatur got $15,000, and his officers and men split the rest. When Downes had this same ship off South America, he entered into a venture that was quite acceptable at the time. In return for a personal fee, he used his public ship as a repository for private money or specie belonging to American merchants in the region. The almost unchecked piracy that flourished during the civil strife was a threat to any merchant who dared carry significant sums on his ship. The navy rationalized that such a service promoted the national economy.

The regulations permitted captains to accept only American specie and to charge no more than 2.5 percent. But Downes was alleged to have accepted British specie and to have charged as much as 6 percent. Another claim asserted that he took $480,000 in American money out of Callao when he left in December 1819. In April 1820 the *Boston Daily*

Advertiser reported that Downes improperly carried $500,000 to Panama for Spanish merchants. Percival felt "called upon as an officer, recently from the Macedonian, to contradict those barefaced assertions, that have not even the shadow of truth for a foundation." According to Percival's letter to the editor on the subject, "there was not one half that amount, and that on account of *Americans*." Such reports "should be received with some doubt, and republished with great caution," he admonished. Mad Jack criticized the British naval captain who made the charge, adding that the Englishman himself had been involved in transporting $3 million in Spanish specie out of Panama. Percival concluded by noting that Downes's "high and deserved popularity may have made him somewhat the object of jealousy," and the allegation "appeared a safe method to aim a shaft at him."[29]

Percival arrived back in Boston from Panama just in time to become a central figure in another unpleasant controversy as well. His involvement centered on his earlier trip to England to promote Baker's Patent Elliptical Pump. He had acted during that trip as agent for the shareholders. Capt. Isaac Hull owned seventy of the five hundred shares. Hull was not particularly pleased with Percival's performance in London. Percival did not write to him for six months, and when he finally did write, the letter was so ambiguous that Hull became angry and told him to sell out and return home. After he got back, Percival charged the company's stockholders $126.83 for travel expenses including $31 for a surtout and pantaloons. Hull rejected the claim, and the two men exchanged harsh words.

At the same time, Lewis Deblois, the yard's purser, questioned the propriety of giving Percival his full service pay of $589 for the time he spent in London. Hull thought precedent entitled Percival to full pay and told him to seek approval from Washington. A Treasury Department official ruled that if Hull considered Percival as attached to the Boston yard during his leave, payment would be proper. Percival thus needed Hull's approval in order to obtain his service pay.

Some weeks later, Percival allegedly discussed the issue with Dr. Samuel Trevett, the yard's surgeon. Percival supposedly told Trevett that he gave up his claim for the $126 in travel expenses in order to get his pay voucher signed, explaining: "In short, I bribed him [Hull]." According to Trevett, Percival cautioned him, "But I tell you this as a brother Mason." In other words, in absolute secrecy.[30]

Hull's refusal to allow his private travel expenses clearly made Percival unhappy. Nor did he soon forgive and forget. He still recalled this dispute when he returned from the Pacific in 1820. And in May 1821 he wrote to his friend Thomas Aspinwall, a native of the Boston suburb of Brookline who had a distinguished military record during the War of 1812 and later served as the U.S. consul in London, "I. H. is a Connecticut man, of course will not let slip an opportunity of getting money. 'Get it honestly *if you can* but *get* money'—Good Lord deliver us from peculators!"[31]

By itself, the lingering disagreement between Hull and Percival was unimportant. But contentiousness was the order of the day in the U.S. Navy. During the War of 1812, the officer corps had increased to more than 1,100, or some 300 percent above the 1801 peace establishment level. After the war and a brief conflict with Algiers, peace again resulted in the unemployment or underemployment of scores of officers. The navy needed reorganization. Just as significant, an outdated and insufficient system of rank held sway. Only three grades existed: lieutenant, master commandant, and captain. The title of commodore was an honorary designation open to misuse. During the war, a number of men were promoted to captain at a relatively young age. And a number of captains who commanded more than one ship at a time thought they were entitled thenceforth to call themselves commodores. Consequently, Boston and other navy stations commonly carried more than one captain and more than one man using the title of commodore. Without an enemy to fight, the officers feuded and squabbled among themselves. Politicking prevailed.

In these conditions, Isaac Hull and William Bainbridge, career rivals, became embroiled in a fierce feud. Percival became a prominent member of the Hull faction. Others, such as Capt. John Shaw, sided with Bainbridge. Linda M. Maloney's biography of Hull, *The Captain from Connecticut*, contains the details;[32] it is sufficient here to say that the unpleasantness began in 1815 and peaked in 1822, and that Percival was right in the middle of it. Secretary of the Navy Smith Thompson sent navy commissioner David Porter to Boston, accompanied by U.S. attorney George Blake, to investigate charges of mismanagement on the part of Hull. The anti-Hull cabal considered Hull's executive officer in Boston, Percival, the key in their effort to get at Hull. In an anonymous and venomous letter they tried to turn Percival against his commandant.

The letter warned that once Porter left, Hull would arrest Percival. If Percival did not join the anti-Hull faction, the letter continued, he would be implicated in the alleged wrongdoing at the yard. Percival disregarded the advice and turned the letter over to Hull.

At the conclusion of his investigation, Porter arrested Lt. Joel Abbot for maliciously conspiring to defame Hull, and advised Hull to arrest Captain Shaw for contemptible, unofficerlike, and ungentlemanly conduct. Hull followed the advice and made the arrest. In Abbot's ensuing trial, Percival set aside his friendship with Abbot and strongly backed Hull. But during the course of the trial the $126 refund to Hull came under scrutiny. Abbot claimed that it amounted to extortion by Hull in return for approving Percival's pay claim. The court dropped the matter when it concluded that the Treasury Department had approved Percival's pay and that he received it some time before he reached his private settlement with Hull.

During the proceedings, the court asked Percival about the anonymous letter he received early in February. He replied: "The purport . . . was to injure Capt. Hull in my estimation. There was some Latin phrases . . . that I could not understand. The advice to me was, to be neutral in this business."[33] Percival also said that he absolved his friend Abbot of involvement with the letter. The court was not as forgiving. After the testimony ended on 6 May, the members of the court took one day to reach a decision. They found Abbot guilty of twenty of the twenty-nine specifications of the main charge as well as parts of four other charges and ordered him suspended for two years. Percival wrote to a friend: "I assure you I was the only Lt. which stuck fast and friendly to Hull in this trying time, notwithstanding all his unkindness to me in my London expedition and on my return. . . . But justice is my motive."[34]

For a few weeks it seemed that the entire affair might be allowed to end with the Abbot trial. Hull remained skeptical. As he expected, the other side did not concede. A newspaper war developed. Abbot appealed to public opinion by publishing a complete transcript of the trial taken down by one of his friends. Hull had no alternative but to request a court of inquiry. Secretary Thompson reluctantly ordered John Rodgers, Isaac Chauncey, and Charles Morris to convene such a court. They came together in Boston on 12 August. Once again, Percival became a key witness and the $126 came under scrutiny.

In mid-October the tribunal rendered its decision. For the most part, Hull was cleared of the charges against him. Percival's leave of absence in London turned out to be an exception. The board criticized Hull for granting Percival a leave to conduct private business in England without obtaining the department's authorization. "But it appears," the court concluded, "there were more than a sufficient number of officers on the station" to attend to business in Percival's absence. And "no injury did, in fact, result to the United States." As for the $126 payment, the court found that the matter "was entirely disconnected" from public business.[35]

After this, Hull knew he had to leave Boston. He wanted sea duty, and he asked Thompson for the Pacific command. On 23 August 1823 Hull left his post to take command of the frigate *United States,* then at Norfolk. Bainbridge arrived the same day to replace him as the Boston yard's commandant. The two antagonists exchanged thirteen-gun salutes, and Hull took his leave, heading for the Gosport Navy Yard in Norfolk. Percival did not want to be far behind.

As soon as he took over, Bainbridge bluntly told Mad Jack to ask the new navy secretary, Samuel Southard, for a transfer. This retribution clearly upset Percival. Mad Jack consulted Hull, who told him to keep steady, do his duty, watch his speech, and have no fear. Hull was working behind the scenes to have his faithful lieutenant transferred to one of the schooners in his Pacific squadron. Before long, Southard transferred Percival to the *United States,* effective 17 September 1823. Since Hull already had Beverly Kennon as the ship's first lieutenant, Percival joined the ship as second lieutenant.

The *Macedonian* disputes and the feuding in Boston demonstrate that quarreling was common in the navy of the early 1800s, as it is in any large organization at just about any time. Mad Jack got into his share of spats; but regardless of the passions of the moment, most of his differences were a passing thing. Despite his hard feelings about the London travel costs, Percival remained a close friend and confidant of Hull. No other officer showed the commodore deeper loyalty. Downes and Percival had their arguments as well, but the air cleared quickly, and the two men were close throughout their lives. Downes, in fact, was probably Percival's closest friend in the service. And Tatnall thought so much of Percival that he later presented him with a handsome engraved silver cup of friendship. Percival's only lasting quarrel involved the Bainbridge clique. Throughout the years, Percival and this group remained bitterly at odds, and the squabble affected his career.

~4~

TRACKING MUTINEERS

I n early December 1823, while he was helping to prepare the *United States* for her Pacific cruise, Percival wrote to Secretary Southard asking for command of the twelve-gun schooner *Dolphin* under Hull. The *Dolphin* was a relatively new ship, built in 1821 as part of a navy program to suppress piracy in the West Indies. Lt. David Conner had her on station. Southard replied that he thought it unlikely that events would lead to the requested assignment. But if the *Dolphin* remained in the Pacific, the secretary was certain that Captain Hull would "place in command . . . the Officer whose rank and services best justify it." He added: "My wish is that the Merchants and others who recommended you may be gratified by your appointment."[1]

In the absence of an outright "no" from the secretary, Percival held on to his hope and went about his work on the *United States*. The department had reactivated the "Old Wagon" for Hull's cruise to the Pacific with directions to protect American commerce in the region and secure respect for the country's flag—a tall order. U.S. commerce was scattered over a vast area, and the western coast of South America remained torn by revolution as Simón Bolívar struggled to break Spain's hold on its New World colonies. Adding to the importance of the mission, in December,

President James Monroe issued the statement advising European powers to cease their colonizing efforts in the American continents that became known as the Monroe Doctrine.

Before sailing, Hull named Percival his first lieutenant. Kennon remained at Norfolk to defend himself in a frivolous court-martial. The *United States* slipped out of Hampton Roads on 5 January 1824 and made Rio de Janeiro in the notable passage of thirty-seven days. After remaining in Rio for a couple of days, she continued southward, rounded the Horn, and anchored at Valparaiso on 27 March, only thirty-nine days out of the Brazilian port. The Americans learned that Spain had recognized Chile's independence, so they moved north to Peru, where the fighting continued.

On 11 April Hull brought the *United States* into Callao. As the ship passed Callao Castle, he ordered a twenty-one-gun salute. The royalist forces manning the castle returned the salute, but with only eighteen guns. Hull immediately sent a detail ashore to find out the reason for such discourtesy. The Spanish quickly made amends by firing three more shots, thereby averting an international incident. Naval officers of the period considered protocol a serious matter, though a few observers such as Herman Melville thought the silly scrapings and bowings it entailed to be "stilted etiquette and childish parade."[2]

Although America professed neutrality regarding Spain's struggles with its colonies, most Americans sympathized with the patriots, associating their cause with the still recent American Revolution. Hull even invited the Liberator to breakfast on board the *United States* on the Fourth of July, and Bolívar expressed great satisfaction with his reception. The Spanish forces, on the other hand, elicited little compassion. Hull's men were hard-pressed to prevent privateers, especially royalist privateers, from seizing and condemning American merchant ships under the guise of combating gunrunning. On one occasion, the crew of the *United States* watched as an armed royalist vessel cowardly made sail and declined to engage a patriot ship. American midshipman Andrew Hull Foote noted that as the Spanish frigate passed, the *United States* was "at quarters, and it would have taken little provocation from her to have been complimented with a broadside from Uncle Isaac."[3]

Hull soon found a way to send Conner home, opening up command of the *Dolphin* for his friend Mad Jack. Effective 30 April 1824, Percival became the skipper, although the ship's log shows him in command as early as 22 April. The *Dolphin*'s first cruise with Percival as her commander was a sail from Callao in concert with the *United States* on 1 May. For a time, Percival was occupied with routine patrol, convoy, and mapping duties. On the night of 25 November he did not hesitate to board the frigate *O'Higgins*, the former flagship of the Chilean patriot navy, to demand a *Dolphin* deserter. A few days later, he took four more *Dolphin* deserters off the French frigate *Maria Teresa*. On 13 December the miscreants paid for their misdeeds. Given the choice of a court-martial or flogging, they elected the cat-o'-nine-tails. Whether the men made the best choice is in question. One seaman reputedly got forty-eight lashes—the most—while one got off with eleven.

A major concern of the Pacific squadron was protecting American whaling interests in the region. At first, Hull had all he could do to protect the American commercial interests along the embroiled coast. He aided whalers only when they were nearby or when they came to him, as the Nantucket whale ship *Lima* did in July 1825. A young man had been seriously injured when a struggling whale stove in his boat, and the U.S. Navy provided the youth with medical care. The young man's father, George Swain, praised Hull warmly for his assistance. In May, however, Hull was forced to pay closer attention to whaling interests when he received orders from the secretary to investigate an alarming incident, one that could not have been news to him; word of mutiny always spread quickly. Hull's small force was busy with other matters and did not respond until August. By the time he set Mad Jack loose to track down the mutineers, the trail was a year and a half old.

On 26 January 1824, only three weeks after the *United States* left Norfolk, a vicious mutiny took place on the Nantucket whaling ship *Globe*. Considered the worst insurrection in the history of American whaling, it occurred in the South Pacific near Fanning Island. Capt. Thomas Worth, twenty-nine years old, left in the *Globe* from Edgartown on Martha's Vineyard late in 1822. He worked the Japan grounds without great success and after a year put in at Oahu. While at the Sandwich Islands, six of the crew deserted and Worth discharged another man. Unable to be too selective, Worth picked six men from the derelicts and malcontents on shore to replace them.

Samuel B. Comstock, twenty years old, a regular member of the crew and one of the *Globe's* two boatsteerers, led the mutiny. He had the reputation of a troublemaker. The third mate, twenty-year-old Nathaniel

Fisher, once thrashed Comstock when the latter lost his temper during a supposedly good-natured wrestling match between the two, and Comstock vowed revenge.

One of the rogues taken on at Oahu provided the spark that set the mutiny in motion. The man was Joseph Thomas of Norwich, Connecticut. Just hours before the uprising, Thomas offended Captain Worth by being tardy in obeying an order of the second mate, John Lumbert. He compounded the offense by being insolent in the process. Worth advised Thomas that if he did not step livelier when ordered, "I will knock you to hell." Thomas snapped, "You will pay for it if you do." In a flash, Worth grabbed Thomas "by the scruff of his jacket and smacked him on both sides of the face."[4] A sullen crew looked on.

Comstock saw an opportunity in this exchange to gain his revenge on the ship's officers. He added Thomas to his band of conspirators, which already included Silas Payne, William Humphries, Thomas Lilliston, and John Oliver—all Oahu replacements. The group got together and began plotting a midnight mutiny. Worth was about to pay for it.

Once the ship settled down to the quiet routine of night, Comstock silently moved aft, past the helm where his bewildered fifteen-year-old brother George stood. He found the captain asleep, and with one blow of an ax crushed Worth's skull. He then raced to help Payne overcome the first mate, Bill Beetle. After a ferocious struggle, the two mutineers fractured Beetle's skull and dispatched him with fatal blows from an ax and a boarding knife.

Comstock grabbed a pair of muskets with bayonets and went after Lumbert and Fisher, who were hiding in their cabin. Oliver and Humphries stood outside the door to prevent their escape. Comstock fired a shot into the room that struck Fisher in the mouth. Sensing success, Comstock crashed into the cabin and attacked the two mates. In the struggle, the murderous boatsteerer lost his weapon to Fisher. The close quarters impaired co-conspirators Oliver and Humphries.

Fisher actually had control of the ship at this point, but did not realize that in subduing Comstock and the others he had effectively halted the mutiny. Comstock played his last card. He boldly deceived Fisher, convincing him that the mutiny was broad-based and the ship was completely in his hands. After being assured that Comstock would spare his life, Fisher returned the gun to him. In a flash, Comstock wheeled and bayoneted Lumbert several times. Fisher, realizing that he was doomed, sighed, "If there is no hope, I will at least die like a man! *I am ready*!!"[5] Comstock put the muzzle to Fisher's head and blew out his brains.

Lumbert remained alive, and Comstock repeatedly plunged the bayonet into the mate's trembling body, screaming his hatred. He then had the two officers carried on deck and pitched over the side. Remarkably, Lumbert grabbed hold of the plank sheer and clung to the boat. Comstock sadistically completed his revenge by stomping on the mate's fingers and breaking his grip. When last seen, the tenacious Lumbert was swimming after the ship.

Now in command, Sam Comstock steered for the Mulgraves. Within three days he began to suspect that Humphries was planning a counterplot. He restrained Humphries and ordered him hanged. Before carrying out the execution, Comstock gave Humphries an opportunity to speak. "Little did I think I was born to come to this," Humphries responded.[6]

Two weeks later the men of the *Globe* went ashore at Mili, the principal islet in the atoll. Comstock schemed to burn the ship and establish a hideout on the atoll. Just three days after the landing, while the crew were busy removing supplies from the *Globe*, Payne quarreled with Comstock, accusing him of plotting with the natives to annihilate the entire crew and set himself up as a lone and innocent shipwreck survivor. Payne acted on his suspicions and, assisted by three others, shot and killed Comstock as he returned from a visit to the native village.

Payne, aided by Oliver, now took charge. The pair soon became careless. Unaware that harpooner Gilbert Smith had conspired to overturn the mutiny from the outset, Payne placed him in charge of the ship on the evening of 17 February. Smith and five others—George Comstock, Stephen Kidder, Peter Kidder, Joseph Thomas, and Anthony Hanson—went out to the vessel while the rest of the men remained on shore carousing. Payne had taken the precaution of removing all of the ship's compasses, or so he thought; one remained on board.

Smith did not trust Thomas and Hanson, who had not been included in his secret plans. Young William Lay and Cyrus Hussey *were* part of his plot, but Payne had kept them on shore that evening. Smith waited as long as he could for the pair to make their way to the ship, but a few minutes past 9:00 P.M. the moon was about to rise, and it was too dangerous to wait any longer. Without Lay and Hussey, Smith cleared the undermanned ship and stood to the east. Though Smith did not have a skilled navigator onboard, he hoped to reach Chile—and so he did, arriving at

Valparaiso on 7 June 1824. Word of the tragedy reached Nantucket in October, and Smith and his crew arrived home in November.

The whaling interests of Nantucket wasted little time in urging the U.S. government to act. In December, William Coffin and 136 others petitioned the president to capture and punish the mutineers and strengthen the U.S. naval force in the Pacific to discourage future outrages of this nature. As Massachusetts's native son John Quincy Adams prepared to head the government early in 1825, Aaron Mitchell and forty-three others from Nantucket dispatched another memorial to the White House. This petition emphasized the importance of the Sandwich Islands as a base of whaling operations and the need to mitigate the restrictions the islands' rulers had placed on their industry. The appeal also noted the existence of more than 150 destitute and lawless deserters there. If the president failed to act, the Nantucket men warned, the islands would become a haven for criminals and pirates. Secretary Southard replied to Mitchell, informing him that Captain Hull would be told to visit the Sandwich Islands as soon as possible. Southard forwarded Mitchell's petition to the Pacific station, as he had Coffin's earlier plea, and ordered Hull to proceed when appropriate in the *United States*.

Not to be outdone by Nantucket, a group of New Bedford whalers led by Gideon Howland petitioned Washington as well. Their memorial informed the president of a popular belief among the Pacific natives that the British had men-of-war to guard their commerce, but the Americans had only merchantmen and whalers—a misconception that could be dangerous to U.S. commerce in the Pacific. Late in May, Southard forwarded the New Bedford communication to Hull along with more specific and urgent instructions to visit the Sandwich Islands and deal with any problems there.

The last communiqué reached the *United States* while she and the *Dolphin* were lying at Chorrillos, just south of Callao and Lima. The department granted Hull the discretion to send one of his smaller vessels on the mission if he elected to do so. On 10 August 1825 Hull asked Percival for an estimate of his needs for such an undertaking. Percival replied that he could sail with sixty-seven men and provisions for six months. On 14 August, Hull concurred with the estimates and told his lieutenant to lose no time in his preparations.

The commodore directed Percival to proceed to the Mulgraves in search of the mutineers, and if he found them to "use such measures as to you may appear best calculated to get them on board your vessel, and to secure them, preferring a mild and friendly course as regards the natives." The specific details he left to Percival's "discretion and good judgement." After providing all the information he had on the culprits, Hull instructed Percival to touch at the Sandwich Islands on the return leg if his provisions allowed it. While there, he was to assess the local government's feelings toward the United States and learn "whether the same privileges are granted to vessels of the United States as to those of other nations." And since the natives owed Americans considerable money, Percival was told to ascertain whether payment could be anticipated. Hull also instructed Percival to contact a Mr. Stewart, a respected and well-informed resident who could be expected to provide useful intelligence. As well, Stewart might have collected plants, seeds, or roots destined for the United States. Hull added that Percival himself should make it a practice to collect worthwhile seeds, plants, vines, and minerals at every stop. "Indeed," he told him, "it is desirable to make your cruise useful independent of the great object for which you are dispatched."[7]

Considerable competition developed among the officers for a place on the *Dolphin*. Lt. Hiram Paulding, twenty-seven years old, secured the coveted first lieutenant's slot. The total crew amounted to seventy men. Percival told his purser, John A. Bates, to purchase a quantity of small articles to be used as presents for the natives they would encounter along the way. The items, personally charged to Mad Jack, included jewelry, ornaments, beads, handkerchiefs, combs, knives, and cottons. Percival added to his store of gifts by purchasing calicoes and fishhooks on his own.

On 18 August the *Dolphin* set sail. The need for haste had prevented Percival from gathering all of the provisions he wanted; nonetheless, he set out with spirited enthusiasm, determined to pick up the missing items along the way. The ship sailed north along the Peruvian coast, touching at Casma, Santa, and Huanchaco. The men found little in the way of supplies until they reached Paita on 26 August. At some expense, Percival filled the deck with livestock and vegtables. He also procured a good supply of water. On 2 September he shaped a northwesterly course into the Pacific.

Percival made his way to the Galápagos Islands, six hundred miles west of the South American coast. After touching there, he set a course for the west-southwest and the Marquesas Islands and then on to Caroline Island. Late in October the *Dolphin* made Duke of Clarence Island, a small group of two-dozen islets located north of Western Samoa. Here the Americans had their first encounter with natives.

When the schooner reached shoal water, Percival sent a boat ahead to take soundings. According to Hiram Paulding's account, a swarm of canoes, "nearly a hundred," came from the shore and encircled the sounding boat. In each of the two closest canoes, a native stood up "with a barbed spear, which he held in the attitude of throwing." The American boatmen discharged their pistols, intending only to scare the natives; however, an errant shot hit one of them. "Seeing the blood flow from the hand of their countryman" and alarmed by the noise, the islanders "discontinued their assault, and retired with precipitation."[8] After this undiplomatic start to relations, the Americans were able to meet with the suspicious natives, but they could not obtain water. A lone canoeist shadowed the *Dolphin* as she continued probing the coastline.

The vessel paused at nearby Duke of York Island and moved on to the island of Byron (Nikunau), arriving there on 9 November. Canoes assembled in great numbers, Paulding noted, "and as soon as we anchored, came along side, the people jumping on board without the least hesitation, talking and hallooing to each other so loud, as almost to deafen us with their noise."[9] Before long, it became apparent that the natives were unabashed thieves. Midn. Charles Henry Davis reported that they swaggered aggressively about the deck armed with shark's-tooth spears and did not leave until sundown.

At daybreak, the natives arrived back on board for a repeat performance. "We were at length," wrote Paulding, "obliged to resort to some little violence to clear the decks of the unruly rabble, whose disposition to thievery and violence became every moment more difficult to repress."[10] When an elderly but athletic chief forcefully embraced Percival and refused to let go, the *Dolphin*'s men passed the bight of a rope around the man's neck and choked him until he loosened his grasp. Then the sailors pitched him overboard. This firm show of force cleared the deck. Paulding commented, "The captain having enough of Indian courtesy, was well pleased to dismiss them."[11]

The *Dolphin* still required water, but when Mad Jack took a boat and attempted to land, the now-hostile natives would not allow it. They first tried to drag the boat onshore, but when American firearms again drew blood, the aborigines gave up and the boat returned to the ship. "Only the great coolness and tact of Captain Percival," wrote Davis, "saved the boat's crew from destruction at the hands of the savages."[12]

Although a number of natives still remained on board, Percival ordered the *Dolphin* to get under way. The crew got one anchor up, but the second hooked on a coral rock. Taking the forward sentinel's musket, Mad Jack directed him to lend a hand to free the embedded anchor. An islander who had been talking to Percival grabbed the musket, which was fixed with a bayonet, and jumped into the water. Prodded by a liberal shower of lead, the thief made his way to land and disappeared into a thicket. As might be expected, Percival revoked the order to get under way and manned several boats. He would have his musket back and teach the local miscreants a lesson. While he was at it, he might find fresh water, too.

Percival landed the lead boat on a reef. Unfortunately, the thundering surf ruined the men's gunpowder. Worse yet, as they attempted to shove the boat back off, the waves dashed it to pieces. Percival ordered the other boats to stay away, electing to remain in his defenseless situation on the reef. Even hostile savages could not force him to risk losing the rest of his boats.

He led his boat crew through three feet of water to the beach and by prearranged signals directed the *Dolphin*'s gunners as they bombarded what appeared to be the chief's hut. At length, a group of natives came down to the water's edge. Using sign language, Mad Jack demanded the return of his musket. In about an hour the weapon was returned, but without its lock or bayonet. Percival demanded these as well, emphasizing his gestures with another barrage of the schooner's guns onto the hut. After a short wait a native returned the lock, but nothing could induce them to surrender the bayonet.

Percival and his crew, forced to withdraw to a hundred-yard-wide bank of coral, found themselves in a perilous situation. Small bands of islanders sallied out and stoned them. Without dry powder, the hard-pressed Americans had to rely on the *Dolphin*'s guns for protection. The hustle of shot and the shattering of coconut trees made an impression, and the natives backed off. Percival became impatient. He moved back onto the island to demonstrate confidence and boldness—and, perhaps, to find a source of water. Followed by his men, Mad Jack stormed inland as the natives retreated before him. After an uneventful hour-long march into the interior, the group returned to the reef without encountering the islanders or finding fresh water.

With nightfall rapidly approaching, Paulding anxiously paced the *Dolphin*'s deck. As soon as his commander reappeared on the shore, the first lieutenant sent a boat manned by two able swimmers to pick up the party. After a lengthy and difficult struggle, the boat made its way back to the ship with the entire crew. In short order, the *Dolphin* "bade adieu to Byron's Island and its inhabitants, whose acquaintance had been productive of little but perplexity and anxiety."[13]

At last, on 19 November, the schooner made the Mulgrave Islands. George Comstock identified the site of the mutineers' encampment, and Percival prepared for a meticulous search. Still plagued by a water shortage, he first sent a detail in quest of this critical need. The crewmen not only found water but also encountered natives who seemed friendly and hospitable. In no time a searcher found a whaler's lance. Now the Americans had more to go on than young Comstock's memory.

The Mulgraves, known today as the Marshall Islands, comprise a thirty-mile-long chain of 102 islets in the west-central Pacific. Percival intended to check every one of them until he found the mutineers. He sent Paulding out in a boat to examine each island while he followed offshore in the *Dolphin*. The process proceeded for several days, hopping from islet to islet, repeatedly spurred by discoveries of items unmistakably from the *Globe*. On 23 November the searchers arrived at a well-inhabited island, unaware that one member of the ill-fated whaler was held captive in a hut there. William Lay later described how the hooting and yelling of the natives awakened him. A ship had anchored at the head of the island. The natives were alarmed while Lay dared to hope. The natives consulted their god, who approved their planned response.

The islanders developed a straightforward plot. They would swim out to the ship a few at a time. When two hundred of them were on board, a signal would be given and they would kill the crew and throw them into the water. The natives readied two large canoes capable of carrying fifty men each. Lay tricked the chief into allowing him to accompany the warriors by declaring that he could not speak the language of the strangers. He knew they were from a different country, he told the chief, because their ship had fewer masts than the *Globe*.

During the night, about two hundred natives massed within a couple of miles of the *Dolphin*. The following forenoon turned squally, so the islanders sat tight. Before long, the visiting vessel moved closer. In the afternoon Percival left for shore in the first cutter. He returned to the ship two hours later after finding whaleboat oars, blue canvas, and other evidence of the mutineers' presence. Such boldness gave the natives pause, and during the second night they fled to a distant islet some forty miles away, taking Lay with them. Lay's fear and disappointment were indescribable.

Over the next few days, the Americans continued to find unequivocal proof that they were getting close. Evidence was all about them. The searchers considered a mitten marked with the initials of Rowland Coffin, a member of the *Globe*'s crew, a key find. On 29 November the navy men reached the islet where the natives holding Lay were hiding.

The *Dolphin*'s logbook indicates that a search team found a skeleton, possibly the remains of Comstock, before they were confronted by a sizable line of threatening natives. The Americans withdrew into a defensive position, but their rain-soaked powder made it necessary to rely on bayonets and cutlasses. Two messengers raced back to the *Dolphin* to report. Percival acted on his growing suspicions. While the Milians had not been especially helpful up to now, this was their first aggressive behavior. Mad Jack organized a well-armed party of fifteen to relieve the threatened crewmen and sent it out under Paulding.

Meanwhile, the natives once again made plans to overcome their visitors. They again consulted their deity, and they conferred with Lay, who thought it advisable to offer to assist in their plot. He assured the head chief that he could deceive the strangers so they would let down their guard. The chief accepted Lay's proposition. Lay hid his joy. He moved to the beach along with about one hundred of the most able-bodied natives. He convinced the band to remain friendly and agreeable until he gave the word. When they reached a spot about fifty-five yards from the shoreline Lay told the warriors to sit down and wait. He stepped down to the edge of the water and shouted to Paulding: "Don't come on shore unless you are prepared to fight. The islanders are going to kill you."[14]

It was immediately obvious to Paulding that this was one of the *Globe*'s crew. He had a wild appearance: his hair tied in a knot on the top of his head, a mat loincloth, and tanned skin. Paulding reported, "I asked his name, which he told me was William Lay and that he was one of the crew of the Globe." Paulding told Lay to come to the boat. Lay did not move, saying he was afraid of the natives. Paulding told him to make a run for it. When Lay remained frozen with fear, Paulding responded decisively. He ordered his men to fire, reload their pistols, and follow him onto the beach. When the charging sailors drew near, Lay ran to the lieutenant. Paulding put his pistol to Lay's chest and asked: "Who are you?" A tearful Lay replied: "I am your man."[15]

The natives, meanwhile, remained immobile. Paulding instructed Lay to tell them that if they rose from their seats or threw stones, they would be shot. One elder ignored the advice. The man, in a sense, had adopted Lay, and he came down to get his boy back. Paulding cut short the discussion and, waving his pistol at the natives, got Lay on board the boat. Midshipman Davis, who like Paulding would one day rise to the rank of rear admiral, called the operation "the boldest act" he "ever witnessed."[16]

As the rescue boat moved away from the shore, the effusive Lay indicated that only one other *Globe* crewman remained alive. Cyrus Hussey, he said, could be found on a nearby islet. Paulding had his crew pull for the place at once in order to beat any native messenger. The swift move took the natives by surprise, and Lay identified the chief named Lugoma who held Hussey as his boy. Paulding got right to the point. He grabbed the chief and threatened to kill him unless the islanders produced their young captive. In a few minutes Hussey appeared, his yellow hair hanging in ringlets. Paulding said: "Well, young man, do you wish to return to your country?" Hussey's eyes filled with tears as he replied: "Yes, sir, I know of nothing that I have done for which I should be afraid to go home."[17] With deep emotion, Hussey bid farewell to his "father" and the rest of the natives with whom he had lived for the past months. Lugoma pleaded with Hussey to promise to return. Paulding suggested it would be up to Hussey's mother. Lugoma understood.

Once on the *Dolphin*, the captain outfitted the two young men and had them shaved and given haircuts. "Our joy and happiness on finding ourselves on board an *American Man-of-War*," they recalled, "and seeing 'the star spangled banner' once more floating in the air, we will not attempt to describe."[18] In 1828 Lay and Hussey published a narrative of their experiences dedicated "To John Percival, Esq. of the U.S. Navy."

Percival took down the two men's initial account shortly after they arrived on board the *Dolphin*. The pair described the fates of the seven other whalers left in the Mulgraves after Smith and his band escaped in the *Globe*. Payne and Oliver provoked the islanders by mistreating one

of their women. And the natives infuriated Payne by stealing his hatchet
and two chisels. Roland Jones was stoned to death while attempting to
recover the tools. The islanders took control of the remaining whaling
men and dispersed them among the different islets. In short order, six
were killed. Lay and Hussey were spared because of their youth and
their good deportment. Lay thought the reprieve would be a short one.
"Knowing that many of the natives inhabiting the Islands in the Pacific
Ocean are cannibals," he wrote, "we were not without fears that we had
been preserved to grace a feast."[19]

Hull forwarded Percival's 7 December 1825 report on the recovery to
the secretary on 2 April 1826. Months passed before it reached Washington. The first news of the *Dolphin*'s success reached Nantucket by way
of Canton, China, on 26 August. A subsequent item in the *Nantucket
Inquirer* mentioned survivors. A week later, a Boston paper said there
were only two or three survivors. On 21 October the *Inquirer* reported
that the returning whale ship *Loper* had encountered the *Dolphin* at
Tahiti, and that there were two survivors. A week later, the Nantucket
paper printed a letter from the American consul at Valparaiso dated 30
July 1826. Consul Hogan said the *Dolphin* arrived on 23 July with Lay
and Hussey, and that both young men were in fine shape. For the first
time, Nantucket learned the complete details of the tragedy.

Years later, Nantucket historian Edouard Stackpole asserted that this
leg of the *Dolphin*'s cruise embellished the U.S. Navy's reputation. Historian Linda McKee believes that Percival and his crew deserve credit
for the fact that the *Globe* mutiny was not repeated in the American
Pacific whale fishery.

Although Percival had accomplished the primary goal of his mission, he
was not through with the Mulgraves. The primary goals of the Pacific
squadron were to protect American shipping and to secure respect for
the U.S. flag. Percival determined to address these points with the local
authorities. On 30 November he hiked to the opposite side of one of the
principal islets, where, with Lay as his interpreter, he had a meeting with
a prominent woman. But he wanted to talk to the leading men. Since
they were absent and were not due back until the morrow, Percival indicated that he would return to see them the next day.

The chiefs did not show the next day, and it was clear to Percival that
they were avoiding him. Mad Jack began to show signs of irritation. He

told the natives on hand that he would wait one more day. If the men were not there when he returned, he would turn to coercive measures. The morning came, and the islanders sent word that the chiefs were available to parley. Percival took Lay and Hussey along and headed for the village. When they arrived, the chiefs were not there. According to Lay and Hussey's account of events, Percival was "very much displeased at this perfidious treatment," and he issued a threat to the natives. If the chiefs were not there by sunset, he would return "with fifty men, well armed, and destroy every person he could find." The ultimatum "threw the natives into a consternation," and they quickly dispatched a messenger to fetch the chiefs. "The natives were so alarmed, that they soon sent off three or four more messengers." The Americans returned to their ship to dine.[20]

Early the next morning, Lay returned to the settlement and found the chiefs present. Lay told them that Percival would come on shore soon to talk to them. Mad Jack later explained that all he had wanted to do was commend the islanders for sparing Lay and Hussey. "I felt it a duty," he wrote, "as well as good policy, to give them substantial proofs of my approbation of their conduct, to induce them to treat any others who might by misfortune be thrown on their islands, with humanity and protection."[21]

Once he got all the native leaders together, Percival explained that his "*Head Chief,*" the president, had told him to look for the men left on their islands by the *Globe.* He took note of the fact that they had murdered all but Lay and Hussey, but "as it was their first offence of the kind, their ignorance would plead excuse." However, if they "should ever kill or injure another white man," Percival warned, the United States "would send a naval force, and exterminate every soul on the Island; and also destroy their fruit trees."[22] He continued to lecture the chieftains, discussing at some length their proclivities for lying, stealing, and general immorality. Having made his main points, Percival altered the tenor of the conference by handing out gifts, including three tomahawks, one ax, a bag of beads, and some cotton handkerchiefs. Two hogs and a pair of cats were released, with instructions to the natives to care for them so that they might multiply. Potatoes, pumpkins, and the like were planted, and guidance for their care provided as well. A few years later, Percival explained his philosophy of island diplomacy to Secretary of the Navy Levi Woodward: "The articles . . . were always given as presents from the

President of the United States, and in conformity with an ancient and universal usage; coeval with the discovery of the islands, and practised by all navigators."[23]

Throughout the ensuing week, the men of the *Dolphin* devoted time to the natural science component of their mission. The officers led a scientific survey of the islands. In the process they uncovered the remains of Samuel Comstock and his cutlass. The men also did what they could to gather fresh stores. Percival and Lay visited the nearby village of Alloo and presented gifts to the inhabitants. The commander had to make a special trip to Mili to rescue the ship's carpenter, who had been sent there to help the natives repair a canoe. The carpenter's work proved so satisfactory that the islanders were reluctant to let him depart on his own.

During the *Dolphin's* time in the Mulgrave Islands, the ship's surgeon died. Percival conducted a military funeral on shore and marked the grave with an inscribed metal plate nailed to a tree trunk. At Percival's request, the high chief made the site taboo. In 1872 the USS *Narragansett* found the grave in good order, and the taboo still in place.

Before leaving the islands, Percival went onshore to say farewell. He returned to the ship with the high chief and two of the chief's aides. Mad Jack told the chief he would fire a demonstration round from one of the cannons if the chief was not afraid. The chief confessed that he did not want to hear it. Feeling it the least he could do for his distinguished visitor, Percival gave orders to beat to quarters and demonstrated the American manner of fighting. Lay and Hussey observed: "Those untutored children of nature, seemed highly gratified with the manoeuvres, but were most delighted with the music, probably the first of the kind they ever heard."[24] For their part, the natives gave the *tamon*, or high chief, as they called Percival, a number of presents, mostly mats. On the following day, 9 December, the *Dolphin* weighed anchor and left the Mulgraves. The principal chief's son pleaded with Percival to be allowed to ship on the *Dolphin*, but the captain refused him.

Two days later the schooner made land to the northwest. Percival, accompanied by Hussey, took the gig through the surf to the beach. Before going up to the local village, he instructed his interpreter not to reveal his knowledge of the native tongue until given the word. The headman treated him civilly but clearly wanted him to leave. Percival played his trump card and told Hussey to use the native language. The chief was surprised but composed himself enough to hear Percival's lecture about the dangers of harming white seamen who might find themselves on his island. Mad Jack emphasized the benefits of friendly relationships by giving the tamon an ax, and then, shrewd Yankee that he was, bartered for coconuts and fruit with beads and handkerchiefs before returning to the schooner.

On 12 December the lookout sighted another island. Percival took one boat, Paulding took another, and the two officers set out to explore the area and add to their provisions. Percival came back with seventy-three pineapples and fifty-four coconuts. Paulding added to the harvest; between them, they collected two hundred coconuts. Happy as he was about the addition to the ship's stores, Percival was happier to find water sufficient for a ship of the line.

Less than a month later, after much stormy weather, the *Dolphin* approached the Sandwich Islands. The passage had been difficult for Percival. Three days before Christmas, after clearing the main boom, he jumped from the trunk and sustained a double hernia. He put up with it, but the injury would bother him more and more as time went by. As a result, in 1837 he applied for and received a retroactive disability pension of $12.50 a month.

Initially, the ship put in at Bird Island, an uninhabited islet of 155 acres. Percival and half a dozen others went ashore to fish. A squall with high winds blew in, and the party was forced to pass the night on the island. They sought shelter in a cavern at the water's edge, but the rising tide drove them out onto the beach. Thoroughly soaked by the rain, the men made their way inland to a drier cave.

The weather had subsided enough by the next morning to attempt a return to the *Dolphin*. But the elements would not give up easily. The storm had left behind large swells, and the thundering breakers smashed his boat. Five of the men swam for the ship and made it while Mad Jack helped a nonswimmer back to the beach. Paulding rigged a breeches buoy and brought the stranded pair through the surf to the safety of the schooner. Their injured captain's concern for one of his men did not go unnoticed by the crew.

Percival wasted little time in getting under way, and on Sunday, 15 January 1826, the *Dolphin* was "standing in for the harbor of woahoo [Oahu]." The ship's log indicates that "the shipping in the harbor saluted" the *Dolphin*, which "returned the Salutes of the merchant ships with 10 guns."[25] In addition to being the first U.S. Navy man-of-war to visit the Mulgraves, the eighty-eight-foot *Dolphin* was the first to put in at a Hawaiian port. A few observers wrongly grant the distinction to Lt. John Gamble of the U.S. Marine Corps and the *Sir Andrew Hammond*. In 1814 Capt. David Porter captured the *Hammond*, a twelve-gun British merchantman. He put the vessel under prize master Gamble and sent her into Honolulu on 23 May 1814. She remained there for three weeks undergoing much-needed repairs. Two days after leaving her refuge, her short American career came to an end when HMS *Cherub* recovered her for the British. Most authorities do not consider the *Hammond*'s visit that of a U.S. warship.

As he brought his ship into port, Percival had no way of knowing that his difficulties up to this point would resemble a picnic compared to what was in store for him at the Sandwich Islands. Grasping traders, zealous missionaries, brawling whalers, and enchanting women were on hand. Adding an ailing Mad Jack Percival to the mix created the potential for fireworks.

❧ 5 ☙

TROUBLE IN PARADISE

*T*he mixed welcome accorded the *Dolphin* when she arrived at Honolulu on Sunday, 15 January 1826, was an omen of what was to come. The log entry for that date reads: "Standing in for the harbor of woahoo, the shipping in the harbor saluted us."[1] The *Dolphin* returned the salutes of the merchant ships with ten guns. The local authorities were not so welcoming, however, when they were contacted to arrange an exchange of salutes. "That is a secular service," they asserted. "We keep sacred the Sabbath, and observe the Word of God."[2] Moreover, personnel from the American Board of Commissioners for Foreign Missions failed to show up at the waterfront and extend the customary greetings to their countrymen.

Mad Jack pondered the correct response to the authorities' message. Hull's written orders for the visit to the Sandwich Islands included the instruction to ascertain whether U.S. vessels visiting the islands were granted the same privileges given to ships of other countries. He knew the islanders had promptly returned Lord Byron's salute in good style when he entered the same harbor in HMS *Blonde* the previous May. Moreover, the fort had saluted the Briton again when he stepped ashore. With this in mind, Percival went ahead and fired a twenty-one-gun salute, "the return of which by permission of the Capt. at the request of

the High Chief was postponed in consequence of the religion ceremonies of the day." The ship's log for Monday the sixteenth notes: "At 9
the Governor saluted us with 20 guns as a return for our yesterdays
salute."[3]

Despite their aversion to cannonading on the Lord's Day, the natives
"could not sufficiently express their gratification at seeing us," noted
Paulding in his journal. "They continued to feast and give us parties every
day for more than a week and until our various and pressing duties made
it inconvenient for us to partake of them."[4] The round of parties included
one on Tuesday aboard the *Dolphin* sponsored by Percival. The missionaries and their patron chiefs declined to attend. The only native of note
in attendance was Boki, the governor of Oahu, who was a great deal more
worldly than the usual islander. Boki had accompanied King Kamehameha II to England in 1824, and his firsthand observations of a less
than exemplary Christian country left him with a properly balanced view
of religion. He resisted the missionaries' efforts to convert him to the
Congregation, maintaining that he was a confirmed member of the
Church of England. He attended Percival's fête dressed in a British major
general's uniform and struck up an immediate friendship with the American officers. When the formalities ended, Percival brought the *Dolphin*
up for repairs. The officers found lodging in town while the crew took up
temporary quarters in another vessel.

When Percival arrived, the islands were in the midst of a constitutional crisis of sorts. A month earlier, the leaders of Hawaii had convened to consider a proposal submitted by the head missionary, Hiram
Bingham, a thirty-seven-year-old Vermonter nicknamed the "Pope"
because of his zeal. Bingham wanted the Hawaiians to adopt the Deca-
logue, or Ten Commandments, as the law of the islands. Kalanimoku,
also known as "Billy Pitt," and his sister Kaahumanu, the dowager
queen, favored the plan. The pair had a great deal of power because
they were the regents for the youthful King Kamehameha III. Their
brother Boki opposed the idea, as did the foreign merchants. Boki
feared that the proposition would give the puritanical Bingham control
of the government.

Boki approached Mad Jack about the matter. Did the U.S. government really send the missionaries to Hawaii to govern local affairs? he
asked. No, answered Percival; it is inconsistent with American policy to
interfere in the civil institutions of any people. There must be a mistake

or misunderstanding, he said. Boki insisted that the missionaries claimed to be agents of the American government. Percival sensed a serious problem here. He determined to remain aloof from the controversy while taking any opportunity to close the breach between the missionaries and the other foreigners.

On his visit to the islands in the *Blonde* in May 1825, Lord George Byron had also noticed that Bingham was an inveterate meddler in public affairs. He intruded in every kind of business, from foreign affairs to local amusements. The British were concerned that Bingham's pervasive intrusion was promoting American interests in the islands over theirs. His profound influence throughout the Sandwich Islands was a serious threat to the aspirations of Great Britain. Ever since an Englishman, Capt. James Cook, had discovered the islands, Great Britain had considered itself their protector. American domination of trade in the region would undermine that relationship—and Britain's power. But the sharp practices of some American traders alienated many islanders, and the native rulers continued to look to London for traditional assurances.

Two years before the *Dolphin* arrived in the islands, King Kamehameha II, Queen Kamamalu, and Boki had traveled to England hoping to obtain a place in the British sphere. Tragically, both the king and queen succumbed to measles in London. The British dispatched Byron to carry the bodies back to Honolulu. Lord Byron participated in the coronation of the succeeding king, Kamehameha III. After going through the august rite, Byron turned to the populace and, brandishing his sword, admonished the people to obey the king.

Byron determined during his visit that the activities of Bingham and his associates went well beyond propagation of the faith. Percival reached the same conclusion soon after his arrival. At the outset, Percival tried to promote harmonious relations with the missionaries, most of whom were fellow New Englanders. His men knew that "he always desired . . . when they went ashore [on Sundays] to go to church first and behave decently and then go and have their frolic."[5] John Newberry, the *Dolphin*'s steward, remembered that his commander gave the missionaries several dozen bottles of wine, but the goodwill gesture was not returned. The secular agent of the mission, Levi Chamberlain, later claimed that the American commander even advised the Hawaiians to pay attention to the missionaries' instruction. Even Rev. William Richards admitted that Percival treated the missionaries with tolerable politeness.

Toward the end of January, however, Percival's resolve to promote good relations with the mission began to break down when Percival and Bingham entered into a discussion about the mission's jurisdiction. Percival thought the mission's policy should be a gradual effort at civilizing the natives, and that the missionaries should proceed slowly with instituting the Mosaic Code. He criticized Bingham for deceiving Boki into believing that the mission represented the United States. Bingham responded that his authority was indeed backed by the U.S. government: the Massachusetts legislature in 1812 had sanctioned the general object of the American Mission Board, namely, to propagate the Gospel in heathen lands. Since the American system is a constitutional government, he rationalized, the charter awarded by Massachusetts represented a grant of legislative power. Percival scoffed at such sophistry. Thereafter, Bingham avoided the man whom he had hoped would be a moral influence for good while ignoring the mission's involvement with local government. Percival tried to keep up the appearance of amity. He directed crewmembers who were on shore on Sundays to attend church. From time to time, he went to Sunday meetings himself.

Nevertheless, the stage had been set. Fundamental and irreconcilable differences had been exposed. It was only a matter of time before the differences became outright hostility. Only one person on the island possessed any degree of legitimate American governmental authority, and that person was John Percival. Authority, to be effective, relies heavily on prestige. And prestige—and therefore authority—is weakened when the person holding the warrant or prerogative allows another to usurp his power. Percival was not about to permit a missionary to encroach on his official primacy, and rightly so.

Another factor, however, carried more weight with Percival than the mission's usurpation of his authority. He did not approve of the mission's activities in the islands. His relationship with and reaction to the American Mission Board's missionaries, the subject of much titillating twentieth-century commentary, is explained to a great extent by his heritage. The settlers of Cape Cod, including his forebears, from the outset resisted the restraints and rigors of Puritanism. Many Cape Codders became dissatisfied with the church and angry at church authorities who fined them for religious offenses such as failing to attend public worship. Over time, the independent element prevailed over the Puritans, and the central church lost control over public affairs and everyday life on Cape Cod.

When he confronted the American Mission Board in Hawaii in 1826, Percival confronted the unbending Puritanism of Plymouth Colony in the seventeenth century. A review of the board's October 1826 statement of purpose makes the point. The mission asserted that its goal was "to introduce and get into extended operation and influence among them [the natives], the arts, institutions, and usages of civilized life and society: above all to convert them from their idolatries, superstitions, and vices, to the living God."[6] Percival felt that the board was overreaching its mandate and thought the islanders and traders had every right to object.

As the differences between Percival and Bingham began to surface, another man from New England appeared onstage. On 21 January Alfred P. Edwards, a merchant captain from New London, Connecticut, ran his ship, the *London,* onto a coral reef off the island of Lanai. Edwards dispatched a message by a local schooner begging for assistance from the *Dolphin* and promising to furnish any stores Percival might need. He blamed the chief of the island, a man called Thunder, for his desperate situation.

Mad Jack received the plea for help on the twenty-seventh and promptly prepared to go to Edwards's assistance. Since the *Dolphin* lay dismasted, Percival chartered the Boston brig *Convoy* from Capt. William McNeil. He put forty-four men on board and, accompanied by several of his officers and Boki, sailed for Lanai that afternoon. A violent gale delayed them, and the voyage took two days. Despite the delay, the merchant expressed thanks for Percival's response. Percival told Edwards that the *Convoy* was the only ship available and that he had rented her for one hundred dollars a day. At the time, Edwards did not question the price. The master of the *London* placed all of his men under the command of the energetic Percival, who began salvage operations. One of the crewmen of the stricken ship claimed that Percival went about the task as if the vessel and its cargo were his own.

The rescue required a showdown with Chief Thunder. Despite the taboo placed by Edwards on his precious cargo, principally sixty-seven thousand dollars in uninsured specie, Thunder and his band plundered the wreck. When Mad Jack threatened to punish Thunder if he did not return what he had stolen, the chief brought back much if not all of the loot.

Percival's problems were not confined to the native element. Some of the *London's* crewmen were intoxicated and refractory. At one point, as Percival was giving instructions to the men, a runaway sailor from Boston named James Cullins demanded to know "who the Devil" he was. "The reply made," Percival later explained, "was that I would let him know and then I struck him 3 or 4 times with a *flour barrel* stave." Cullins ran away, but several of the navy men caught him and tied him to a spar. About half an hour later, Percival released Cullins and ordered "him to behave himself, to go to work."[7] Cullins later claimed that from that point on, "I always avoided meeting Percival, through fear that he would lay violent hands on me."[8]

Edwards later professed that "Lieutenant Percival was extremely profane, very abusive in his language, and of a most ungovernable temper." Percival's method of command, he continued, "was more like that of a man destitute of his senses, than that of an officer of the United States Navy." Edwards added, "He constantly bestowed upon himself the appellation of '*crazy Jack*' and '*mad Jack*' *Percival*, saying he would be d—d, if he did not teach them (meaning the seamen) *who crazy Jack was.*"[9]

Regardless of any misgivings Edwards may have had at the time, the salvage operation proceeded without conflict between the two skippers. Although Edwards had the specie under the heaviest guard he could muster, he thought it would be safer on the *Convoy* and allowed Percival to take the money. Percival promptly sent the specie to Honolulu in the *Convoy* under Lt. William H. Homer. Percival's clerk, Alfred Whitney, went along on the mission. Homer arrived without incident on 3 February. Percival and the others returned to Honolulu two days later. As soon as Edwards got in, Purser Bates presented him with a bill for eight hundred dollars for the *Convoy's* charter. Percival retained the specie as surety on board the *Dolphin*.

The *London* affair did not end there. The *Convoy's* charter bill remained unpaid while Edwards contrived to get his insurer to cover the cost. At the moment, however, Percival had more pressing issues to handle, such as the problem of sandalwood debts. Sandalwood, a close-grained, yellowish heartwood, is prized for its fragrance and its suitability for cabinetwork and ornamental carving. Yankee merchants found an eager market in Canton for the Hawaiian wood and stripped the Sandwich Islands to satisfy the Chinese demand. Sandalwood became scarce on the islands by 1826, and income from its export declined sharply as a result. Extravagant chieftains accustomed to the payments thoughtlessly overextended their credit and imported goods beyond their diminished means. When the *Dolphin* arrived, the chiefs owed an estimated $200,000 to foreign traders, mostly Americans.

Percival gathered detailed information from the complaining merchants and, pursuant to his orders from Hull, met with the local authorities. He arranged entertainments for the young king and the chiefs that provided a forum to deal with the claims. Through his exertions, Percival got the locals to acknowledge their debts and offer assurances that they would liquidate the obligations promptly. The merchants remembered this accomplishment. In the controversies to come, they sided with Percival almost to a man. Self-styled U.S. consul John C. Jones commended Percival in a letter to Secretary of State Henry Clay.

At this point the unmistakable hand of Bingham reappeared. The missionary attempted to postpone the islanders' payments on their debts. The angry merchants scurried to Percival with tales of their myriad grievances with the mission. Some mission practices affected their businesses—as, for example, when local leaders forced able-bodied men to attend the mission schools rather than work for them. Missionaries, furthermore, took advantage of the natives' good nature and generosity. The merchants cited an incident involving Mr. Chamberlain to make the point. When Chamberlain sold some slates to a native for $1.50, he denied that greed had played a role. Chamberlain explained: "As I persevered in declining to take the money, he put it in my pocket" and refused to take it back. "Being pleased with his perseverance, I concluded to sell him a couple."[10]

Other allegations against the mission trickled in. If even half of them were true, Percival thought, the American Mission Board ought to be expelled from the islands. The most common complaint involved the newly adopted restriction that deprived visiting seamen of the society of females. The mission's campaign against licentiousness received official backing in September 1825 when the chiefs instituted a taboo to prevent women from visiting ships. This prohibition above all others aroused the temper of the mariners. A mob from the British whale ship *Daniel* threatened Rev. William Richards, demanding that he repeal the irksome law. Other incidents of this nature followed. The decree continued in effect, however, and the naive missionaries seemed to think it actually checked immoral behavior. There is ample evidence that it failed to curb the practice and that the guards placed on the beach to stop the women were ineffective. The carefree and unrestrained women of the islands had been a key attraction since the time of Captain Cook, and visiting mariners viewed the restrictions advocated by the mission as an infringement on a fundamental right.

Percival entered the controversy when two longtime white residents, Messrs. Crown and Pease, asked him to intercede on their behalf. Both men had taken Hawaiian wives some time ago, but Kaahumanu, the ponderous regent—often referred to as the queen or queen mother and occasionally as the "Old Bitch"—had confined the women because they refused to leave their husbands to attend the mission school. Their children were now motherless. Percival's compassion was aroused. He went to the queen and asked her to reconsider. She released the two wives.

From this point on, the missionaries associated Percival with the liberals opposed to the mission's reforms and activities. In their book recalling the time they spent in the islands, Lay and Hussey passed over the events of the next few days except to note that they could not discern the reason for the growing ill will. Paulding's journal mentions only a "most unpleasant occurrence . . . which was afterwards greatly misrepresented."[11] The missionaries, however, with considerable enthusiasm and boundless resources, promulgated detailed accounts of their version of what took place. Most of what has appeared in print over the decades draws from these biased accounts. Percival understood what was at stake. "A victim was wanted," he said, "and they considered it no difficult matter to gather sticks for the altar."[12]

The mission's doctor, Abraham Blatchley, offered his share of sticks. He swore there were up to eight women at a time on board the *Dolphin*, and that some seamen contracted venereal diseases as a consequence. Blatchley also claimed that when he voiced concern over the influenza epidemic on the island, Mad Jack responded that it was traceable to the fact that the natives were not bathing as often as they had before the taboo was instigated. "Now these girls," Percival allegedly said, "who swim off and on to my Schooner half a dozen times a day, have nothing of the influenza."[13]

As the issue of female visitation developed and played out, Percival was drawn deeper into the controversy. Certainly in the accounts that followed Bingham focused on Percival's conduct. The head missionary claimed that Mad Jack sought an audience with Kaahumanu and young King Kamehameha III to discuss the matter. The king was indisposed, and Kaahumanu declined to meet with Percival. According to Bingham, she prepared a somewhat conciliatory statement on the subject, crafted to counter Percival's strange argument that a prohibition on lewd women amounted to an insult to the American flag.

The missionaries reported that Percival was angered when he wrongly thought the locals had favored HMS *Blonde* over the American ships by allowing women on board during her visit a few months earlier. Whether he held this view or not is as unclear as most of the complaints lodged against him. But it is a fact that the *Blonde* left Honolulu three months before the ban was imposed. And the firsthand account of the British ship's visit notes the physical attractiveness of the scantily clad and promiscuous young island women.

In any event, Bingham asked Boki to carry Kaahumanu's statement to Percival. Boki agreed, though he feared Mad Jack would be *"huhu loa"* (extremely angry). Boki returned and allegedly reported, "The man-of-war chief says he will not write, but will come and have a talk [with Kaahumanu], and if Mr. Bingham comes, he will shoot him." Boki added, "He is ready to fight, for though his vessel is small, she is just like fire."[14] Percival later explained his failure to offer a written response by saying that he favored oral discourse over written communications with unlettered savages. More important, he did not want Reverend Bingham to act as his interpreter, which formal protocol would have permitted if both the regent and Percival had communicated in writing. Nor did he want to magnify Bingham's importance in the eyes of the natives and otherwise assist his proselytizing.

On the following day, 22 February, Percival met and talked with Kaahumanu. The early reports of what transpired are from the pens of the missionary group. They indicate that Percival threatened to blow the town down if the prohibition was not repealed. Bingham reported on the discussion in some detail even though he was not present. In fact, he showed uncharacteristic disinterest by failing to appear. Although he explained his absence as being due to the fact that both parties had not put their views in writing, there is reason to suspect that it stemmed rather from fear that Mad Jack really would shoot him. Bingham was not one to miss such an important meeting because of adherence to rigid standards of negotiation.

Percival scoffed at the allegation that he had threatened the town. In fact, the charge had an altogether innocent basis. The islanders were expecting the death of an ailing chieftain, and there was some fear that the death might precipitate civil unrest. Some island authorities had suggested that the foreigners arm themselves. Percival let it be known that if any commotion occurred, apprehensive Americans could seek refuge on the *Dolphin*. "Notwithstanding their fort of 30 pieces of Cannon," he said, "I could rattle it in a few minutes about the ears of the Natives."[15]

On Saturday evening, 25 February, Percival again conferred with the queen regent, supposedly railing at her for an hour. The two did not reach an agreement. As Mad Jack departed, Kaahumanu, also strong-willed, told him, "I have seen men-of-war before. I have seen men-of-war from England, and from Russia, and from France, and from Spain, but I have never before seen such a man-of-war as you are!"[16] After the navy officer disappeared down the path toward his hut, Kaahumanu allegedly waddled over to Reverend Richards's house and asked him if Percival really was an American officer or a pirate.

On Sunday afternoon, rain dampened the usual recreational activities around the port and the seamen on liberty found their frolic curtailed. Some thought that if Bingham and his gang had kept to school teaching, sailors could have found entertainment without even going ashore. An idle group with time on their hands decided that getting rid of the taboo would be appropriate Sunday sport. Reverend Richards said the band of sailors numbered at least 20, while Bingham, who had a fleeting opportunity to count while looking back over his shoulder, calculated the mob's size at 150 men.

The angry seamen broke into a prayer meeting at Prime Minister Kalanimoku's house and demanded the young women. Failing to receive a satisfactory response, the men hurled stones and swung clubs until sixty-seven of the premier's windowpanes were broken. "Thus commenced a riot," wrote Bingham, "which occupied the time and place of the expected divine service."[17]

Reverend Bingham diverted the rioters at this point when he made a dash for his nearby home. His flight is described in an emotional letter sent by Mrs. Bingham to a friend in Springfield, Massachusetts. The letter, reproduced in a number of American newspapers under the heading "Abominable Transactions at the Sandwich Islands," has Mrs. Bingham hustling across her living room to bolt the door as the gang approached, while at the same instant Mr. Bingham was sprinting across the front yard for the same door and the safety it offered. Mrs. Bingham reached it first and unwittingly locked out her husband. "I experienced for a moment the agonizing feeling that my friend was gone," she wrote. "But to my great joy, I soon caught a glimpse of him, and in a few moments unbolted the door for him and Mr. Chamberlain."[18]

Paulding's journal indicates that the riot peaked within a few minutes. Bingham was briefly in peril, but the tide began to turn when the natives jumped in and defended him. Stones and clubs flew through the air.

"When I first heard of the affray," Percival later claimed, "I ran to the spot and there exerted myself to suppress the tumult."[19] Two *Dolphin* midshipmen and several whaling captains helped. As he approached the scene, Percival roared at the rioters, "I'll teach you to disgrace us!"[20]

Edward C. Barnard of New Bedford reported that one of the missionaries—he thought it was Mrs. Bingham—later told him of Percival's exertions. Mad Jack leveled the first man he encountered with a blow from his umbrella. He continued to swing away and knocked three or four more rioters to the ground. The riot stopped at that point, and the missionaries credited Percival's interference. Percival cleared the field of battle and ordered a score of bound men taken to his schooner and placed in irons. Bingham expressed concern for one sailor who appeared to be dead and remembered Percival replying that he wished all of the hooligans had been killed. But Richards recalled that Percival was in a much different mood and said he could not blame the seamen.

Whatever his feelings in the heat of the moment, Percival met with the island's chiefs Sunday evening and assured them the guilty men would be punished. Bingham, who was present, "immediately entered into a conversation upon the profanation of the Sabbath," Percival recalled. The minister, he went on, felt "great utility . . . would flow from a strict regard of it among the natives." Percival expressed doubt that the natives were prepared for the change. And he told Bingham this was the reason he "had better not meddle any further. Just confine yourself to instruction."[21]

As the debate shifted to the taboo itself, Percival declared some doubt that the chiefs acting alone had instituted the restriction. Some heat was generated on this point, noted Percival. Prior to leaving the meeting, the lieutenant did agree that the rowdy sailors had gone too far and pledged that he would have the wrongdoers repair the damage, which he did. He also asked Dr. Blatchley to come onboard the *Dolphin* in the morning to administer aid to the injured. Some serious wounds had been inflicted during the riot.

Before the night passed, Boki declared his agreement with Percival. The constant presence of four to five hundred seamen in port made the law against lewd women unenforceable. The governor lifted the ban. A host of native women reportedly hastened to the ships and their old practices. The missionaries claimed that when the first group of women paddled out toward the ships, a triumphant cheer rang through the harbor. Bingham and his band considered the turn of events a victory for their opponents. Without question, the loose women benefited. In bygone days, the local government had assessed an income tax on their ill-gotten earnings. But now, under the influence of the American Mission Board, the chiefs believed it ungodly to tax sin.

Bingham came aboard the *Dolphin* on Monday morning to help Percival identify the culprits. The clergyman examined the prisoners and selected several he had noticed in the riot. These men were flogged for their lawlessness; others were confined for a period of days. Percival always believed that Bingham backed the flogging to an extent wholly inconsistent with his calling. Apparently a little squeamish when the time came, however, he left just before the punishment was administered. As he took his leave, he declared, "I hope they lay it on well."[22]

Dr. Blatchley also declined to witness the flogging. He remained belowdecks attending to the wounded men. He did hear the strokes and the cries, and he understood that six men received from eighteen to thirty-six lashes. Four *Dolphin* crewmen—Blodjet, Green, Miller, and Smith—got a dozen lashes each.

For the remainder of the *Dolphin*'s stay, Percival did not allow her crewmen on shore except for a few mechanics and those who served the officers. Mad Jack wanted the other shipmasters to impose similar restrictions. On 3 March he circulated a letter throughout the port addressing the outrage and asking the captains to limit shore leave for their crews, thereby reducing the missionaries' anxiety.

Before the month passed, he followed up with a more stringent regulation. In concert with the local officials, he declared that crews would not be permitted to remain on shore after sundown. Men found onshore after that time without a liberty letter attesting to their steadiness and temperance would be apprehended, confined, and assessed a penalty of six dollars before being released to their ships.

Percival's problems did not end with the abolition of the visitation ban. Other troubles continued to beset the *Dolphin*. Illness was a major problem. Many men were on the sick list while at the Sandwich Islands. John Newberry, one of the *Dolphin*'s crew, said his commander rose to the occasion, providing kind and humane care for the sick. He even gave the sick men wine from his private store. And when it came to fresh provisions, crewmen received the same rations as officers. Such benevolence throughout his career made Mad Jack as beloved as any officer of the period and promoted a high degree of loyalty among his men. Before long, he found it necessary to draw on this reserve of devotion. The quarrel with Edwards over the *London*'s salvage was about to take center stage again.

For a month, Edwards had been trying to obtain a certificate from Percival that would enable him to charge the hire of the *Convoy* to his insurance carrier. Insurance covered the cargo and materials on the *London,* but not the large amount of specie on board. If Percival would certify that he had gone to Lanai to save the money as well as the insured items, Edwards could charge the total expense for the salvage operation to the distant insurance company. Percival wanted no part of such a petty scheme. When Edwards continued to evade paying for the charter of the *Convoy,* Percival decided to meet the bill by charging a commission on the specie he still held in safekeeping, and he deducted the amount from the whole. The Connecticut trader disagreed with Percival's method, and a vitriolic battle of words erupted. Edwards claimed that whenever he attempted to confer with Percival about the matter, the navy officer abused and insulted him. During one confrontation, Edwards said, Percival shouted, *"You are a d—d Connecticut, deceptive, lying son of a bitch."*[23] "The opprobrious term of liar which was used came from himself," responded Percival, "and instantly I punished his insolence."[24] He grabbed Edwards, apparently intent on throwing him over a banister. Edwards said that his clothes were torn in the scuffle.

Finally, after deciding that the commission charged by Percival would amount to upward of $2,200, well above the cost of the charter, Edwards tried to settle the matter by paying the $800 charter bill. Percival rejected the tardy offer, insisting that self-respect required it. For several days in early March, Edwards badgered Percival without success. Finally, he threatened to abandon the money rather than submit to robbery. Edwards claimed that Percival "prayed to God" he would follow through on his threat, because "he knew 'd—d well' how to employ it to good advantage on the coast of Peru."[25] Realizing at last that the navy men were determined to get the money owed to them, Edwards decided to prevent a total loss and succumbed. On 11 March, Bates brought the money up on the *Dolphin's* deck and turned it over to Edwards, less $999.35 (the $800 charter fee plus the 1.5 percent holding fee demanded by Percival). The New London skipper took his money and left, but the incident, and the friction, did not end there.

Edwards hired the ship *Becket* and made arrangements to continue his voyage to Manila. Just before he left, he spread word ashore that Percival had stolen a mattress from the *London*. The Connecticut shipmaster even had a clandestine search for the mattress made at Percival's quarters. Percival was incensed. Accompanied by Lieutenant Paulding, he hastened to the *Becket,* intent on redress. Edwards claimed that Percival began to abuse him while Paulding assumed a defensive posture. "If you have the least spark of a gentleman you'd come on shore" and disavow the false accusation, Mad Jack shouted.[26] When Edwards refused, Percival felt compelled to take the next step. He rapped his detractor's bare head with his whalebone cane.

Edwards escaped aft and began to throw belaying pins and stanchions at Percival and Paulding. Edwards found the cook's ax and a gun rammer, faced Percival, and swore he would split his head open. Percival calmly told Edwards to crack away. "But if you do—it'll be the worst thing you've ever done!"[27] When Edwards made an ineffectual attempt to carry out his threat, Percival ordered several of his boatmen to grab Edwards and take away his weapons. This they did, and Percival, his honor redeemed, plowed back to the *Dolphin.*

Although the incident may strike modern readers as bizarre or ridiculous, it was a common practice in those days for a man to defend his good name by physical means if necessary. Even the practice of dueling remained an option. Indeed, in 1820 Commo. James Barron killed Commo. Stephen Decatur in a duel. And one of Percival's later acquaintances, Congressman Jonathan Cilley of Maine, died in an 1838 duel with a Kentucky congressman. Percival handled the affront to his honor in the accepted way—and in a manner not at all atypical today, one might add.

Mad Jack planned to leave the Sandwich Islands at this time, but thirty-six whaling masters drew up a petition asking him to delay his departure for a month if at all possible. The whalers felt that Percival provided a great service by preventing desertions, protecting their property, and in general maintaining law and order within the port. One of the most persuasive pleaders was a commercial agent named Jones, who was also Percival's most ardent supporter on the islands. Coincidentally or not, Jones was for some time also the most outspoken and determined opponent of the mission. A fair amount of correspondence passed between the two men, with Jones repeatedly telling Percival of the benefits his presence produced. Among other things, Percival had succeeded in bringing port duties levied on Americans into line with the lesser charges assessed on vessels of other nations. Lord Byron had promoted some reform during his visit. Percival, of course, wanted to eliminate discriminatory assessments on U.S. shipping altogether.

Lavish entertainments continued to be a feature of Mad Jack's negotiations with the chiefs. On 3 April he put on a spectacular entertainment for the young king. Navy men spent much of the morning borrowing signals from the other ships in the harbor in order to dress up the *Dolphin* in style. A fine meal was served to the king, and the schooner fired general salutes before and afterward. During the feast, discussion centered on the regulation that charged American ships 30 percent more than English ships. Percival negotiated an agreement to repeal the unfair regulation. He also got a firm assurance that no advantage would be granted to the ships of other nations over those of the United States.

Before he departed, Percival made one more lasting enemy. Acting—as a U.S. Navy captain was supposed to do—in an enforcement capacity in an almost lawless environment, Mad Jack had encounters with a number of people. Most did not carry a grudge. Capt. William B. Jackson of the Boston brig *Harbinger* was of this ilk. A store clerk named Samuel B. Gibbs recalled a dispute between Jackson and Percival in which strong words were exchanged and a scuffle ensued. Both men made light of the incident and never mentioned it thereafter.

But Capt. Leonard Sistair was not of such a forgiving nature. He refused to forget his encounter with Mad Jack. Percival went after Sistair because he had been ordered to do so by Commodore Hull, acting under orders from the secretary of the navy. Sistair had been the master of the *Adonis,* a merchantman owned by the Hammond and Newman Company of Baltimore. Some months before Percival arrived at Oahu, Sistair sold the *Adonis* without the owners' permission, kept the money, and settled down to a life of ease in the islands. The owners authorized Hull to seize two chests of money held by Sistair.

Percival did not have difficulty finding Sistair. He was an ally of Edwards and a close friend of Stephen Reynolds, a prominent merchant. Reynolds, in fact, held one of the chests at his store. Mad Jack simply sent one of his officers and several of his biggest men to the store to confiscate the chest. They also brought Sistair back with them to the *Dolphin.* Sistair, fearful that he would be placed in irons and returned to the United States for punishment, bargained for his release. He authorized Percival to go on the ship *Mersey* and seize the second chest of money. The navy eventually turned over all the recovered money to Hammond and Newman in Maryland. Sistair blamed Percival for his misfortunes, and for years he did not miss an opportunity to smear and vilify him, often in concert with Edwards.

Among his other positive accomplishments, Percival prevented the wrecking of the American whale ship *Commodore Perry,* and he rendered opportune aid to the brig *Tally Ho.* By the end of April, however, most of the whalers were gone. Many had sailed for the recently discovered grounds off Japan. On 3 May, Mad Jack began to prepare the *Dolphin* to depart on the eleventh. On 10 May, anticipating the morrow, a dejected Jones wrote to Percival expressing keen disappointment over his departure. Reverend Bingham held another view. He limited the *Dolphin*'s accomplishments in the islands to the acquisition of "the proud name of 'the mischief making man-of-war.'"[28] Reverend Richards wrote, "This is certain, that if any more such vessels as the United States' schr. Dolphin visit the islands, there will be no hope for our lives."[29] Peter Cornelius, one of the navy crew, recalled that the natives "were much affected, howling and making gestures" when the *Dolphin* got under way.[30] Bingham interpreted the demonstration as an impromptu thanksgiving; Percival felt the islanders were indicating their sorrow at his departure.

One point seems indisputable. Percival had taught the Hawaiian gunners something about the age-old practice of firing salutes. The *Dolphin*'s log entry for 11 May 1826 indicates that as the ship "got under way the fort fired a Salute of 21 Guns which was returned with the same number."[31] The *Dolphin* stood out to sea and shaped a course for Chile.

Lt. John Percival about 1817, from a painting by Ethan Allen Greenwood owned by the U.S. Naval Academy. *Courtesy of U.S. Department of the Navy*

The USS *Peacock* defeating HMS *Epervier* on 29 April 1814 off the east coast of Florida. *Courtesy of U.S. Naval Academy Museum*

The U.S. frigate *United States* under full sail. Percival served as the ship's first lieutenant on the Pacific station for periods between 1823 and 1827. *Courtesy of U.S. Naval Institute*

The U.S. schooner *Dolphin* under John Percival, the first American warship to visit Hawaii, departing Honolulu on 11 May 1826. *Courtesy of Raymond A. Massey*

Capt. John Percival, from a painting by Henry A. Wise now in the possession of the U.S. Naval Academy. *Courtesy of U.S. Department of the Navy*

Capt. John Percival, from a painting by Marshall Johnson once owned by
Charles Lee Frank. *Courtesy of U.S. Department of the Navy*

Image commonly said to be of John Percival, possibly in error. Features of the subject vary from those in definite likenesses, and the garb appears to be from an earlier period. More significant, the man is not in uniform. All of Percival's certain portraits show him characteristically in uniform. *Courtesy of U.S. Department of the Navy*

The sloop *Cyane*. Percival commanded the twenty-gun vessel on the Mediterranean station in 1838–39. *Courtesy of U.S. Naval Historical Center.*

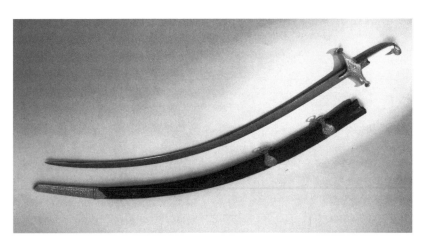

Sword presented to Percival by the sultan of Muscat in Zanzibar during the *Constitution*'s round-the-world cruise. *Courtesy of U.S. Naval Academy Museum*

The *Constitution* leaving Honolulu, 2 December 1845, to join Commo. John Sloat's Pacific squadron off Mexico. *Courtesy of Raymond A. Massey*

One of two known photographs of Percival, by J. W. Black of Boston, about 1860. Percival is holding the sword presented to him by Congress for his role in the *Peacock* vs. *Epervier* fight. *Courtesy of U.S. Department of the Navy*

The West Barnstable (Mass.) Congregational Church, the center of Percival's hometown during his lifetime. He was buried in full uniform from this church on 20 September 1862. *From the author's collection*

Percival's grave site in West Barnstable, Massachusetts. His gravestone is behind the memorial tablet. *Courtesy of Scott Thompson*

~6~

THE TRIALS

*T*he Pacific cruise of the *Dolphin* clearly boosted the standing of the U.S. Navy in the eyes of the nation. American traders and whalers were rapidly expanding their activities in the region at that time, and the U.S. naval presence was reassuring. Prior to Percival's voyage, the postwar navy had limited its overseas activities to the Mediterranean, the Caribbean, and the South American coasts. Percival proved the feasibility of operations in the Pacific. The *Dolphin,* in short, was in the van as the American navy carried law and order around the Horn and into the wide expanses of that ocean. By any measure, the cruise amounted to a significant chapter in the history of the service.

While enhancing the standing of the navy, Percival thought it appropriate to honor one of the service's notables—Isaac Hull. On 7 June 1826, toward the end of the return passage, the *Dolphin* discovered an uncharted atoll of four islets, and "in compliment to the commander of our squadron in the Pacific ocean" Percival named it Hull's Island. Lieutenant Paulding's journal notes that the discovery was set down on the charts "in latitude south 21 degrees 48 minutes and longitude by chronometer 154 degrees 54 minutes west." The uninhabited island was "a little more than a mile long, and from a hundred yards to a quarter of mile wide. It was everywhere very low."[1] Hull's Island eventually became part of French Oceania, and France changed its name to Maria Island.

Farther east in the Tubuai chain, Percival brought his schooner to anchor on 12 June and remained until 22 June. The *Dolphin's* mainmast required repairs, and the crew also attended to the continuing need to replenish the ship's wood and water stores. A month later the American schooner made Mas Afuera Island, and four days after that had Valparaiso in sight. The *Dolphin* beat up the Chilean harbor and came to anchor early on 23 July. Learning that Hull was in the vicinity of Callao, Percival obtained the necessary supplies and headed north. On 20 August, Mad Jack found his commander at the island of Lorenzo and joined the flag. In a few days the *United States* and the *Dolphin* passed over to Callao.

At the beginning of September 1826, Hull transferred Percival back to the flagship to act as his executive officer. Lt. Beverly Kennon, who was senior to Percival, had rejoined the squadron in Percival's absence and received the *Dolphin* command. Hull assured his loyal friend that the change "has not been done with a view that the least possible censure can be attached to you," adding "on the contrary, so far as your conduct has come to my knowledge and particularly during your long and interesting cruise . . . , it meets my approbation."[2] Hull wrote to Secretary Southard to tell him that the cruise of the *Dolphin* had been a success. Actually, Percival welcomed the relief. That common maritime hazard of the period, shipboard sickness, had plagued Percival for much of the voyage between the Sandwich Islands and Chile.

Hull remained on the coast throughout the fall months. Finally, he put into Valparaiso on 6 January 1827 and set about getting ready to leave for New York. In the past two years he had developed a liking for the *United States*. He was as proud of her as he was of Old Ironsides. There was not an English man-of-war in the Pacific capable of catching her. When the U.S. frigate *Brandywine* appeared on the scene and Hull heard her officers brag about her swiftness, he set up a good-natured contest. The vessels were similar in most respects, with two important exceptions. The *Brandywine* was only two years old, while the *United States* was thirty; and the 1,726-ton *Brandywine* was heavier than the 1,576-ton *United States*. Hull had provisioned his ship by the latter part of January and was ready to sail for home—after first taking on the *Brandywine*.

On 23 July, Mad Jack ordered the boatswain to call all hands and up anchor. Although the actual race would not begin until both ships were out of the harbor, it was important to rouse the crew from the outset and set the proper mood. Percival had perfected the art of inspiring seamen, and he went about the task with vigor. Agile sailors scaled the rigging like spiders, and in seconds the sounds of falling and rising canvas filled the air. As Hull's ship passed out of the harbor, HMS *Cambridge* gave three cheers, which were returned with three times three. The Americans returned the British salute gun for gun. Indicative of the cordial Anglo-American relations at the time, the British ships were in full dress with their yards manned to bid good-bye to the *United States.*

Several months later, *Niles' Weekly Register* noted that the men of the American man-of-war *Vincennes* and those in the English squadron at Valparaiso were anxious to know which ship won the race. They related how the *United States* stood out under topgallant sails while the *Brandywine* remained under topsails until her rival had passed ahead and dropped her a mile. Before both frigates came under full sail, they were five miles apart. The general impression at Valparaiso held that the *Brandywine* was gaining rapidly, but the ships were hull down in a short time. The unnamed correspondents added, "the United States has beaten everything in this sea, and there can be no doubt of her *heels.*"[3]

By August, *Niles'* was able to report the outcome. The race was in doubt for only a few minutes. The *United States* showed the *Brandywine* her stern in short order. In an hour, she clewed up the gallants and royals to let the *Brandywine* come alongside. The crews gave three cheers, and the officers took a social glass together aboard the victor. The superiority of the *United States* over anything in the Pacific was acknowledged.

High summer resulted in an uneventful passage around the Horn. The *United States* reached Bahia on 6 March, and Percival anticipated a happy return to his wife and home. However, his Honolulu foes—the American Mission Board and Captain Edwards—were plotting to dampen his homecoming. In addition to their own publications, the American Mission Board utilized regular newspapers to publicize lengthy and intense complaints against Percival and the *Dolphin*'s officers and crew. On 30 December 1826 *Niles'* summarized the missionaries' allegations. During his time in the Sandwich Islands, Percival had insisted on a repeal of the visitation taboo, threatened to shoot a missionary, permitted some of his men to riot, and bullied the chiefs. "This," *Niles'* observed, "is the amount of what fills a whole column in the *New York Commercial Advertiser* of the 22d inst. [of this month]." But the paper closed judiciously by saying, "When lieut P. shall be present to defend himself, we may have another version of this affair: he is represented as a very worthy man and an excellent officer, and should not be condemned unheard."[4]

The *United States* arrived in New York on 24 April 1827. On the twenty-fifth, the navy detached Percival and put him on a leave of absence. He needed the time away from active duty. Edwards had obtained an indictment charging Percival with extortion by color of office (i.e., extortion by an officer under the pretense that it is within his authority), and the authorities arrested Mad Jack as he left the ship. He spent nine days in jail before being released. Tired of reading newspaper accounts unfavorable to Percival, a self-described friend of justice sent a contravening version to the *Baltimore American* in his defense. Hezekiah Niles, as an act of justice, printed the reasonably accurate report in his 30 June 1827 edition because Percival's actions seemed justifiable and because it was the paper's policy to consider the reputation of naval officers public property. In addition to Niles's deep interest in maritime matters, the impending litigation was of local interest in Baltimore, his newspaper's hometown. Captain Sistair, it will be recalled, had attempted to defraud a Baltimore commercial house before Percival apprehended him. The discredited Sistair accompanied Edwards before a New York grand jury and became one of the key prosecution witnesses.

In the middle of June, while at his father-in-law's home in Trenton, New Jersey, Percival received an encouraging note from his attorney in New York, Robert Emmet, reporting on his talk with one of the judges of the U.S. Circuit Court. Percival could relax; Emmet thought the extortion charge farcical, and the judge seemed to agree. On 2 July, Percival appeared before Circuit Court Judge Samuel R. Betts and put up recognizance of two thousand dollars, and John Low Jr., a New York merchant, pledged one thousand dollars. Both amounts were subject to forfeiture if Percival failed to appear at the next term of the court.

On Monday morning, 5 November 1827, the U.S. Circuit Court for the Southern District of New York convened to hear the extortion case of *United States v. John Percival*. U.S. Attorney Tillotson opened for the prosecution. Attorney O. Hoffman began the defendant's case. On the following day, both sides summed up, the court charged the jury, and the jury promptly returned a not-guilty verdict. Percival had won the first round.

In October 1827, spurred on by the fervor of Edwards, the American Mission Board intensified its campaign against Percival at the organization's annual meeting in New York. Through such publications as its *Missionary Herald,* the board detailed its complaints against the Massachusetts officer's behavior in the Sandwich Islands. Percival had interfered with municipal regulations; claimed that America and England permitted prostitution on their ships; demeaned the missionaries; described himself as a high authority and the missionaries as people without regard in their own country; asserted that the missionaries interfered in local government; kept Bingham out of meetings, and threatened to shoot him if he attended; shamefully refused to put his requests in writing; terrorized the natives; conducted himself in a manner certain to lead to rioting; and permitted an unusually large number of men on shore on the day of the riot, supposedly encouraging them to do violence.

In fact, criticism of the missionaries' interference in commercial and political activities in the islands was intensifying, and the board found itself on the defensive. The complaints were the subject of a public hearing at the islands in December 1826. Lt. Thomas ap Catesby Jones of the U.S. sloop-of-war *Peacock,* who attended the gathering, thought the forum completely vindicated the missionaries. Although Jones was highly critical of Percival's approach, before he departed from Honolulu in January he advised the mission to proceed slowly with reforms because coercion was seldom productive.

At about this point, the mission's strongest ally and most influential convert, Kaahumanu, fell ill, reportedly with venereal disease. Reverend Bingham could not suppress the damaging rumor. Boki, hopeful of overthrowing the queen regent, became increasingly hostile toward the American mission. The governor displayed his disdain for Bingham's group by cultivating the friendship of the newly arrived French Catholic mission.

In August 1827 a crisis of lesser import developed. A New York newspaper carried a slanted version of the *Daniel* affair of the previous year, portraying Capt. William Buckle, the ship's master, as a villain. When he returned to Honolulu in October 1827, Captain Buckle blamed Reverend

Richards for the article and threatened to strike back. Kaahumanu stepped in and called a council to hear the complaint against the churchman. The chiefs hesitantly dropped the charge leveled against Richards. But the underlying reason for the continuing discord remained: the mission regularly aired its grievances in American newspapers and journals. The mission defended this one-sided practice by claiming that the Christian public had a right to know about the threats and violence to which missionaries were exposed. Under strong pressure to alter its style, the American Mission Board diverted attention and criticism to a vulnerable target—John Percival—the only public officer to openly question the missionaries' methods. His status as a government employee made him particularly susceptible to criticism and censure.

In April 1828 the American Mission Board called a hearing in New Bedford to gather evidence to support its case against Percival, who showed up uninvited and was astonished to find a large crowd. He was informed that the testimony sought by the board would be taken in public, and neither Percival nor anyone acting in his behalf would be allowed to cross-examine those who testified against him. A furious Mad Jack declared that the board's conduct was unconscionable, but the missionaries proceeded with the hearing nevertheless.

As a result of the joint efforts of Edwards and the American Mission Board, by the spring of 1828 Secretary Southard had received a score of letters and affidavits asserting that Percival conducted himself improperly while at the Sandwich Islands. Capt. Josiah Chester of the New London whale ship *Connecticut* offered a common accusation when he claimed that Percival was profane and blasphemous. Jebez Gillespie of Windsor, Connecticut, master of the brig *Manilla Packet,* said Percival "had a tongue as well calculated for abusive language as ever I heard." Percival's "reputation at Oahu," Gillespie continued, "was very low." Curiously, Gillespie also noted that he "commonly . . . dine[d] at the same table" with Mad Jack, despite his distaste for the man.[5] Capt. Alexander Bunker of the whaler *Ontario* out of Nantucket summarized the various complaints when he charged that Percival was ungentlemanly and unofficerlike.

As early as the previous April, Percival had submitted a request for a court of inquiry to clear up the charges against him. The secretary replied that he would give the subject due consideration. On 13 May 1827 Southard sent Percival a copy of Edwards's accusations, and on 2 July 1827 he forwarded the initial allegations of the missionaries. At the end of the year the secretary instructed the navy commissioners to look into the matter. In March 1828 the navy informed Percival that a court of inquiry would convene on 1 May at the Charlestown yard in Boston. Southard appointed Commo. Charles Morris, Capt. Alexander Wadsworth, and Capt. John O. Creighton to the task.

Edwards and the American Mission Board took thirty-one days to present their now familiar complaints. During this time, Percival heard that one of the defense witnesses had vowed to give Edwards a thorough beating. Prudently, on 28 May, Percival wrote to Morris asking the court to provide Edwards with all the protection within its power. He feared such an assault would be attributed to him, and he would suffer the consequences.

Percival's chance to address the court and answer the charges against him finally arrived on 12 June. Prior to answering the specific charges, Mad Jack voiced his displeasure with the breadth of the complainants' testimony. The board had permitted his opponents to present their perceptions of his religious beliefs and other private thoughts and opinions. He asserted that he was accountable only for his overt and public acts, and he would not respond to charges that fell outside his official conduct.

Percival chose to deal with the *London* incident first, charging that Edwards's claim that he was mercenary was without truth. He denied the existence of an agreement to deliver Edwards's money without charge, stressing the fact that Edwards could not produce a witness who could testify to it. It was unfortunate, Mad Jack acknowledged, that he had to physically chastise Edwards, and he agreed that the assault on board the *Becket* required an explanation, if not justification. In plain terms, he argued that anyone low enough to accuse him of stealing a mattress deserved a thrashing. Edwards's persistent demeaning of Paulding, who was not involved other than by his presence, was further proof of his mean spirit. Percival closed his rebuttal of the Edwards phase of his trial by drawing the court's attention to Edwards's boast that he could always fall back on the satisfaction of having kept Percival in jail for nine days.

Moving to the missionaries' charges, Percival answered the important complaint that he interfered with the local government at Hawaii by asserting that in reality it was the missionaries who had interfered. He described his initial attempts to establish good relations with the mission, his role in suppressing the riot, and the various conversations that took place between himself, the native authorities, and Bingham. Percival admitted that one of the talks did indeed deal with prostitution in America and England. Boki, he recalled, had observed that English women were allowed to visit British ships; when he was in England he often saw them on board the men-of-war anchored at Portsmouth. Regardless of its propriety, Percival said, the court knew the practice was common.

Percival responded to several allegations by questioning their materiality. Even if certain charges were true, he said, they did not amount to improper conduct or criminal behavior. Rather, they related to a permissible exercise of judgment, such as when he kept Bingham out of his meetings. Mad Jack next moved on to a more serious allegation, claiming it was difficult to speak calmly about the outrageous charge that he instigated the riot. Only the usual number of men was ashore on liberty at the time, he insisted, and he had ordered them to behave. He described how he raced to the mission compound and quelled the disturbance. "Yet in the face of these notorious facts," roared Percival to the court, "the allegation of instigating the Riot is unhesitatingly brought against me. On what ground, upon what pretext is this done!"[6]

Several defense witnesses justified Percival's use of profanity in different ways. John Newberry from the *Dolphin,* for instance, claimed he never heard Percival swear except while getting the ship under way. James C. Swain of Providence took the step of writing to the navy secretary to say, "I have heard Lt. Percival sware [*sic*] when any one has attempted to impose upon or deceive him, but not blasphemously." Swain added, "I never heard him make use of gross or obscene language. His language was decisive and his conduct prompt and energetic."[7]

Percival's own candid explanation could stand without support. Anyone acquainted with the navy and knowledgeable about maritime affairs, he told the court, "must be aware that duty cannot, or at least it is very generally believed that it cannot, be carried on without the use of some expletives." He acknowledged that regulations prohibited profane swearing, but he was innocent of that offense. He summarized, "I do sincerely believe that I am as little addicted to this custom as any officer I ever sailed with."[8] The body language of the members of the court indicated that they agreed with Percival's review of the subject. Before he closed his defense, Percival felt compelled to speak out against the unjust tactics of the missionaries, especially their New Bedford hearing convened just days prior to the earlier scheduled court of inquiry, which, he felt, had polluted the pending judicial process.

Five days later the inquiry ended, and Percival left for his Cape Cod home and a rest. Morris, Wadsworth, and Creighton held his career in their hands. The trio sent their findings and recommendations through channels. The secretary would not announce his decision for another six months.

Captain Edwards would not wait. The scoundrel, as Percival described him, continued his vendetta. Capt. John Butler of New Bedford claimed that Edwards dogged him for days trying to elicit his support in the attack against Percival. Edwards, Butler said, thought himself the greatest captain, a brother the greatest judge, and another brother the greatest statesman in the United States. Others around Charlestown heard Edwards declare that he would return to New York and bring more suits against Percival. He made good on his threats. During the May 1828 term of the U.S. Circuit Court for the Southern District of New York, he filed a suit charging Percival and Paulding with assault and battery. Percival, his fellow *Dolphin* officers Paulding and Edward Schermerhorn, and Purser Bates were named in a second complaint, charged with trespassing and conversion (i.e., the unlawful appropriation of another's property) during the salvage operation at Lanai. The quartet posted bail on 10 June and awaited a November trial.

Beginning on Thursday, 6 November 1828, the first suit against Percival and Paulding was heard before a jury in New York City. W. S. Johnson, attorney for the plaintiff Edwards, opened by introducing now well-used testimony. Defense attorney Emmet responded after raising an objection to the indictment itself. The next day, Emmet and Hoffman summed up for the defendants. Edwards's attorneys followed. The court thereupon gave the charge to the jury, which retired with directions to seal its verdict and return the next morning.

Before calling the jury back in on Saturday, the court overruled Emmet's objection. The jury returned a not-guilty verdict for Paulding but found Percival guilty of the assault charge. The court assessed damages of one hundred dollars with six cents' cost. Of all the charges lodged against Percival, he admitted sufficient facts to support just one—the assault on Edwards. There is little doubt that if the situation had arisen again, Mad Jack would have responded in a similar manner.

The trial on the second indictment was anticlimactic. When Johnson opened for Edwards, the court plainly saw that the testimony did not implicate Paulding, Schermerhorn, and Bates. The judge charged the jury at this point, and it found the three men not guilty. The ensuing Percival trial took little time to cover considerable ground. The jury just as quickly found Percival innocent of the second complaint.

After a few weeks in New York, Percival traveled to Washington to renew an effort to change and improve his relative rank. While he was there he finally received the decision on the navy court of inquiry. The mass of details as well as Edwards's suits had occasioned the delay. The department determined it unnecessary to convene a court-martial. In January 1829 the secretary wrote to Percival saying that the complaints were without merit, but "the Executive has not been able to approve the whole of your conduct while at the Sandwich Islands." Percival should have shown more restraint in front of impressionable Hawaiians. Secretary Southard regretted the absence of "proper caution." In closing, he tempered the rebuke by saying he was pleased "to add that your conduct does merit approbation by its zeal, energy, and attention to the interests and wants of some of your fellow citizens whom you found at the Islands, and in the repression and punishment of improper conduct on several occasions."[9]

After a year and a half of litigation and inquiries, Percival could put his Sandwich Islands troubles behind him. Historians, however, would not forget the events there. Almost every history of Hawaii mentions the *Dolphin*'s 1826 visit, highlighting the Sunday riot. James Michener in his 1959 novel *Hawaii* even loosely patterned a key character, Captain Hoxworth, after the missionaries' picture of Mad Jack. Early writings on the subject largely drew from the acrimonious and sometimes titillating accounts published by the missionaries. More recent writers have unfortunately tended to rely on these secondary sources. Percival's version never made it into print, although his side of the controversy is documented in various archives. A rich source of information is the John Percival Papers at the Massachusetts Historical Society in Boston. As in most controversies, a review of archival material indicates three sides to the story: the missionaries' and Edwards's side, Percival's side, and the truth.

In the final analysis, the judicial system achieved substantial justice. Even when the rough, coarse, and turbulent environment in which the events occurred is considered, Percival did commit an undeniable assault on Edwards, as the civilian court found. However, the facts did not justify action against Percival on the myriad other assertions and charges, some clearly unfounded and many involving matters of form instead of substance. By today's standards, Percival's actions in Hawaii may seem unpolished, if not severe—but the same was true of 1826 Hawaii.

~7~

CAUGHT IN ANOTHER CONTROVERSY

With the Edwards trials behind him, Percival turned his attention to a long-standing grievance while he awaited the report of the court of inquiry. When the navy made him an acting lieutenant in November 1814, he was designated number 13 on the list. When the Senate confirmed the appointments in December, a clerk appended a note to the list intimating that the relative ranking of the names on the list was not set. The next two Naval Registers (1815 and 1817) continued the initial order. However, the register for 1818 dropped Percival to number 32. That setback by itself was disappointing, but it rankled Percival even more because a number of those placed ahead of him had been young midshipmen when he was a sailing master. As well, he had more time in the service.

Certainly, his career path had been unusual. Normally an officer progressed from the entry position of midshipman to lieutenant. Percival entered the service in 1800 as a master's mate, made midshipman, and was discharged in the 1801 cutback. Eight years later he left the merchant service to return to the navy as a sailing master, a rating outside the normal sequence of officer grades. All of this set him apart from most officers and contributed to his mystique. He came in through the hawsehole, so to speak, not through the cabin window.

At the time of the change in the 1818 Naval Register, he had asked Secretary Benjamin Crowninshield to reverse the ranking and put it back as it was in the earlier registers. Although precedent existed for such changes, Crowninshield did not act on Percival's request. In 1823 Percival again asked for relief without result. Now, in late 1828, he renewed his quest. Secretary Southard reviewed Percival's memorial of 1823 and other documents and in December told Mad Jack he could not make the change. The problem, he said, originated when the officer nominations had been sent to the Senate for confirmation. Percival had petitioned the Senate for redress without result. As long as he held the grade of lieutenant, he would have to live with what the secretary agreed was a possible injustice. Just as important, the alteration delayed later promotions and affected his relative standing as a master commandant.

This was a trying time for Percival—conducive, perhaps, to fatalism. One of the many Percival anecdotes is traceable to this difficult period. Legend has him taking passage on a Boston-to-Barnstable packet. The vessel fought heavy seas as it labored throughout the afternoon and into the evening. Mad Jack ignored the weather and turned in after supper. Well behind her normal seven-hour schedule, the packet struggled as the winds intensified to full gale force. At midnight, an apprehensive mate roused the veteran naval officer and confessed that the crew feared the vessel would founder before daylight. Completely unconcerned, Percival replied, "Well, I've got ten friends over there to one in this world." Grumbling, "Let her go," he rolled over and slept soundly until they were inside the lee of Barnstable Harbor.[1]

Spring found Percival acting the part of a gentleman farmer, a common pursuit of returning Cape mariners. Hemmed in by the Great Marshes to the north and by hills covered with oak and pine to the south, his native West Barnstable was an agricultural community. Local tradition credits Percival with planting the row of horse chestnut trees that still shade the old King's Highway in front of the former Bursley homestead in the village. According to a Bursley descendant, Percival probably did plant some of the exotic trees about the farm, notably an English walnut.

When the winter weather of 1829–30 halted his horticultural activities, Percival turned increasingly to that other addiction of mariners: spinning yarns. He found that his fellow Cape Codders were prone to listen to him whenever naval topics were discussed, for by now they

regarded him as the area's authority in the field. When the talk shifted
to a more general maritime subject, however, such as the navigational
hazards encountered in the Strait of Magellan, everyone had an observation to make.

Daniel Webster took note of this trait. The great number of mariners
on the Cape who were as familiar with the Galápagos and Sandwich
Islands as with the inland counties of Massachusetts impressed him. He
once argued a case in the Barnstable court that centered on the harbor
entrance to Honolulu. The opposing lawyer called for an expert witness
to describe the hazards of the entrance. Webster sensed the meaning of
one juror's smile. He asked the judge to poll the jurors. Seven out of the
twelve rose and said they were quite familiar with the place, having been
there often. Hence, when Mad Jack talked in the village or down at the
harbor about the infernal schoolmasters who dominated the Sandwich
Islands, in all likelihood at least one other man in the gathering could
enliven the conversation by offering views on the matter as well.

Mad Jack remained on leave of absence until the following summer. In
August 1830 Secretary of the Navy John Branch ordered him to report to
Norfolk and prepare the U.S. schooner *Porpoise* for a cruise against the
persistent pirates in the West Indies. In September the secretary told
Percival to proceed to the West Indies and report to Commo. Jesse
Elliott. Percival took the twelve-gun schooner out of the Virginia port on
19 October and headed for his station. During the next sixteen months
the *Porpoise* teamed up with the sloops-of-war *Erie, Fairfield,* and *Vincennes* and the schooners *Grampus* and *Shark* to suppress piracy in the
Caribbean. Pensacola, Florida, served as their base station.

Another tale that perhaps defines Percival as well as any other is traceable to this time. One of his men was derelict and repeatedly drunk. Mad
Jack ordered several crewmen to prepare the offender for corporal punishment. Just before the flogging commenced, the transgressor pleaded,
"Pardon, me, sir. I'm also from Barnstable—your own hometown."

"You deserve a dozen more lashes for disgracing the place—you rascal," roared Percival in reply.[2] Regulations prevented a more severe punishment, but Mad Jack made his point.

While he was relentless in disciplining shirkers, Percival possessed an
unusually soft heart. When he heard that fire had desolated Fayetteville
on 29 May 1831, for example, he initiated a collection on board the *Por-

poise. The crew responded by contributing two hundred dollars for the relief of the victims.

Percival devoted much of his time in the Caribbean to assisting American maritime interests there. On 21 May the *Porpoise* aided the Bath, Maine, merchantman *Java,* which had wrecked on the north coast of Cuba. Capt. Nathaniel Jellerson praised Percival for saving much of his cargo. Percival split the six-hundred-dollar reward among the crew, exclusive of the officers. In August he rescued nine men stranded on the Salt Keys. The *Barnstable Patriot* reported that the men were starving and about to perish. In October he came to the aid of the Portland, Maine, brig *Rodney* and received the thanks of the captain and the insurers.

Another action involved the American ship *Corsica,* which grounded at the British Virgin Islands in early November 1831. The officers and men thought their lives were in danger from lawless blacks in the vicinity and fled to Saint Thomas, which was then under Danish control. Percival had the *Porpoise* in port at the time, and the U.S. consul asked him to lend a hand in salvaging the *Corsica*'s cargo. When he arrived on the scene, he found the British merchant vessels *Catherine* and *Trial* and some black boatmen picking over the American wreck, and fired a signal gun. Capt. William Walpole of HMS *Ranger* reported that the Americans actually shot into the *Catherine.* In any event, the band of boatmen fled and the captain of the *Corsica* went on board the British salvage vessels. Percival reported that the captain and the British masters adjusted the salvage, and the latter gave up half the *Corsica* property they held.

Captain Walpole vigorously complained that Percival's actions were against all law and usage. Since the *Corsica* was abandoned and cast away on a British shore, he insisted, the agreement or compromise was improper. He wanted all the property back. Percival retorted that the *Corsica* had wrecked two leagues from the shore and more than ten leagues from any magistrate or public official. According to precedent in Admiralty courts, he continued, the *Corsica*'s captain became the agent the instant his ship wrecked. Therefore, the compromise agreement was proper. Warming to the subject, Percival went on to say that he had neither insulted the British flag nor used violence. He cited English Admiralty authorities again to support his refusal to return the recovered property when he noted that a mere quitting of a ship to obtain aid ashore does not constitute abandonment. He concluded: "No civilized nation now considers wrecks as forfeited because they may be cast upon its shores. This vice of a barborous [*sic*] age has been long abandoned. . . . Misfortune is no longer treated as a crime."[3] In an earlier report to Elliott he admitted: "The subject has caused me much solicitude as it was one from which I could derive *no interest,* except that of zealously performing my duty."[4]

A year later, Secretary of the Navy Levi Woodbury forwarded a grateful letter from the *Corsica*'s lawyers and added his commendation. In a second letter Woodbury declared himself pleased with Percival's efficiency and said that his efforts deserved the highest credit. Otherwise, the cruise turned out to be routine even though the *Porpoise* required close attention. If handled just right, the ten-year-old schooner proved rather fast. Percival resisted the urge to drive her hard. Her full bow and large rigs tended to drop her stem, which could be dangerous. A succeeding commander was not so cautious. The *Porpoise* was wrecked on this station a year after Percival left the ship.

In August 1831 Percival's health began to fail and he asked the secretary to place him on leave once again. While in port at Havana in November, he received approval. As soon as it could be arranged, Lieutenant Armstrong would replace him. The change of command took place in Pensacola on 11 February 1832.

Before he left, Percival demonstrated once again his deep concern for the welfare of sailors. He reported to Woodbury that two deserters from the U.S. frigate *Potomac* had surrendered to him before he left Saint Thomas. The two men had expressed contrition and behaved themselves while on his ship, he told Woodbury, and they hoped this would be to their favor. Percival added the following postscript: "Mr. Woodbury I would most respectfully add my supplication to you in favor of the above Seamen, believing as I do, that they have been more sinned against than intending to sin."[5] This kind of interest in the condition and well-being of ordinary seamen typified Percival's career. Time and again he extended himself on behalf of those who served under him.

Once again, Percival headed home to West Barnstable. Though he was not in vigorous health, his eighty-eight-year-old mother, Molly, needed his help around the farm. In May 1832 he asked to be continued on leave because his health remained indifferent. In January 1833, still at West Barnstable, he asked for another extension, explaining that he was taking medicine for a liver problem.

Soon after he settled down to agrarian living Percival received pleasant news from Washington. President Andrew Jackson, on 27 April 1832, signed a commission promoting him to master commandant, or commander. Curiously, the promotion was made retroactive to 3 March 1831. Ten other lieutenants—Slater, McCauley, Newell, Valette, Spencer, Aulick, Taylor, Mix, Dulany, and Stringham—were promoted at the same time. A longhand entry on Percival's commission indicated that he was to take rank preceding John H. Aulick.

The more than thirteen months between the presidential action and the effective date has led to some confusion about this promotion. U.S. Navy records indicate that he was promoted on the March 1831 date. His own gravestone, perhaps prepared under his direction, reflected the later April 1832 date. When the town of Barnstable replaced his weathered, almost illegible stone in 1965, the 1832 date was retained.

Later in the year, Percival sought some special relief from Washington. He wrote to Woodbury asking for remuneration for incidental expenses incurred while in command of the *Dolphin*. He noted that he had made an original request for reimbursement in December 1827, but was advised that the law did not cover his situation. When he learned that Lt. Thomas ap Catesby Jones, who followed him to Hawaii within the year, received compensation for similar expenses, Percival decided to reopen the matter. Explaining the apparent tardiness of his petition, Percival said the trials and inquiry of 1827–28 had left him little leisure to look into the matter at the time.

In his reply, Woodbury acknowledged that several officers had received reimbursement for similar expenses, but as of 1828 such claims had to be sent to Congress. Thus, with Woodbury's tacit approval, Percival contacted Congressman John Reed, a Cape Cod friend. Reed introduced a petition in Congress. To support his claim, Percival swore that his expenses amounted to $500. Articles used as gifts to the native islanders cost him $170, and entertainments for the Hawaiian chiefs and extraordinary expenses came to $330.

The next step involved communicating with Congressman John Anderson of Maine, who sat on the Committee on Naval Affairs. Percival provided Anderson with supporting details and justification, including a statement from Purser Bates verifying the $500 figure. Percival stressed that William Finch of the *Vincennes,* another officer who followed him to the islands, had received $5,000 for expenses from the last session of Congress. Anderson's report to the full Congress made special note of the fact that Percival claimed much less than the officers who had succeeded him. The House accepted the findings, and on 19 June 1834 Congress passed a private act directing the secretary of the treasury to pay Percival $500. Percival's reputation for frugality certainly helped him in this matter. Congress as well as others recognized his thriftiness. In another decade, this attribute would gain him a coveted command.

By March 1833 Percival was ready to get back to work. The navy gave him command of the receiving ship *Columbus* in Boston. He promptly regretted asking for the assignment. His old nemesis Commodore Bainbridge still headed the Boston Navy Yard. Percival asked Secretary Woodbury to excuse him from the position, explaining that the department was familiar with the friction that existed between the two men as well as its origin in the Hull controversies. A superior officer could make things quite difficult for a subordinate even if the latter did his duty, he added.

Percival's concern was short-lived. In another week he learned that Bainbridge planned to vacate his post due to illness. On 22 March, Mad Jack informed the secretary that the circumstances had changed and asked if he could retain the command and if the department would excuse his apparent fickleness. The request came too late. The department instead assigned him to administrative duties and set him to work overhauling the *Independence,* a sister ship of the *Columbus, Franklin,* and *Washington.*

During the March exchange of correspondence with the department, Percival made it clear that Dorchester, Massachusetts, was his place of residence. This would be the case for the rest of his life, although he forever remained attached to West Barnstable and visited there often. His mother continued to live there until her death in 1841.

In May 1833 Percival asked the secretary to appoint him to the vacant master commandant's post at the Gosport Navy Yard in Norfolk. He felt sure that Lewis Warrington, the head of the yard, would concur. Mad Jack did not mention that he held the new Boston commandant, Jesse Elliott, in low regard; many did. This request was denied, as was his plea to take over the *Vincennes* in the Pacific. Percival remained in Boston.

On 15 November 1833 Secretary Woodbury called all midshipmen in from leave and ordered them to report to Boston, New York, or Norfolk and attend naval school. Woodbury directed the yard commanders to furnish the young men with suitable accommodations and professional training. Percival found himself back in charge of the training ship *Columbus*. Built in 1819, the *Columbus* displaced 2,480 tons and carried a 780-man crew at sea. Barely exceeding the *Franklin* in weight, she was the largest ship Percival ever commanded. The U.S. Navy did not have any ships larger than the 74-gun class until the great *Pennsylvania* was launched in 1837.

Bitter political contention at the national level marked this period in the nation's history. The dominant issue involved the merits of the Bank of the United States, which was up for recharter. Despite its name, the bank was not owned by the U.S. government, and its profits went to private stockholders. President Andrew Jackson, always suspicious of privilege, led the opposition to the bank some called a "monster." The matter became central to his presidency. Jackson favored the establishment of a government-owned bank with greatly limited powers to prevent a monopoly, and possibly to prevent violations of the Constitution as well.

The president of the Bank of the United States, Nicholas Biddle, had tried to circumvent Jackson's opposition by urging Congress to pass an early recharter bill. In July 1832 Biddle seemed to have succeeded when Congress passed such a bill. But Old Hickory wasted little time in vetoing the measure, and Congress sustained his veto. The electoral campaign of 1832 made much of the issue. Despite the bank's financial support of Henry Clay's candidacy, Jackson won reelection by an overwhelming majority. Thus supported by the masses, he continued his uncompromising war against Biddle. In September 1833 Jackson ceased depositing federal funds in the bank. The controversy peaked during the winter of 1833–34 after a contest of many months. Despite considerable maneuvering by Biddle, Jackson eventually emerged victorious. The wealthy were humbled, and the bank died in March 1836.

In New England, there was a great deal of local interest in the issue. Bostonians protested and signed memorials supporting both sides. Editors scolded and lampooned the participants. Politicians hurled charges and countercharges. A fair amount of anti-Jackson sentiment existed in Massachusetts during the controversy. Just as it began to subside in early 1834, Jesse Elliott thoughtlessly fanned the flames of discontent. Jackson had made a popular tour of New England the previous summer. Invited to Massachusetts by the legislature, the president received a

Lafayette-like welcome in the Hub, and staid old Harvard awarded him an honorary doctor of laws degree. Not all New Englanders were that hospitable. The ex-president and Harvard graduate John Quincy Adams headed the show of disdain. Still miffed over his 1828 defeat by Jackson, he refused to witness the disgrace of his alma mater when it conferred the high honor upon the barbarian from the backwoods.[6]

Elliott's actions seem to suggest that he had been out of touch with public opinion in recent months. In fact, he was a Democrat, and his political loyalties clouded his judgment. He put the inflammatory bank question out of his mind. All that seemed to matter to him was Jackson's success in New England the previous summer. He thought the president deserved a special honor to commemorate it. Many could agree in principle, but Elliott's specific method struck Bostonians as blasphemous. He arranged to adorn the stem of the frigate *Constitution,* which was undergoing repairs in the new Charlestown dry dock, with a full-length likeness of the old warrior. The original *Constitution* figurehead, a likeness of Hercules, was shattered in a collision with the *President* during the campaign against Tripoli. The second design, a characterization of Neptune, gave way to a billet head in the shape of a scroll. Elliott decided to replace the scroll with a fourth version. He commissioned a local craftsman named Laban S. Beecher to produce a Jackson figurehead.

An uproar erupted over this profanation of the idolized *Constitution.* "There had been a difference of opinion about breaking her up," Ira Hollis noted in a subsequent *Atlantic Monthly* article, "but there was a very rancorous difference about the propriety of Andrew Jackson as a figurehead."[7] Elliott's unthinking action so close on the heels of the bank fight resulted in a war of words of a magnitude seldom experienced anywhere, including politically active Boston. Elliott, always a stormy petrel, was roundly scorned in the Massachusetts capital. "The removal of the deposits having raised the Bostonians from their genuflections into an attitude of 'resistance to a tyrant,' it became their new policy to abandon shaking hands with Captain Elliott as *the President's particular friend,* and to denounce him as the *tyrant's* subservient tool," noted Russell Jarvis in a biographical note about Elliott published shortly afterward.[8] The curses came loud and clear from the very people who a short time before had cheered Jackson. Elliott belatedly concluded that the *Constitution* belonged not to the United States but to the North End of Boston.

The protestors circulated incendiary handbills throughout the city. One of the most indignant wondered if Bostonians would consent to place the figurehead of a landlubber on the bows of Old Ironsides. Hull, Decatur, or Porter would deserve the honor, but not Jackson! The call went out to save the ship from a foul disgrace. The regular press, including the normally pro-Jackson newspapers, quickly joined the crusade. The *Mercantile Journal,* for example, claimed, "It will be in time to ornament our vessels with busts of any man, when *History* shall have established his character."[9] A letter reproduced in a later edition of the paper wondered: "Why will not our fellow citizen stuff the wooden effigy, with combustibles, give it a slow match, and swear it went off by self-combustion. This would be entirely in character and a consummation likely to befall the original."[10] *Niles' Weekly Register,* published in distant Baltimore, viewed the excitement in Boston with more objectivity, although no less displeasure. The editor thought that, politics aside, it was improper to place the head of a living person on a national ship. The *Constitution,* he felt, ought to remain in appearance as she was when she humbled the British.

Elliott did have supporters who argued that there were precedents for a Jackson figurehead. During the presidency of John Adams, for instance, his likeness appeared on the corvette *John Adams.* George Washington's image was placed on the *Washington,* and Benjamin Franklin's on the *Franklin.*

Late in March, Beecher informed Elliott that several prominent Bostonians had offered him a fifteen-hundred-dollar bribe if he would permit them to carry away the nearly completed figurehead. Jesse Elliott decided to remove the head to the safety of the navy yard. Mad Jack appeared on the scene at this point and became the favorite of the Elliott critics. On 21 March, Elliott sent Sailing Master Hixon to Beecher's shop. Hixon boxed the head, placed it in his launch, and made his way to Charlestown without incident. Elliott concealed the image in the steam engine house. By nightfall he became anxious. Handbills and rumors suggested an attempt to take the head from the yard might be forthcoming. Elliott sent for Percival and told him to quietly arm his men and prepare to thwart any move against the figurehead.

There are different versions of what happened next. In a letter to the secretary of the navy, Elliott said that when he directed Percival to receive on the *Columbus* boarding pikes and cutlasses, Mad Jack accepted the order without question. But when the gunner actually appeared with the arms, Percival allegedly refused to take them without a written order from Elliott's executive officer, Lieutenant Smith. The gunner could not locate Smith, so he went to the commandant with his problem. Elliott promptly sent for Percival and demanded an explanation. Elliott later said that Percival's only response was that he would not receive an order from a gunner. Elliott promptly suspended Percival from duty and turned over the *Columbus* to Lieutenant Varnum.

The *Mercantile Journal* jumped to Percival's defense, praising his foresight in recognizing the "disastrous consequences" of arming his men "to secure the public tranquility." The paper thought he "very properly requested a *written* order to that effect, which was not given,"[11] and that his arrest was unjust. Another incendiary handbill took up the fight. The bill described Percival as a brave and distinguished officer who knew he did not have to arm against the good people of Boston. The flyer called Elliott a "bloodthirsty and petty tyrant." The exaggerated and inflammatory bill, signed "TEA PARTY—Cradle of Liberty, March 27, 1834," concluded by calling for a coat of tar and feathers for Elliott.[12]

The newspapers continued to stir the pot, but on 28 March the *Journal* admitted that some of its coverage of Percival's involvement was in error. Percival actually did receive the arms and distribute them to the regular crew, the paper said, but he refused to arm the inexperienced and undisciplined yard workers. A number of these laborers were billeted on the *Columbus*. When the gunner appeared with cutlasses and pikes for the civilians, Percival told him to leave the weapons and go to Smith and ask him to send a written order to cover the situation. The gunner could not locate Smith but did find Lieutenant Babbitt, one of Percival's subordinates, who told the gunner to take the arms away. As the man left, he encountered Elliott and told him that Mad Jack had refused to accept the weapons. On this evidence alone, Elliott sent for Percival and relieved him of duty. Both Elliott and the *Journal* agreed that on the following day, Percival gave a satisfactory explanation of his conduct and Elliott restored him to his post. Elliott's biographer, Russell Jarvis, acknowledged that Percival had a "shadow of pretext; a color of right."[13]

Within a few days the image of Jackson—complete with a scroll proclaiming "The Union, it must be preserved"—appeared on the *Constitu-*

tion's bow. As a precautionary measure, Elliott moored the frigate between the *Columbus* and the *Independence.*

On 5 April 1834 Percival asked for a fifteen-day leave to deal with some personal business. On 5 May the department directed him to prepare the sloop *Erie* for the Brazil station. As a consequence, his role in the figurehead caper ended at that point. But another Cape Codder was on hand to bring down the curtain. Samuel W. Dewey, a merchant captain from Falmouth, Massachusetts, arrived in Boston with a load of sugar from the West Indies at the height of the controversy. After he disposed of his cargo, Dewey visited the office of his employers, Henry and William Lincoln. The men were discussing the figurehead, and Dewey claimed it would be an easy matter to remove Old Hickory. The Lincolns promptly issued a challenge, offering one hundred dollars if he could carry out his boast. Dewey told them to consider the task done.

A violent thunderstorm broke over Boston during the night of 2 July. Dewey made his move. He quietly rowed across the harbor to the yard and pulled himself up onto the *Constitution* by her manropes. Three sentries—one on the wharf, another on the *Columbus,* and yet another on the *Constitution*—failed to detect him. He cut away much of the figurehead and stole back to the Boston shore carrying his prize, which he subsequently hid in a shed at his mother's house on School Street. Once again, the community erupted. Depending on one's politics, the mutilation was either heroic or cowardly. Elliott was incensed. He decided to take the *Constitution* to New York and safer waters. Besides, no carver could be found in Boston brave enough to make another Jackson head for fear of losing his own. As he sailed out of Boston Harbor, Elliott directed a parting slap at his antagonists. He draped what remained of the Jackson effigy with an improvised five-stripe flag, a derisive reference to the infamous attempt by New Englanders to secede and establish a five-state republic during the War of 1812. Elliott procured a substitute figurehead in New York.

Back in Boston, Dewey hid the figurehead until the uproar died down. When things were quiet again, he packed it up and brazenly set out for Washington. He planned to present the head to Jackson himself, but the president was sick so he had to settle for Vice President Martin Van Buren. The audacity of it all greatly entertained the vice president, and he sent the prankster and his prize to Secretary of the Navy Mahlon Dickerson. The secretary was not amused and threatened to arrest him.

Dewey convinced Dickerson that no jury in Boston would convict him, and the matter was dropped.

By the time the figurehead farce played out, Percival was deeply involved in his preparations on the *Erie*. He wrote to the secretary on the importance of having a capable carpenter on the ship and asked for Amos Chick, an able mechanic from Portsmouth, New Hampshire. The secretary denied the request, explaining that Elliott, acting within his delegation, had already appointed another man. The yard commandant was in a foul mood and felt it necessary to assert the authority so publicly questioned in recent days.

The continuing tension between Elliott and Percival was obvious and did not disappear quickly. Earlier in January, for instance, Percival had had to appeal directly to the secretary for a cook and steward for the *Columbus* because Elliott would not provide the customary servants. This incident aside, Percival simply had little use for the man. Many in the navy disliked or disrespected Elliott, who had committed the ultimate sin during the Battle of Lake Erie on 10 September 1813. Elliott held the second command to Oliver Hazard Perry but did not come to Perry's assistance until almost three hours after his commander became engaged with an enemy of superior numbers. Even the most charitable observers said that he failed to act decisively. Several years after the 1834 uproar at Charlestown, Elliott once again found himself in murky water when the navy charged him with cruelty and transporting animals without the proper authority during a cruise of the *Constitution*. A court-martial handed him a four-year suspension. The department eventually remitted part of the sentence, restored him to duty, and placed him in charge of the Philadelphia yard. He served there for a year until his death in 1845.

On 13 June 1834 the navy secretary instructed Mad Jack to get the *Erie* under way as soon as he could, proceed to New York, complete his crew, and await sailing orders. A week later Percival informed the secretary that Elliott had said that he alone would decide when the *Erie* was ready to sail. Four days after that, Percival informed the department that he had reported to the ship. "I would most respectfully represent that I find the ship and stores in such an unarranged state as almost to preclude the hope of my being able to proceed to sea for at least ten or twelve days," he reported. He complained that he had neither a boatswain nor a boatswain's mate; nor did he have sufficient crew to handle the ship. He promised to make "every exertion" to remedy the situation.[14]

The next day, Percival wrote the secretary, "I shall be unable, I fear with all my exertion to sail before the 5th or 6th of July," adding the assurance that "on my honor as a seaman and what I hold as sacred my gratitude to you . . . no exertions shall be wanting on my part to get to New York as soon as possible." His strong desire to leave the yard was very much in evidence.[15]

While looking for men to complete his crew, the nurturing side of Mad Jack surfaced. He asked in behalf of a "respectable family in this vicinity" to have Frances Reed assigned to the *Erie*. Young Reed had joined the navy against his family's will and was, said Percival, "a little disposed to be wild." In addition, Percival asked for Franklin Baxter, "a distant relative of mine who is one of the inconsiderate & improvident but an excellent seaman who has a deserving family." He especially wanted to "have some control" over Baxter to "correct his habits as to induce him to provide something for the support of his family."[16]

The secretary got right back to Percival, telling him not to take the *Erie* to New York before she was completely ready. He added: "As you and Comt. Elliott have differed on that point—and as the responsibility for the safety of the vessel rests on you, after you take the command, Comt. Elliott is instructed to place as many men on board as you may require."[17]

Percival was finally ready to sail by early August. On the second, Acting Secretary John Boyle gave him his orders. Percival was to go to Rio de Janeiro and report to the commodore at that station. He was to give particular attention to aiding and protecting American commerce in the region. Since the station commander, James Renshaw, did not arrive until 1835, Percival was his own boss for a while.

❧ 8 ❧

THE VERY PATTERN OF
OLD INTEGRITY

*T*he U.S. sloop-of-war *Erie* was built in Baltimore during the War of 1812 and lengthened and rebuilt at New York in 1820–21. Percival's yearlong South American cruise in the ship provided considerable fodder to feed the legend of Mad Jack. Until Renshaw showed up in the spring of 1835 and took over as commodore, the *Erie* operated alone and Percival answered directly to the secretary.

One of Percival's first major reports to the secretary covered the fate of the brig *Mexican* out of Salem, Massachusetts. It seems that pirates had plundered five thousand dollars from the ship and taken refuge on the Portuguese island of Saint Thomas off the African coast. The mate of the pirate vessel gave a large sum to the island's governor to obtain protection. Percival sensed that the governor feared what the authorities in Lisbon might do if he were implicated in piracy and thought that energetic measures by an American man-of-war might recover the money. If the United States did not act, he knew that Capt. Henry Trotter of HBM brig *Curlew* was prepared to respond. He offered his services to the *Mexican*'s owners, saying he was quite familiar with Saint Thomas and "the character of the lawless inhabitants, as well as their more guilty rulers, who are convicts of a greater or less shade of depravity."[1]

The department did not receive Percival's report until April, and did not reply until 8 June. Some weeks passed before Percival received the response from Acting Secretary Boyle, at which time he learned that the department wanted him to act on his February report. Boyle instructed him to proceed to Saint Thomas as soon as he could get ready and demand restitution for the stolen money from the governor. The department gave him the added assignment of cruising north along the African coast to suppress the slave trade before returning to Brazil. A companion letter of the same date urged prompt attention to this special task.

Unfortunately, Commodore Renshaw had arrived on station in the meantime, and irreconcilable differences had developed between the two men. Commodore Renshaw was not disposed to favor Percival with the mission. Acting under his authority as station commander, Renshaw told Comdr. William Salter to carry out the mission in the *Ontario*. Salter left in August and returned in January 1836, having failed to clear Brazil. He blamed unseasonable weather and shipboard sickness for his default.

Another of Percival's February reports summarized a more serious chain of events. He arrived in Pernambuco on 12 January 1835 and communicated with the U.S. consulate there, inquiring about the state of the province and the adequacy of local protection for U.S. commerce. Consular Agent L. G. Ferreira reported that everything was in good order. But a day later, on the fourteenth, he asked Percival to delay his departure because he saw signs of a revolution, or at least of serious unrest. On the fifteenth, Ferreira told Percival that he had consulted with American property owners and that it was safe for the *Erie* to depart. The local government had taken effective and decisive measures, he told Percival, and Pernambuco was now tranquil. As it turned out, Ferreira was too optimistic. After his departure, Percival informed the department, a disturbance took place and several lives were lost.

Percival got to Bahia on 19 January, just in time for another uprising. Blacks revolted on the twenty-fifth and nearly succeeded in carrying the day. Some seventy-five people were killed or wounded. Percival offered all the foreign consuls the asylum of his ship. The consular community reacted with gratitude. John Parkinson, the British consul, thought the prompt and handsome offer was reflective of cordial Anglo-American relations. The French consul, the representative of the Netherlands, the German vice consul, and the Russian agent in Bahia all sent letters of appreciation. The Sardinian vice consul, A. J. Armando, was the only official to accept Percival's offer of protection. He did so, he explained, because of his young family and his own poor health. More than two dozen British merchants thanked Percival on the twenty-ninth for his generous concern.

Before he left Bahia, Percival dispatched a detailed report on political conditions in the area to the Department of the Navy. He also passed on a complaint commonly voiced by American merchants: direct trade between the United States and Brazil had declined within the past two years. British and other foreign bottoms were transporting American flour. The British, in fact, were well on the way to eliminating U.S. carriers in the region. On 23 April the secretary acknowledged Percival's reports on civil and commercial conditions in the Bahia region and indicated the president's satisfaction with his diligence.

The *Erie* left for Rio on 13 February. The French were building up their naval forces in the area, and Percival passed this news on to the department. This intelligence was of more than passing interest in Washington. For years, Americans sought damages for U.S. property seized by the French during the Napoleonic Wars. Negotiations broke down in 1834, and the two countries flirted with war before resolving the matter in 1836.

At Rio, the rift between Renshaw and Percival came out into the open. The underlying cause for their enmity is obvious. Renshaw was part of the Bainbridge circle, and Percival was still considered a Hull man. In fact, Renshaw was so close to Bainbridge that he named his son born in 1816 William Bainbridge Renshaw. Moreover, like Percival, Renshaw was passionate if not high-strung. In 1808, when he was a lieutenant, Renshaw was charged with and tried for challenging another man to a duel.

Renshaw gave Mad Jack a cool reception when he returned from Bahia. Percival took exception to the affront. A few days later, he undertook a spot inspection of the U.S. naval storehouse. The thrifty Percival was appalled at the mess he found there. Waste and mismanagement were obvious. Renshaw fired the storekeeper, but it is likely that he resented Percival's uninvited intervention.

Perhaps to get him out of the way, Renshaw sent Percival to Buenos Aires to check on conditions there. Mad Jack found the Argentine dictatorship anything but friendly to Americans. He agreed with the U.S. consul, E. R. Dorr, that the Argentines were jealous of America's prosperity and "extremely vain from their success over the ill managed expedition of the English General Whitlock and the imbecile effort of the Brazilians to subdue them in their late war." The shallow waters of the local harbor and its entrance prevented men-of-war from getting closer than six miles from the city, he noted in his report to the secretary, but he thought the Argentine authorities "would comprehend and understand . . . a small and efficient force within point blank range." He suggested that four to six schooners—"to cost about 5000 dollars each and to carry each two long 24 pdrs and about 35 men and officers each; to *not draw more than 9 feet of water*"—might deal nicely with the situation. Such a squadron would provide the necessary protection for U.S. interests and would be a "much more competent and efficient force."[2]

Fiscal accountability and the well-being of his midshipmen, always two of Percival's major concerns, came together in June. Purser Grenville Cooper interpreted a recent departmental financial instruction to mean that midshipmen could draw part of their rations in whiskey. Mad Jack could not believe the department had really intended this result. He wrote to the secretary: "On board this Ship there are Eight modest, temperate, unassuming, talented young Midshipmen, calculated to adorn any society, and do credit to any profession." A daily ration of half a pint of whiskey was too much of a temptation, he argued, and "would prove the Apple of Seduction to Intemperance, and consequent improper conduct and degradation and result in blasting the fond hopes and just expectations of their paternal guides."[3] Percival said that he had enforced an earlier standing order that kept whiskey out of the hands of midshipmen. Secretary Dickerson responded to Percival immediately sanctioning his position.

Later, while on station at the entrance to the Río de la Plata in July 1835, Percival asked the department to clarify the status of the ship's schoolmaster. An act of 3 March 1835, passed after the navy had appointed him, expanded the duties and increased the pay of ships' schoolmasters. Percival felt that his schoolmaster should be paid the amount stipulated when he was hired and asked the department for a ruling so he could correctly pay the man. "I am very anxious that all accounts approved by me, as also all acts of mine, should be correct," he stressed. The purser wanted to grant the schoolmaster full pay, but Percival was not sure. "We occasionally differ in opinion on those subjects," he noted, "which is the lot entailed on the imperfections of human judgement."[4] In time, the secretary approved Percival's strict interpretation. In order to get full schoolmaster's pay, a man had to be appointed after 3 March 1835. The *Erie* professor had obtained his post before that date and therefore could not receive the higher rate of the revised position.

Percival's difficulties with his station commander were more serious. In early August the breach between the two became complete. The particular incident involved their accommodations. Renshaw had been using the *Natchez* as his flagship. He made a change, carrying his pennant to the *Erie* and ousting Mad Jack from his cabin. In order to make room for his son, secretary, clerk, and servants, the commodore extended the bulkhead forward. Percival believed this reduced the fighting capacity of his ship, and he said as much.

By 3 August it was apparent that Percival would soon be leaving his command. Eleven American merchants at Rio de Janeiro sent him a letter of appreciation and a gift. *Niles' Weekly Register* published the compliment, originally reported in the *Army and Navy Chronicle,* with the expectation that it would be received with gratification by the friends of a creditable and worthy officer. Touched by the kind words and farewell gift, Percival thanked the merchants for their flattering gesture and told them that zealous performance of duty was a principal object of those in the navy.

On 10 August, Percival sent the secretary a copy of his commendation from the American merchants. The next day Renshaw relieved him of command of the *Erie* and assigned Lt. John Pope to the post. Percival tried to get Renshaw to permit him to carry out Boyle's orders of 8 June to go after the pirates at Saint Thomas, but Renshaw insisted that his own order took precedence.

Within a few days Percival obtained passage to New York, where he arrived in early October. He reported his return to the department and asked Secretary Dickerson for permission to visit Washington "to show the reason why I was refused permission (if not the right) to execute" the 8 June order, "the execution of which *my honor* as an Officer and *my rectitude* as a man was deeply interested."[5] Dickerson placed Percival on leave and gave him the permission he requested. Percival met with the secretary for an hour in November and outlined his case, but the department did nothing to rectify the wrong he felt had been done to him.

On 15 December 1835, still on leave in Boston, Percival asked to command a sloop-of-war near the Gulf Stream. Marine interests had petitioned the department for such coverage. Mad Jack did not suppose other officers of his grade would object since it would be a winter assignment and he would be limited to the coast. The navy never made the assignment.

On 4 January 1836, his leave having expired, Percival asked to be considered awaiting orders in Boston. Still unassigned in March 1836, he wrote to the secretary to express in greater detail his views regarding his differences with Renshaw and his desire to be utilized by the navy. He reminded Dickerson that in an earlier meeting the secretary had promised to find him employment. Actually, Percival hoped he had found a post on his own. His longtime friend John Downes commanded the Boston yard, and an opening existed there. He asked for the spot and went on to say that if he were left unemployed any longer, censure would be implied. "My health and indeed I almost might say my existence depends on active and energetic employment,"[6] he asserted.

The department took some time in responding. In the recent past, Percival had made plain his view that assignments should be based on merit. Nonetheless, he recognized that as long as Andrew Jackson was in the White House, a Yankee might not receive the same consideration granted to a southerner. Downes supported Percival's request for the Boston berth, so there was no obstacle there to the appointment. Finally, on 14 May, the department told Mad Jack to report to Charlestown on 1 July to take the place of Master Commandant George Budd. Percival acknowledged the assignment within the week.

On 29 June 1836, just before Percival returned to duty, a train of the Boston and Providence Rail Road Corporation crashed, and a score of sailors en route from the Brooklyn Navy Yard to the Boston Navy Yard were injured, four of them seriously. As the Boston yard's executive officer, Percival stepped in to act in their behalf.

The entire affair was routine, and by itself unnoteworthy. More than a century and a half later, however, a professor specializing in diplomatic and naval writings concluded that Percival stole more than twelve thousand dollars entrusted to him for the benefit of the most seriously injured sailors. This careless charge of criminality is utterly false. It is so baseless, in fact, that if Percival were alive, he would have a cause of action for libel.

mostly the latter—the late David F. Long claims in his book *"Mad Jack":* *The Biography of Captain John Percival, USN, 1779–1862* that an insurance settlement totaling $12,862 was turned over to Percival as trustee for Joshua Howell, Thomas Murdock, James Thompson, and Charles White. Professor Long assumes that Percival followed the recommendation of an attorney and invested all of the money in a Massachusetts Hospital Life Insurance Company policy.

At about this point, inexplicably, Professor Long introduces the 1862 "Executor's Inventory" attached to Percival's will into the story. The list includes the following notation: "Cash deposited in the Mass. Hospital Insurance Co. & due on their policy no. 3196—$12,761.10." "This is surely close enough" to the rail settlement total, the professor asserts, "to bring about the inescapable conclusion" that Percival "had robbed unlettered and impoverished seamen of their little recompense for their suffering."[7] He concludes that the facts lead to "an inescapable judgment: a damning indictment of Percival's character."[8] Percival "deliberately kept control of the principal, outlived the sailors, notified none of their relatives about their deaths and what was coming to them." Then he "appropriated the money for himself, surely the worst blot on a generally honorable life."[9]

Ironically, before presenting this original and damaging conclusion, the professor comments on "the oddity that almost half" of the Percival Papers deal with this trust, which was an "apparently unimportant" incident in Percival's life. "Why would he fill and file away four folders crammed with its correspondence and receipts?"[10] The answer is obvious. Percival was meticulous in accounting for any funds entrusted to him. He foresaw that someone would question his handling of such a large sum and kept detailed records of the account. Although not every receipt or piece of paper relating to the fund is present, an audit trail exists. And on every key point, Professor Long is wrong. Granted, the trust papers are ponderous and sometimes approach illegibility, but lurking therein is an altogether different story.

To begin, a receipt dated 26 January 1837 shows that $8,350, not $12,862, was entrusted to Percival. Just as important, Percival invested this money in Phoenix Bank of Charlestown stock, not with the Massachusetts Hospital Life Insurance Company, where he invested his own money. The award amount runs throughout the trust documents, most prominently in the four individual account ledgers. The court awarded Howell $3,000. Thompson and Murdock each got $2,250, and White received $1,500. Two other sailors, John Cummings and Benjamin Ransom, received awards of $175. The total award thus amounted to $8,350.

The men had to pay for lawyers and other legal expenses out of their base awards. There were unusual trial expenses as well. For example, Mad Jack had to dip into Howell's account for $3.50 to pay "a constable to take Joshua Howell when drunk during the trial from Boston to the Navy Yard in carriage."[11] In the end, Percival had $2,351.47 to invest in behalf of Howell, $2,193.75 apiece for Thompson and Murdock, and $1,462.50 for White. He recorded these amounts in the individual ledgers he began for each man's account.

Percival paid Cummings the entire amount awarded to him, which came to $150 when adjusted to account for costs. He made out the check to Thomas Williamson, cashier of the Bank of Virginia, in behalf of Cummings, who was then at Norfolk. The papers at the Massachusetts Historical Society do not include any record showing how Ransom received his money.

The record shows that Percival invested a total of $8,201.47 in behalf of Howell and the three others, not an even $8,350. The difference is due to the immediate costs of setting up the trust once the court established the final awards. The several account ledgers detail these expenses. Cummings's payment did not come out of the $8,350.

The trust agreement gave Percival complete control of the funds and directed him to invest the money "in his own name . . . in some stock or securities that he may think safe & productive." He explained to his friend Charles Chauncey that he took up the task because the men were "pennyless sailors, maimed and crippled without friends." He assumed the duty, he added, only after making certain that he was "fully and clearly exempted from all trustee and other vexatious suits—by artful and designing landlords and landladies."[12] Percival was ordered "from time to time" to pay the four men "the income . . . & also portions of the . . . principal in such manner as he may think best."[13] The court authorized him to deduct administrative costs from the principal or income.

Within a month Percival began making income payments to the men. Almost as quickly, the men began to try to get hold of part or all of their shares of the principal. White asked for $200 to help him get into a business or trade. Howell and Murdock made identical pleas. Percival rebuffed most of these requests and based the periodic payments to the men on the fund's earnings. Thompson tried another approach. He gave a Brooklyn lawyer power of attorney, and the latter unsuccessfully tried to gain control of his client's trust funds.

Thompson's sister, Mrs. Mary Roache of Brooklyn, also got into the act. She needed at least $200 to take care of her brother, she wrote to Percival. She was "very bad off," with "every thing going out and nothing coming in." Her brother, she added, gave her "power to receive whatever money is coming to him."[14] Percival was unmoved. During the preceding two months Thompson had managed to get hold of nearly $120 from his trust fund, and Percival felt that was sufficient reason to deny another advance. "I know my duty and shall do it," Percival declared. Ever one to watch his pennies, he admonished Mrs. Roache: "When you write me again, pay the postage."[15]

Professor Long's biography indicates that the last correspondence on the trust was dated 4 August 1840, when Murdock asked for part of his principal to buy some land. "No reply from Percival is extant," Long notes, "but undoubtedly his negative was unequivocal."[16] This, too, is untrue. Percival replied to Murdock less than a week later, on 10 August, advising him that selling the stock in order to get at the principal would "cause a sacrifice of from eight to ten per cent if not more." Mad Jack agreed to sell the stock only if Murdock declared that he understood the implications "before a proper authority, say the Mayor of Brooklyn." He also invited Murdock to Boston early in September to settle and close his account. His letter to Murdock closes, "you will have an opportunity to see how well you can manage and take care of the ample provision *obtained by me* for your support."[17]

By this time the trust was breaking up. Howell died at a Boston boardinghouse, and his executor, Robert W. Casey, settled the estate with Percival. Howell's balance in the trust was $1,071.99, and on 16 March 1840 Percival issued a Phoenix Bank check to Casey for this amount. White also demanded a payout. Since he had but $300.82 in the trust, Percival obliged. He paid White the total amount, and White signed a receipt on 13 August 1840. Murdock took Percival's offer. On 7 September 1840, Percival closed his account and Murdock affirmed receipt of the balance of $876.94.

James Thompson died late in 1840. Peter Turner and John Mansfield of Brooklyn were his executors. After an exchange of legal documents, on 15 June 1841, Percival settled the Thompson account with an $800 payment to the two executors.

With a cautious eye to the future, Percival gathered up the trust documents in his possession and secured them under a cover sheet reading: "The accts of Thos Murdock, James Thompson, Joshua Howell, and Charles W White settled & signed & sealed, thank God—J Percival." The evidence should end any belief or speculation that John Percival violated and defrauded a trust. The record, in fact, shows that he administered the Howell et al. Trust with honesty, prudence, and fairness, just as everyone at the time expected him to do. Percival had his faults, but improbity was not one of them.

Delighted to be back at work, Percival threw himself into his regular administrative duties at the Boston yard. Always watchful of his midshipmen, in July 1836 he sent a report to the department providing details on one who arrived twenty-four days late for duty on the sloop *Boston*. In November he complained to Secretary Dickerson that the shameful nightly desertion of recruits from the station was due to the lack of supervising officers. He placed just as much blame on inadequate, inconvenient, and uncomfortable quarters, noting a prejudice among sailors "against being confined in Stores, which by them, is considered analogous to a Jail." He recommended "a proper Receiving Ship" to solve the problem.[18]

The receiving ship letter did not require an immediate response. But Percival's agitation about another matter later in the month elicited an immediate reaction from Secretary Dickerson. A former employee of the yard, John D. Howard, complained in writing that Percival had ordered the lower masts of the exploring vessels then in the yard to be cut off. Percival responded that the charge was "*utterly untrue, & false & without foundation.*" As well, he denied causing one to two thousand dollars' worth of damage to sails. Interestingly, he did admit the truth of one of Howard's charges: "To the *sobriquet* of 'Mad Jack' which he is as careful as to mention; I plead guilty, & in this unhappy predicament, my only consolation is, that I am not unaccompanied by many of the first & most distinguished men of the Country."[19]

Percival blamed Howard's charges on the man's personal vendetta against the officers and mechanics of the yard. At one time the Boston yard had employed Howard as a caulker. But one day, Percival explained to the secretary, Howard appeared "upon the stage in the respectable character of a smuggler of spiritous liquors into this Yard." And "if the Sailors can be believed did vend it at a *Dollar a pint.*" Elliott, the commandant at that time, fired Howard for this offense. Percival thought Howard unworthy of "the serious notice of any gentlemen" and closed his letter to the secretary by suggesting, "If you have a shadow of confidence in the reports of Howard, I request you will direct a legal investigation."[20] The secretary responded to Percival's letter immediately, indicating that his explanation was fully satisfactory to the department, and dropped the matter.

In March 1837 Percival forwarded a special request, through Downes, to Dickerson. On the eve of his departure from the *Erie* he had promised the crew, most of whom were natives of the Northeast, that he would pass on their request to end the cruise in Boston. He begged the secretary's pardon for his presumptuousness in making such a request. Within the week the secretary told Percival he would take the matter under advisement.

On 7 April Mad Jack received a special assignment from the Board of Navy Commissioners. An ongoing dispute dragged along on Cape Cod about the need and best location for a lighthouse or lighthouses on Nauset Beach in Eastham, one of several "graveyards" for shipping along the Atlantic coast. A dangerous gap existed between Highland, or Cape Cod Light, in North Truro and the pair of lights to the south in Chatham. Mariners wanted something done. A small band of men employed in the wrecking business, however, was stubbornly resisting a new lighthouse; the more wrecks to salvage and plunder, the better their business. The board wanted someone with intimate knowledge of the coast and a sterling reputation to study the situation and make recommendations. Nobody was better suited to the task than Percival. He left for the lower Cape to look into the matter.

Advocates of action had presented a plan to the board calling for three fifteen-foot towers, and the board directed Percival to determine the plan's feasibility. He talked to Cape mariners and walked the ground at Nauset. At the site that had been proposed for the towers, neither the Chatham lights to the south nor the Cape Cod Light to the north was visible.

Percival strongly recommended the three-tower plan, which, he believed, would identify the spot unmistakably for mariners and reduce marine accidents. Ten vessels had been wrecked on Nauset beach within the past eight years, at a loss of many lives and about half a million dollars. The beach was too low to be discernible from the deck of a ship; the high ground one-half mile inland overshadowed the shoreline. Percival included a sketch of that part of the coast in his May report locating the proposed towers and marking the sites of the disastrous wrecks of recent years. Percival determined and staked out the exact position for the towers and advised that there should be no deviation from his placements.

The board accepted Percival's 20 May 1837 report and recommendations and forwarded the material to Congress. Congress passed a ten-thousand-dollar appropriation, and the authorities engaged Capt. Winslow Lewis of Wellfleet to build the towers. The Three Sisters Lights, completed in July 1838, were distinctive because they stood 150 feet from one another. The three brick towers continued to operate for more than fifty years. In 1892 coastal erosion destroyed the bluff they stood on and the lights crumbled to the beach below. Three wooden towers replaced them in the same year. In 1911 lighthouse officials retired the wooden structures and moved one of the Chatham towers in as a replacement.

On 8 June 1837 Percival, fresh from the lighthouse business, asked to be returned to his prior post, and within several days the secretary instructed him to resume his Boston duties. He did so, bumping Lt. Edward Carpenter from the executive officer's slot. Carpenter, with feelings bruised, headed to Washington to obtain a suitable new assignment. Somewhat typically, Percival wrote a favorable letter of recommendation to Dickerson on behalf of Carpenter. He apologized for taking the liberty to write privately but said, "If you would look into my heart I am sure you would not condemn me." He said he was "not so burthened with the bump of Self Esteem as to suppose I have any influence," but he did want to recommend Carpenter for an assignment with the Ordnance Department under Captain Shubrick. Percival had had difficulty with Carpenter more than once, he wrote, but the two always settled matters. He closed: "I have felt it a Christian duty to make this frank statement & I have *no private interests, ambition or enmities* to gratify."[21]

A few days before he wrote the Carpenter letter, Percival had one of his most memorable encounters. Nathaniel Hawthorne visited the yard, accompanied by Congressman Jonathan Cilley of Maine, a fellow alumnus of Bowdoin College. Hawthorne lived in the seafaring city of Salem, Massachusetts, and was comfortable around the waterfront. Among his other occupations, he had worked in customhouses.

Like so many writers of that period, Hawthorne kept a journal or diary, which he called a notebook. From June 1837 to June 1853, when he sailed to Liverpool to take up his post as consul, he recorded his observations on Americana. Some were no more than curious facts he noticed or gathered from reading. Some of his thoughts became ideas for essays or tales. Many entries were just one or two sentences. Among the entries in the notebook is one recording a meeting between Hawthorne and Percival.

Hawthorne and Cilley sat down to dinner aboard the revenue cutter *Hamilton* with Col. Isaac Barnes, the officer in charge of the Boston Custom House. After they had finished their meal and settled down to a glass of champagne, the waiter informed the cutter's captain that Percival was sitting on the deck of the anchor hoy smoking a cigar. The captain sent Mad Jack a glass of champagne with his compliments. When the waiter returned, the captain asked about Percival's reaction. The man replied, "He said, sir, 'What does he send me this damned stuff for?'—but drinks, nevertheless."[22]

"The captain characterizes Percival as the roughest old devil that ever was in his manners," Hawthorne later wrote in his notebook, "but a kind, good-hearted man at bottom." Before long the steward entered the cabin and warned, "Captain Percival is coming aboard of you, sir." "Well, ask him to walk down into the cabin."[23]

Mad Jack made his way below, and Hawthorne gathered material for perhaps the most perceptive description of Percival ever recorded. Since it is the only extended sketch describing the man himself and not a fictional character based on him, Hawthorne's portrait merits repeating in its entirety. The man who joined Hawthorne's company was

a white-haired, thin-visaged, weather-worn old gentleman, in a blue, Quaker-cut coat, with tarnished lace and brass buttons, a pair of drab pantaloons, and brown waistcoat. There was an eccentric expression in his face, which seemed partly wilful, partly natural. He has not risen to his present rank in the regular line of the profession; but entered the navy as a sailing-master; and has all the roughness of that class of officers. Nevertheless, he knows how to behave and talk like a gentleman. Sitting down, and taking in hand a glass of champagne, he began a lecture on economy, and how well it was that Uncle Sam had a broad back, being compelled to bear so many burdens as were laid on it,—alluding to the table covered with wine-bottles. Then he spoke of the fitting up of the cabin with expensive woods, of the brooch in Captain Scott's bosom. Then he proceeded to discourse of politics, taking the opposite side to Cilley, and arguing with much pertinacity. He seems to have moulded and shaped himself to his own whims, till a sort of rough affectation has become thoroughly imbued throughout a kindly nature. He is full of antique prejudices against the modern fashions of the younger officers, their moustaches and such fripperies, and prophesies little better than disgrace in case of another war; owning that the boys would fight for their country, and die for her, but denying that there are any officers now like Hull and Stewart, whose exploits, nevertheless, he greatly depreciated, saying that the Boxer and Enterprise fought the only equal battle which we won during the war; and that, in that action, an officer had proposed to haul down the Stars and Stripes, and a common sailor threatened to cut him to pieces if he should do so. He spoke of Bainbridge as a sot and a poltroon, who wanted to run from the Macedonian, pretending to take her for a line-of-battle ship; of Commodore Elliot as a liar;—but praised Commodore Downes in the highest terms. Percival seems to be the very pattern of old integrity; taking as much care of Uncle Sam's interests as if all the money expended were to come out of his own pocket. This quality was displayed in his resistance to the demand of a new patent capstan for the revenue-cutter, which, however, Scott is resolved in such a sailor-like way to get, that he will probably succeed. Percival spoke to me of how his business in the yard absorbed him, especially the fitting of the Columbus, seventy-four, of which ship he discoursed with great enthusiasm. He seems to have no ambition beyond his present duties, perhaps never had any; at any rate, he now passes his life with a sort of gruff contentedness, grumbling and growling, yet in good humor enough.

He is conscious of his peculiarities; for when I asked him whether it would be well to make a naval officer Secretary of the Navy, he said, "God forbid, for that an old sailor was always full of prejudices and stubborn whim-whams," instancing himself; whereto I agreed.[24]

Some may question Percival's criticism of Bainbridge as recollected by Hawthorne. Mad Jack had firsthand knowledge of Bainbridge's drinking habits, so that observation is reliable. Critics may challenge the *Macedonian* reference, however, because Bainbridge never faced that ship, and may disparage Percival for not knowing better. Of course he knew better. Clearly, his remark referred to Bainbridge's handling of the *Constitution* in 1812 when he met HMS *Java*. When the British ship was spotted, Bainbridge did believe it was an enemy ship of the line, and he did turn away to avoid being trapped in pro-British Brazilian waters. When the *Java* closed faster than a liner could move, he concluded she was only a frigate and turned back and thrashed her.

In making his general point about lack of courage, Percival had Bainbridge's early career in mind. In the Quasi-War with France, Bainbridge surrendered the schooner *Retaliation* without firing a shot and became the first U.S. Navy officer in history to surrender his command. In 1803 he grounded the *Philadelphia* and lost her to the Barbary pirates. This kind of conduct was abhorrent to men like Percival, who would certainly never forget it.

After Hawthorne's death in 1864, his widow, Sophia, edited his journals and published them in 1868 as the *American Note-Books*. His meeting with Percival is described in this book.

Although Hawthorne was the first novelist to write about Percival, he was not the first to publish such a description. Herman Melville has that honor. In 1843 Melville shipped as a regular seaman on the *United States* in the Pacific. He put his experiences and observations into a novel entitled *White-Jacket; or The World in a Man-of-War*, which was published in 1850. A central figure in the book is heroic Lieutenant Mad Jack, a character patterned after John Percival.

The connection between the author and the officer is clear. Percival's lifelong friend Lemuel Shaw, Chief Justice of the Massachusetts Supreme Judicial Court at that time, was intimate with the Melville family. In his youth he was betrothed to Nancy Melville, the daughter of Maj. Thomas Melville of Revolutionary War renown. Although she died soon after they became engaged, Shaw remained close to the Melvilles. In 1847 his daughter, Elizabeth, married Herman Melville, the grandson of the major. Melville dedicated his 1847 novel *Typee* to Chief Justice Shaw. After his marriage, Herman Melville lived in Pittsfield, Massachusetts, and was on friendly terms with his neighbor, Nathaniel Hawthorne. Thus, Melville almost certainly had firsthand opportunities to observe Percival as well as the benefit of reliable secondhand commentary. His description of the fictional Lieutenant Mad Jack is worth repeating at some length.

> Mad Jack is in his saddle on the sea. *That* is his home; he would not care much, if another Flood came and overflowed the dry land; for what would it do but float his good ship higher and higher and carry his proud nation's flag round the globe, over the very capitals of all hostile states! . . . Mad Jack was expressly created and labelled for a tar. Five feet nine is his mark, in his socks; and not weighing over eleven stone before dinner. Like so many ship's shrouds, his muscles and tendons are all set true, trim, and taut; he is braced up fore and aft, like a ship on the wind. His broad chest is a bulkhead, that dams off the gale; and his nose is an aquiline, that divides it in two, like a keel. His loud, lusty lungs are two belfries, full of all manner of chimes; but you only hear his deepest bray, in the height of some tempest—like the great bell of St. Paul's, which only sounds when the King or the Devil is dead. Look at him there, where he stands on the poop—one foot on the rail, and one hand on a shroud—his head thrown back, and his trumpet like an elephant's trunk thrown up in the air. Is he going to shoot dead with sounds, those fellows on the main-topsail-yard?
>
> Mad Jack was a bit of a tyrant—they *say* all good officers are—but the sailors loved him all round; and would much rather stand fifty watches with him, than one with a rose-water sailor.[25]

Five years after *White-Jacket* came out, another novel appeared with a character based on Percival when Henry A. Wise, using the pen name Harry Gringo, published *Tales for the Marines*. Percival appears as the central figure under the nom de guerre "Jack Percy." Wise began to gather material for his book when he served as a midshipman under Percival on the *Erie* cruise. He gathered more material when he shipped as a midshipman on Percival's 1838–39 cruise in the *Cyane*.

Wise's title traces to the common superstition that every detail of a fanciful or scholarly nature that occurs on a ship is immediately passed on to the marines. The book became a prime vehicle for spreading and perpetuating the Percival legend. In fact, it is responsible for generating some of the myths about the man. The tale involves the often fantastic, always entertaining cruise of the imaginary U.S. corvette *Juanita* as she chases down West African and South American pirates. The story is almost entirely fictitious, but the descriptions of sea life and, significantly, the skipper are accurate. Therefore, Wise's characterization of Percival, alias "Percy," was, and should be, widely repeated. He was, said Wise,

> as straight and proper a man in build, as you would care to see. . . . He seemed to have been born a sailor, as he had been bred one, for even his enemies—and they were not few—admitted that he was a very paragon of a seaman. He appeared to perceive by intuition all the exigencies and requirements of his profession, and in the five years that I sailed under him, I positively aver that in those matters I never knew him to make the smallest error in judgement. He was not a man of education, but of excellent natural parts, which enabled him always to appear creditably and make his flag respected. His temper, like that of all the old vikingirs, was not to be relied upon; in other words, he was subject to the most ungovernable passion at times, chiefly about trifles; but on occasions of real danger, he was as cool as marble, his faculties at full command, and his iron will the devil himself could not shake. Notwithstanding his very severe and often harsh conduct towards his crew, they fairly worshipped him; for they felt the master spirit of the sailor in his composition, and knew that he never gave an order that he could not perform himself. This is but a very imperfect outline of our captain, John Percy by name, but better known among sailors and in the service generally as Mad Jack.[26]

The book is rare in modern libraries. The Bursley family has a copy presented by Percival to William T. Bursley. Other old Cape families value their copies.

Pirate Waters, written in 1941 by Edwin L. Sabin, is almost as hard to find. *Pirate Waters* could be called a modernized version of *Tales for the Marines*. Sabin admitted using a good deal of material from Wise's breezy tale. Sabin never met Percival, of course, so his depiction of "Mad Jack Percy" is redundant and of less value.

The similarity between Melville's Lieutenant Mad Jack, Wise's Captain Percy, and Sabin's Mad Jack Percy and the man himself is obvious. Not so apparent to readers is James Michener's use of the Percival personality in his 1959 novel *Hawaii*. His Captain Rafer Hoxworth is clearly, though loosely, fashioned after the onetime *Dolphin* commander.

~9~

THE OLD, GOUTY DEVIL

With the arrival of 1838, the pull of the sea once again controlled Mad Jack. Although he was almost fifty-nine years old and not in robust health, these drawbacks were not enough to defeat his purpose. His primary object seemed to be to restore his reputation after his dismissal by Renshaw. He had a particular ship in mind for himself: the second-class ship sloop *Cyane*, then preparing for sea at the Boston Navy Yard. Completely rebuilt at Boston in 1836 and rated for eighteen guns, the *Cyane* in fact carried twenty. A period account lamenting the lack of fast ships in the U.S. Navy said the *Cyane*'s sailing qualities were unremarkable. With this major exception, however, she was among the finest ships in the world.

Percival wrote to Congressman William Parmenter seeking his help in gaining the command and reiterating his belief that Renshaw's motive in relieving him of command was jealousy of the praise showered on him by the commercial community in Brazil. Percival noted that the secretary of the navy had spoken favorably of him to the president—in Percival's presence. He added: "I feel it is but an act of common Justice due me, that I should have the Command as the Antidote to the Poison administered to me by the unjustifiable conduct of Commodore Renshaw."[1] He wrote other letters seeking assistance as well. One went to former secretary

Woodbury. On 19 January, Secretary Dickerson acknowledged receiving Percival's application for the command of the *Cyane* and promised that his request would receive attentive consideration.

In addition to restoring his reputation, Percival had another goal in seeking a sea command. He needed more sea service to be eligible for promotion to the grade of captain—the highest grade in the U.S. Navy at that time. The navy's ranking system was not without critics. Melville, for one, thought the reluctance to follow the English plan, with its additional flag officer or admiral grades, originated with republicanism. In any case, a promotion would put Mad Jack at the top of his profession.

Percival understood that he could enhance his chance of getting the command by offering something in return. The reconstructed *Cyane* was a rather new design, and Percival told Dickerson that he was anxious "to establish its qualities and character as a Seaboat and Sailor." He also told the secretary that he wanted to show by example of a "rigid economical expenditure, how much the expenses of an efficiently conducted Sloop of War might be reduced per annum." He closed his letter with the point that his reputation was "my *only estate.*"[2]

Early in April he got the good word. Effective 14 April, the navy ordered him to prepare the *Cyane* for a cruise to the Mediterranean. For the next two months Percival busied himself putting together a crew and provisioning the ship. Dickerson told him that officer selection would be based on the rules and on officers' standing on the Naval Register. As a result, Lt. John Marshall initially received the first lieutenant's post. The navy soon relieved him, however, and offered the post to Lt. Samuel Lockwood, Percival's second choice. Since Lockwood accepted, the secretary could not offer a slot to Percival's first choice, Lt. Albert E. Downes.

Percival made other crew suggestions as well. As a favor to Commodore Downes, he asked for Acting Midn. John Downes Jr. He also requested his former purser, John Bates. Pen in hand, Midn. Henry A. Wise made it aboard. Mad Jack asked to have Midn. John L. Worden placed on the ship, too. "He is the son of an industrious farmer on the Banks of the Hudson," explained Percival. "He says he has no friends to aid him."[3] Worden got the assignment. He went on to meet Percival's expectations of him and eventually made naval history.

During the first week of May, Mad Jack informed the secretary that by "extraordinary exertions, in an emergency," he could get the *Cyane*

ready for sea in ten to fifteen days. He described the crew as "principally
. . . young & green hands," which slowed the preparations.[4] There were
still a great many details to be dealt with. His boatswain suffered a
shock, necessitating a replacement. The marines assigned to the ship
showed up without a drummer and fifer, and Percival asked for the two
he had had on the *Erie*. They were unavailable, and the department
authorized him to enlist two men for the positions. He asked Rev. Francis Parkman for thirty Bibles to distribute among the crew.

Early in June the navy issued sailing orders instructing Percival to
carry Thomas Carr, the U.S. consul to Tangier, to Morocco along with
his physician. Because of the considerable American commerce in the
area, Percival asked for permission to touch at the Canary and Madeira
Islands to check on the status of U.S. trade there. Dickerson granted
permission to make the stops on the way out. By 24 June the *Cyane* was
at sea off Boston Light sailing east.

The primary source of information about this cruise other than official correspondence and logs is young Midshipman Wise's journal. With
increasing frequency, officers on navy ships were maintaining private
journals about their voyages. Wise's *Cyane* journal is one of the most
entertaining, best written, and perceptive of them all. Although the two
men, both stubborn and opinionated, were often at odds, and Wise did
not hesitate to record his captain's faults, his underlying affection for
Percival is generally evident. The journals kept by Midn. John Downes
Jr. and Reed Werden also survive, but both are of the officially mandated
style patterned after a ship's log.

Wise's notebook indicates that on 5 July crewmen from the *Cyane*
boarded the distressed English brig *Isabella*, 122 days out of Sydney, New
South Wales. A Spanish brig had stopped and boarded the *Isabella* the
day before, and the pirates had robbed and maltreated the crew and
abused the three women onboard. The Americans resupplied the *Isabella*
and went after the pirate ship. In a 24 July report Percival said he pushed
on to the Azores, suspecting the pirates might have called there target-
ing American whalers. The *Cyane* arrived at Faial on 7 July. Because she
was the first U.S. man-of-war outside of the *Porpoise* to visit the place
in twenty-two years, the inhabitants treated the Americans as celebri-
ties. The consul gave a ball in town for the officers. Wise was not always
complimentary, but on this occasion he had kind words for his skipper.

Percival, he wrote, "with his usual desire of affording us every indulgence, gave permission for *all* to leave the Ship—remaining aboard himself & doing the duty." He added, "let me observe that there are few officers or Captains in the Navy who often exhibit such a mark of their consideration."[5]

The *Cyane* moved on to Santa Cruz de Tenerife, arriving on the twenty-second. There Percival found a brig at anchor corresponding to the one described by Capt. William Ryan of the *Isabella*. Working through the British consul and local authorities, Mad Jack had the brig's captain and crew arrested after a search of the vessel uncovered stolen property implicating the men in the attack. If he had fallen in with the pirate brig at sea, which nearly happened, Percival was prepared to capture her and send her into Gibraltar. There, the outcome would have been certain. "What the result will be in the dilatory and procrastinating tribunals of this place," he speculated, "where the delinquent as in the present case, possesses property it is difficult to say." Percival continued on his way, "confident Her Brittanic Majesty's consul will thoroughly prosecute this matter."[6] The new secretary of the navy, James K. Paulding, expressed his complete satisfaction with and approval of Percival's actions.

As the *Cyane* sailed east, Percival planned his arrival at Tangier. To Carr he stressed the importance of form and ritual in countries such as Morocco and suggested a ceremonious landing. Carr liked the idea. Percival also offered the consul the option of stopping briefly at Gibraltar before landing at Tangier. Carr liked that idea, too, and the ship put into Gibraltar Bay on 21 August. With appropriate formality, in keeping with protocol, Percival arranged a meeting with Horatio Sprague, the U.S. consul at Gibraltar. The diplomatic and naval niceties carried over into the next day. An Austrian frigate pulled in with Archduke Frederick aboard, and the shore batteries saluted, as did the *Cyane*.

The ship soon moved on to Morocco, arriving in the Bay of Tangier on 2 September. Percival contacted the Swedish consul, who was acting for the United States in the absence of an American consul, for advice on introducing Carr. Expressing his regret that severe illness confined him to his bed, Mad Jack left the arrangements in the hands of Lieutenant Hitchcock. Things went well. Her yards manned with sailors, the ship saluted Carr as he left. Fifteen officers escorted him ashore in the ship's boats. Upon landing, the foreign consuls received him, the locals rendered a salute, and the group proceeded to the palace of the dey. All of this impressed the local inhabitants. The next day, the head of the town and some relatives of the sultan asked for and received permission to visit the *Cyane*. When Paulding learned the details of the visit, he was pleased.

With this part of his mission accomplished, Percival returned to Gibraltar en route to Mahón, the chief port and town on the island of Minorca. One of the most repeated tales of the Old Navy is said to have originated at this time and place, although it may be apocryphal. The version that follows is from an article by D. B. Conrad published in 1892.

Shortly before Percival's ship arrived at the British fortress of Gibraltar, some of the officers of the garrison became embroiled in a debate over the character and courage of U.S. military personnel. Several men claimed that Americans were cowards and slackers; one disagreed. The argument became so heated that a challenge was issued and accepted. Early the next morning, the duelists fatally wounded one another, leaving the issue unresolved.

When the *Cyane* showed up, several of the younger British officers thought their answer was at hand. They boated out to the American man-of-war, sent up their cards, and were received on board. The men were from either the "Bloody Eleventh" of Devonshire or the "Blind Half Hundred," the Royal West Kent regiment. Time and frequent retellings have obscured the outfit's identity. Whoever they were, the officers refused to visit the captain's cabin. When Mad Jack appeared on deck, the senior Briton handed him a note demanding satisfaction—not for personal reasons, but on general grounds. Percival received the message "with his peculiar grim courtesy." Before accepting the challenge, Percival asked the British lieutenant for the names of every officer in his regiment, listed in the order of rank and seniority. The list was put together and handed over. Mad Jack advised his visitors that they would "hear from him shortly" and dismissed them.

He gathered his officers in his cabin and declared that he would not allow the American colors to be insulted or himself to be bullied. Noting that the British had some twenty officers, he growled: "As we have only a captain and four lieutenants, I will give the midshipmen the rank of acting lieutenants, which will give us a sufficient number." The youthful middies shouted their approval, as pleased with the prospect of a scrap as they were with their sudden promotions. A cartel was drawn up and sent on shore under a flag.

The challenge jolted the British regimental commander and many of his officers. Most had been unaware of the challenge issued by their fellows and were "not at all willing to be thus unceremoniously dragged into a duel of other people's making." The foolhardy officers, of course, were unaware of the reputation of the American naval officer they had chosen to defy. Fortunately for all involved, the local governor interceded and saved the day. When he got wind of the affair, he immediately placed all of the regiment's officers under house arrest. They remained restricted until the *Cyane* moved away the next day.[7]

Wise recorded an entertaining description of the ship's departure from Gibraltar in his usual droll style.

> I never saw so much humbugging in getting a ship underway, as there was aboard the Cyane this afternoon. The old skipper was in a devil of a rage but having been confined with the gout for the last fortnight *unfortunately* couldn't hop about according to custom, but the way he hove "back rations" into the main topsail was a caution.
>
> "Give her more cable, Sir, don't you see She's dragging her anchor."
>
> "Brace up the Main yard you smuggling rascals."
>
> "Steer true you lubber—another man at the wheel. This frenchman don't know nothing." . . . "Starboard. Steady quick you *potato digger*. Mr. —— *will* you use your feet a *little* faster," . . . etc. etc.[8]

In this fashion the *Cyane* pushed into the Mediterranean. She arrived at Mahón during the night of 12 September 1838. The trip went well until the *Cyane* ran aground while working her way into the harbor. "Tore off a few pieces of the Copper," reported Percival. "*No other* injury *whatever* was received." Writing to Commo. Isaac Chauncey, president of the Board of Navy Commissioners, the mortified Percival said, "I felt it my duty to make this early communication to you, & state *the facts* to prevent misconstruction from rumour or malicious reports, to the disparagement of this splendid sloop." He stressed: "It is not my custom to let vessels I command touch the bottom."[9]

Wise also ran into trouble in Mahón. He disobeyed an order from Lieutenant Lockwood and was relieved of duty. Wise turned to Percival, his old commander on the *Erie*, for relief. He was not pleased with Percival's response, which he considered evasive, and concluded, "He is getting in his dotage—cross, crabbed and gouty. . . . He is so infernally obstinate."[10]

Capt. Jesse Wilkinson, who commanded the Mediterranean station at the time, ordered Percival to visit Marseilles, Genoa, Leghorn, Naples, and Messina, contacting the American consuls at these ports and making the customary exchanges. His primary mission was that of the squadron—to advance American commercial interests in the region. The American warship entered Marseilles on 21 September. Wise noted that Percival took an unaccountable but fierce dislike to the place, as he did to all Mediterranean ports. To Mad Jack, one place was a damn hole, and the next, a hellhole.

On the following day, in the Gulf of Lyons, the ship experienced the first gale in days. Wise's journal notes that it was "blowing hard enough to blow the geese off the officers' buttons." On that same day, Wise spent some time setting down his basic impression of his captain. His description sums up the nearly universal opinion of Percival so well that it bears repeating.

> There is not a better sailor in the world than Cap. Percival or a man of better judgement in the qualities requisite for a Seaman. . . . I have seen him in the River Platte shame the oldest pilots in his predictions of the weather. One would suppose from his impatient & passionate temper, that in case of danger he would lose all command of himself. On the contrary no one is cooler or more able to fulfill the duties of his station. To give the devil his due—I would rather trust my life to his charge in case of emergency at Sea than any other man in the United States Navy.[11]

Despite his high praise for Percival's seamanship, Wise continued to be annoyed with his captain. When Lockwood restored the midshipman to duty on 2 October without any scolding, Wise was disappointed. He was ready to argue. Percival granted his wish, calling him in for a stern lecture about conspiracy. A week or so later the two were at it again. "The old gouty devil of a Captain & I have had another *make up* and another *break out*—both every day occurances [sic]," wrote Wise. Demanding, "Do you belong to the ship or do you *not*?" Percival ordered Wise to send "every loco foco, logical, town meeting son of a bitch off the birth deck." Wise quickly carried out the order.

Percival seemed satisfied and reduced the tension by admiring his midshipman's white gloves.[12]

A few days later, Wise was in trouble again. "I am destined to be overwhelmed with difficulties in this good ship Cyane," he complained to his journal. Wise had accompanied Lockwood ashore "to purchase a few little articles for the men" and had failed to meet the lieutenant at the time set to return to the ship. Mad Jack admonished Lockwood for the delay, and this led to another suspension for Wise. "Captain Percival has some ill feelings towards me, for some ridiculous causes which he himself cannot explain," young Wise groused. His captain, he mused, was "less influenced by merit than subserviance & fawning & his own fantastic & fevered imagination."[13]

The *Cyane* reached Naples late in October. As in the other Italian ports, Wise noted, the ship was "deluged with . . . every ragamuffin in Naples, some smuggling rum, others selling knicknackery." He continued, "A couple of old women favored us with a *howl* until the Captain threatened to heave a shot in their boat & they made sail."[14]

Another elderly woman got a different response. Her Britannic Majesty's ship of the line *Hastings* pulled into the harbor on 1 November carrying the dowager queen of England, Adelaide. Her husband, William IV, had died a year earlier, and her niece, Queen Victoria, now occupied the throne. Percival thought it proper to show Adelaide every mark of respect. Despite the wishes of the *Hastings*'s captain, who could not return the salute, the Americans on the *Cyane* manned the yards, fired a twenty-one-gun salute, and gave three cheers as the British ship passed by on the way to the landing. The ceremony was performed in an elegant manner, according to Wise, and the next day the British minister told the American chargé d'affaires that Her Majesty expressed high satisfaction with the unexpected show of respect.

Before long, the *Hastings*'s captain repaired to the *Cyane* with a summons from the queen. Percival was invited to dinner on the British ship at 1:00 P.M. on the twelfth. The royal family of Naples also attended the feast, but Percival was the center of attention. He exhibited great pleasure in the ostentatious display. "Quite an honor," observed Wise. "Old Jack is in luck. Took a pirate and dine with a Queen all in one cruise."[15]

While at Naples, Wise found another reason to complain about his captain. Percival left the ship to take the sulfur baths at a nearby spa and took along the midshipmen's steward, despite having promised not to do so. Once he was finally off the *Cyane,* Wise swore, he would not have anything more to do with Percival.

Percival planned to leave Naples in company with the *Hastings,* but the English ship was delayed and the *Cyane* left alone on 14 November. A week later, the two warships got together at Messina. When they got under way to leave that port on the twenty-third, they exchanged salutes. Percival showed great displeasure with the quartermaster for displaying a white Cross of Saint George at the fore instead of the correct Union Jack. Wise considered it a minor mistake. Mad Jack, however, did not consider this breach of etiquette to be a little thing.

Before he left Messina, Percival dispatched a number of letters to the Department of the Navy. A 19 November letter to the secretary typifies his concern for the welfare of American seamen. He told the secretary that consuls abroad commonly asked him to receive destitute American sailors, many unfortunate and deserving of help, others insubordinate and mutinous. Percival received them all aboard his ship and gave them a ration until he could send them to the United States. Commerce sustained the navy, he said, and the navy ought to protect it, including American seamen in distress. Greedy landlords were ever ready at home or abroad to seduce and plunder sailors, and many men fell to misfortune through no fault of their own. He closed by asking the department to confirm his practice.

In his response Secretary Paulding thanked Percival for his attention to the distressed seamen. In the absence of any law or fixed precedent on the topic, the secretary saw no objection to receiving such men and providing them with a ration. He told Percival not to pay them, however, unless they actually entered the service.

While Yankee sailors were always a major interest, Percival had downright paternalistic feelings for his midshipmen. Before the U.S. Naval Academy was established in 1845, the primary means of training and educating young men for the officer corps was on the job at sea. All the reports indicate that Mad Jack took this part of his work seriously. A man who knew him said that Percival could be relentless with drivellers and laggards who did not give their best efforts.

Most of the time there were fourteen midshipmen on the *Cyane,* although there were a few changes to the roster over the course of the cruise. The *Cyane*'s instructor, or professor of mathematics, was James Major. Professor Major was responsible for the classroom aspects of the program. In addition to algebra, geometry, plane trigonometry, and the like, he taught courses in more useful subjects such as Bowditch's *Practical Navigator,* plane sailing, parallel sailing, middle latitude, Mercator sailing, mensuration of heights and distances, and surveying coasts and harbors.

Professor Major prepared a quarterly progress report on his students, ranking the midshipmen in order of merit. His first report, dated October 1838, placed the midshipmen in the following order, from top to bottom: Archibald McRae, Reed Werden, Gustavus V. Fox, George B. Balch, David Williamson, Charles W. Place, John Downes Jr., Edward F. Tattnall, Frederick W. Colby, Charles H. B. Caldwell, Robert A. Knapp, John L. Worden, Edward Allen, and Henry A. Wise. Specific assessments appeared next to each name. McRae, for instance, was "very industrious and persevering." Fox was "very intelligent." Tattnall was "disposed to be idle." And Wise, "owing to sickness or some other cause," was said to have "learned very little indeed."[16] It is interesting to find the journalist Wise at the bottom of the list. His naval record suggests that sickness was indeed the likely reason for his low academic rating for the first three months. He was often in poor health. But before he died at age fifty he advanced to the rank of captain.

Mad Jack moved quickly to address the problems raised by Major's report. In a letter to Secretary Paulding, he said he had curtailed liberty for the poor performers. He did not think the measure would impair their health or morals, and it was the only coercion he could employ with effect. Indeed, the restriction was a great inducement for improvement. In his reply, Paulding approved of Percival's measures. The department, he said, believed that midshipmen did not benefit from lengthy shore leave in the Mediterranean.

Before Percival left Messina, he sent Paulding a detailed report on American commerce in the cities he had visited. For the most part, he found U.S. commercial activity in decline or nonexistent. He also enclosed copies of his correspondence with the various consuls he had visited. Washington once again appreciated his attention to the public interest.

Midshipman Wise remained ambivalent about Percival. In his journal for 29 November, for example, he wrote: "Had another small 'snap' with the Captain this afternoon. Came off second best this time." Percival had been "whacking the men over their 'calibashes' with his crutch. Very dignified certainly for a Captain in the Navy. 'It's a way he has though of getting along!'"[17]

Earlier in November, Commodore Hull's flagship, the *Ohio,* sailed from New York under Capt. Joseph Smith. A native of Hanover, Massachusetts, Smith was one of Percival's closest naval friends. Smith's ancestors had preceded Percival's to the Barnstable and Sandwich section of Cape Cod. Like Percival, Smith entered the navy for a brief period during 1809 and permanently in 1812. He brought the *Ohio* through the Strait of Gibraltar on 29 December. Six days later, Hull found Percival at Mahón, where he had been waiting since 10 December. For the time being, Hull's squadron consisted of the *Ohio* and the *Cyane.*

During January and part of February 1839, turbulent midwinter weather restricted the ships' activities. The forced idleness left the men with free time on their hands. Percival took the opportunity to write letters. Midshipman Balch, otherwise considered attentive and studious, received a note from Percival "requesting his reasons in writing for that 'vile practice of swearing.'" The opportunity was too much for Wise. He told Balch to "state in reply that he contracted the habit from the 'example set him by his superior officers.'"[18] Balch unwisely followed Wise's recommendation. As soon as Mad Jack received this reply, he sent for Balch and demanded to know "the author of so great an insult. Balch told him Mr. Wise!! Whew. He stuck his tongue on the top of his head." Young Wise was in trouble again.[19]

A few days later Wise asked permission to go ashore. "No, Sir, not upon any consideration," replied Percival. Wise promptly went below and wrote a letter to send through channels requesting a transfer to the *Ohio.* When Percival got the request, he sent for Wise and the two met for an hour. "At first he tried to frighten me," Wise reported. Percival then said, "The child who gives the mother the most trouble she sets most by." Such trash, wrote Wise, went in one ear and out the other. In the end, Percival promised to give Wise permission to go ashore, and Wise withdrew his application. "I'll swear, he was perfectly astounded at my audacity," Wise concluded. "He is so anxious to have other people believe that his officers like him—forlorn hope. Today he has been almost too kind."[20]

Percival's compassion was real, however, and it was not a passing thing. Over the course of his career he repeatedly showed tenderness toward those in need. A case in point occurred on 25 January when crewman Nathaniel Sidney departed this life. Sick at some length with tuberculosis, Sidney spent his last days in the captain's own cabin.

For some time the conduct of the young officers in the lower grades had been bothering Percival. Some of the men were profligate spenders, and many were in debt to local merchants. The winter layover only added to the problem. Late in February he received confirmation that the department supported him in his efforts to uphold the character of the service. Secretary Paulding expressed concern with the "disgraceful practice" of indebtedness by the men of the squadron. "The liberal pay allowed to the officers of the Navy," he told Percival, ". . . is amply sufficient to maintain them in the rank of gentleman if not wasted in extravagance and debauchery." He vowed to put a stop to it, and he appreciated Percival's efforts.[21] Paulding also wrote to Hull about the men's indebtedness, telling him he had learned about it from unimpeachable sources and asking the commodore to adopt stern measures to end the problem.

Hull knew immediately the identity of Paulding's unimpeachable source. He was already a bit peeved at Percival's penchant for writing numerous and detailed reports. Earlier in the month, word got back to Mad Jack that Hull was not happy with him. "I apprehend," Percival wrote to Hull, "from a remark I have heard, that you have the impression that I am disposed to multiply correspondence." He went on to assure Hull that he would adhere to his commander's intentions when these were known, and above all that he had no object apart from duty. "I have no petty ambitions to subserve, or little envies to satisfy, or paltry little vanities to gratify." Percival stressed, "I assure you, after an acquaintance of twenty four years with you, one third or more of that period under your command, my friendship is unabated." He continued: "I have always felt a desire . . . to the utmost of my feeble abilities, to sustain the honor of your flag." He closed by saying that "blunt frankness of character and profession" was his lot, and when someone asked for his opinion, he offered it "without consulting the feelings or wishes of any one. Were I not to do so, whatever the opinions might be, they would not be mine."[22]

The disagreement turned out to be a trivial and passing thing. Percival cleared from the headquarters harbor and stood for Marseilles to the north. Arriving on 8 February, he gave critical assistance to the Newburyport brig *Powhatan*, which was experiencing difficulty entering the

French port. He found the American trader in a bad way. Percival dispatched three boats under 1st Lieutenant Lockwood and 2d Lt. Robert Hitchcock, who in a seamanlike manner and at much risk to themselves quickly relieved the *Powhatan* from her plight. Percival thought the timely help saved the brig from wrecking.

Percival remained at Marseilles for two weeks, then moved down the coast to Barcelona, where he contacted the U.S. consul, Joseph Borras. From the consul he gathered information on U.S.-Spanish trade and acquired intelligence on the status of the Spanish civil war. Commercial issues were not paramount at that time, however. The old quarrel about impressment had resurfaced. In January, Capt. Robert F. Chase complained to Borras that the British had forcibly removed a crewman from his ship, the *Canton Packet.* A report reached Hull, and he told Percival to look into the potentially explosive situation.

Although for the most part the War of 1812 ended impressments of American seamen, the Treaty of Ghent did not prohibit the practice. Great Britain insisted on retaining it as a legitimate method of recruitment. The Royal Navy felt that impressments were essential to maintaining its readiness. Yet the English did make an effort to avoid antagonizing the emergent American navy. They remembered too well the late war in which the ill-prepared, ill-equipped, and outnumbered U.S. Navy had sheared the British navy of its glory. When Mad Jack got into Barcelona, he informed the alleged offender, Lt. John Simpson of HMS *Weazle,* "I have been directed by the Commander in Chief of the United States Naval Forces in the Mediterranean, to call on you for the reasons for your having violated the Sovereignty of the United States."[23] A major incident loomed. "Rather a serious business I take it," noted Wise, "and one like to hold Mr. John Bull mighty uneasy."[24]

Simpson admitted to having a man from the American vessel on his ship, but he seemed to be able to justify his action. Percival contacted Borras for his side of the story. The American agent told him the British had impressed one of Chase's crew because the man's name did not appear on the articles of the *Canton Packet,* and consequently he was fair game. Added inquiry uncovered the fact that the seaman, William Bruce, had appeared before the British consul at Barcelona and declared himself a native of Yorkshire, England. Bruce further alleged ill treatment at the hands of Captain Chase and indicated a preference for the British service.

Percival forwarded this information to Washington, which contacted Great Britain about the matter. Lieutenant Simpson insisted all the while that Bruce had come to the *Weazle* of his own accord. On the day in question there had been a major disturbance on the *Canton Packet*. Seamen were beaten, and Bruce escaped to the *Weazle*. "The affair was so disgusting that during my long service of 36 years I never saw the like," said the British lieutenant, "and I felt it due to humanity to advise the American Master to a better system of discipline."[25] Percival seemed to be satisfied with the British version, and the *Weazle* sailed without his interference. Adm. Sir Robert Stopford forwarded Simpson's remarks to Hull, emphasizing that Chase's complaint was groundless. Authorities in the United States accepted the explanation and dropped the matter.

Back on the *Cyane*, the midshipmen and their captain were again at odds. Percival told the group he intended to take their steward once the ship returned to Mahón. Wise was so upset that he thought of renewing his request for a transfer. A few days later, Acting Midshipman Fox submitted a brief note to Hull, through Percival, asking to be shifted to the *Ohio*. In forwarding the request, Percival wrote that Fox's father had appealed to him to care for his son and keep him out of trouble. Percival asked Hull to deny the request because it stemmed from the fact that Fox was permitted to go ashore only once a week. "I am not desirous to obtain the popularity of midshipmen at the expense of discipline and their moral benefit," he wrote to Hull.[26] Hull went along with Mad Jack, and their decision helped Fox in the end.

When Acting Midn. John Downes Jr. likewise applied for a transfer to *Ohio*, Percival recalled a letter his friend and former commander, the elder Downes, had sent to Hull in November. Downes had asked Hull to take his son onto the *Ohio* if Percival left the *Cyane*. However, as long as Percival enforced rigid discipline, he wanted the youth to remain with him. Percival told Hull he had recently received two letters from the senior Downes "urging upon me a vigilant care of his son, and to keep him strictly to his studies and duty and allow him to visit the shore but seldom."[27] Hull, of course, denied young Downes's request. Although Hull had supported Percival, Wise thought the requests for transfer had nonetheless disturbed his skipper.

The *Cyane* arrived back at Mahón on 1 March 1839. Percival occupied the crew's spare time in port by training them in seamanship. He also had them exercising the great guns, small arms, pikes, and cutlasses. In addition, he seemed to devote time to personal relations. Young Wise would have none of it. "The Captain has commenced his blarney again," he wrote in his journal. "I don't like soft soap, there's too much *lie* in it."[28]

A more basic matter than his relations with his midshipmen concerned Percival at this time, however. On 2 March he wrote to Paulding and asked to be relieved of his command by the middle of August due to continuing poor health. Gout kept him on crutches more than a third of the time. Nothing else could induce him to make the request, he said, because his primary object of demonstrating the opportunity for reducing operating costs remained unmet. He closed his letter in typical fashion by noting that news of possible conflict with Great Britain prompted him to qualify his request. "Though on crutches I am ready to strike a blow for the honor of my country and its flag," he said. If war broke out, he wanted his request set aside because he was prepared to continue, "whatever may be the result to my health, life, or limbs."[29]

Indeed, another war with England seemed a distinct possibility. Continuing border disputes strained Anglo-American relations. During 1837–38, civil strife broke out along the New York–Ontario border. Another boundary question in early 1839 involved the border between Maine and New Brunswick. Percival could not understand, he wrote to his friend John Payson, why the two countries could not settle a question involving "a piece of spruce land some where the other side of Sundown and which has remained over two hundred years unknown to whom it belonged & to what province or district attached."[30] The so-called Aroostook War was the immediate result of the squabble. The United States and Great Britain assembled forces in the north woods about the Saint Johns River. Although actual hostilities did not occur, the unofficial reports reaching the Mediterranean station concerned Hull. He did not want to be blocked inside the Strait of Gibraltar if war broke out with Great Britain, so he decided to move the squadron.

The *Cyane*'s crew prepared her to sail. Her requisition list tells much about navy life at the time. While she took on 372 gallons of beans, she accepted almost an equal amount of whiskey—352 gallons. Once provisioned, on 15 April Percival set sail for Marseilles. On the way out, the *Cyane* and the *Ohio* had a friendly sailing contest. Once again the *Cyane* prevailed, although the *Ohio* had the reputation for greater speed.

At Marseilles, Percival went ashore to pick up American dollars for the use of the squadron from Fitch Brothers and Company, which was under contract with the U.S. government to supply funds to its ships. He looked around for someone to take along on the endeavor. As usual, Wise observed and commented. He wrote in his journal: "Old Jack asked Hazard on the poop just now who spoke French? 'Wise' said Hazard, 'talks very well.' 'Who. Wise? Why he don't speak it worth a damn—not better than I do and I won't have him.'"[31]

The sparring between the two men continued unabated. A few weeks earlier Percival had sent Wise a bottle of wine. He even offered to lend the midshipman a chicken if he was out of grub. Wise thought he smelled a rat and rejected the offer.

Coming to anchor at Marseilles, Mad Jack and the pilot had a row, as usual, and "unusually the pilot gave him as good as he sent," recorded Wise with delight. "It was 'go to hell . . . etc.' Beat old Jack with his own weapons." The two men patched things up after the ship was safely anchored, though, and the pilot accepted a glass of brandy from Percival.[32]

The American sloop remained at the French port for more than a week, then retraced her path to Mahón on the way to the Spanish seaport of Cartagena. Percival's stop at Málaga was gratifying. In coming to anchor, the crew handled the ship with perfection before they dropped the hook abreast the brig HMS *Wasp*, Capt. D. W. Pelham commanding. "Old Jack went on board and it appears that Captain Pelham was once a prisoner of old Percival's in the War," Wise reported.[33]

The *Cyane* touched at Gibraltar before vacating the Mediterranean for Lisbon. Percival, who suffered a case of acute tonsillitis, had a wretched trip. Worse, the *Cyane* grounded off Trafalgar, much to Wise's satisfaction. "I'm a Prophet," declared Wise. He was in his berth, half asleep, when a commotion erupted on deck. "'Damn and blast that son of a bitch of a leadsman,' says Old Jack. 'Lost the Ship by God!' . . . By the old skipper's usual foolhardiness in standing to close inshore," Wise wrote, "he ran the old Ship again high and dry." A rising tide, a favorable wind, and some effort carried it off. "Quite fortunate. But I feel confident that this will gain him a lesson," added Wise. "He was repeatedly warned of his proximity from the Fo'castle. But too stubborn by half to be told *when* to 'tack Ship.'"[34]

Percival reached the Portuguese port in time to attend a state dinner aboard the *Ohio* on 25 May with the queen of Portugal as the honored guest. Even these festivities did not soothe Mad Jack's temper. Continual ill health had made him cranky. He told Hull that the *Cyane* had only two-thirds of its authorized personnel, and many of them were unfit for duty due to illness or injury. In the event of war, he continued, a man's reputation would be in danger. Furthermore, he declared, "this crew is without exception the most inferior and indifferent ever attached to a vessel of this class which ever left the United States."[35]

Acting Midshipman Allen was a case in point. In his 25 May correspondence with Hull, Percival included a complaint from Allen. The midshipman claimed that back on 9 February, while at Marseilles, "Captain John Percival did apply to me the epithet of an Infernal Rascal in presence of the Officers & Crew. And he has upon several other occasions treated me with contempt."[36] Mad Jack responded that on entering the French harbor it had been necessary to carry out the warps with dispatch. Percival assigned Allen to the boat undertaking the task "to prevent the men from desertion, more than for any assistance he could render, being ignorant then, and still is, how to conduct a boat." Some poor management occurred, and Percival directed severe epithets at the boat's crew. "I did not apply it to Acting Midn Allen, whose ignorance of, and known incapacity to perform the duty, precluded the possibility of holding him responsible for what he was incompetent to execute," explained Percival.[37]

Percival thought it noteworthy that Allen had let the matter remain unaddressed for 105 days because he knew the reprimand did not apply to him. The *Cyane*'s commander suggested that his young officer's hurt feelings were revived because four of his companions were under suspension for insubordination. Mad Jack believed that Hull should also know that Allen was so incompetent that he had to ask Fox to write his protest. The day after forwarding his explanation, Percival sent Allen, along with a report on his studies, to see the commodore. The February progress report indicated that Allen was forgetting things faster than he learned them. In any event, Hull soothed Allen's hurt feelings. Allen withdrew his complaint and returned to the *Cyane*.

When Percival arrived at Lisbon in May, he acquired important intelligence that he passed on to Hull. According to letters from authoritative American sources, war with England was unlikely. Two days later, the *Ohio* and the *Cyane* turned back for the Mediterranean. The return trip went more smoothly than the outbound one. On 15 June, Wise noted:

"The Captain and I am the best possible friends. Told me the other day that he did believe I had something more than *lice* in my head. Complimentary certainly. He let's [*sic*] me do and say everything."[38]

A week after that, Wise told his journal, "The Captain says that his Midshipmen have got a damned *redundancy* of knowledge. And he intends to resuscitate [*sic*] them."[39] Apparently he did, because on the twenty-fifth Mad Jack sent a brief update to the secretary in which he commended his midshipmen, including Henry Wise. They were attentive to their duty and demonstrated good moral conduct, he reported.

Percival next sailed for Leghorn, a principal port on the west coast of Italy, thence down to Sicily. This period appears to be the setting for one of the most repeated Mad Jack tales. Whether the yarn is true or not is unimportant; the fact that Percival attracted such treatment is what matters. At any rate, steamships began to make an appearance at this time, and masters of traditional sailing vessels often called on the steamers to tow them out of harbors, through narrow passages, and the like. Folklore has it that Percival spotted a steamboat as he was about to enter the Strait of Messina, the mythical realm of the female monster Scylla. Since the weather was rough and a terrific sea was running, he signaled for a tow. The steamer captain reluctantly took on the chore. The crews fastened a hawser from one ship to the other, and the pull began. Little progress resulted. After some time had passed, the frustrated skipper of the steamer signaled to Percival: "Unless the wind and tide abate, I cannot tow you through the strait." Never at a loss for words, the irritated Percival picked up his trumpet and bellowed: "As long as you've got wood and coal, Tow away, God bless your soul!"[40]

After contacting the U.S. consul at Palermo, John Marston, the *Cyane* beat back up the coast of Italy to Naples. Percival wrote to Hull that he did not perceive any overt turbulence in the city. However, he remained there until the festival of Santa Rosalia, a likely time for conspiracies, passed. The Italians kept the peace, but the midshipmen did not.

Percival sent a report to Secretary Paulding on 25 July detailing his repeated problems with the group. Nineteen-year-old Allen had improved somewhat, not because of propriety but because he feared the consequences. He could not be recommended for a warrant. Williamson, from North Carolina, was another difficult youngster. Percival thought he was more interested in getting into instead of out of debt. More important, he had been involved in an act of insubordination. He challenged another to a duel despite the fact that all the midshipmen had been ordered under no circumstances to try to settle disputes in that manner. Consequently, Mad Jack could not recommend him for a warrant either, and Williamson wanted to resign.

Percival went on to complain that he had had little difficulty with his midshipmen until the *Ohio* arrived on the station and set a poor example for them. The *Cyane*'s midshipmen could not remain on shore after sundown without special permission, but their *Ohio* counterparts could stay as they saw fit. Percival had taken every precaution to protect his young men from the vice and depravity on shore, he said, but despite his best efforts, three of the youngsters had contracted venereal disease. He added that it would be helpful if all ship's surgeons were required to report the disease truly instead of being allowed to list it as opthalmia or some other innocent ailment. In short, he thought the liberalized modern discipline was creating the problem. Nevertheless, Percival said he did not believe an equal number of subordinate, moral, and attentive midshipmen could be found on any other ship in the navy.

Recently assigned warranted Midn. Charles S. McDonough, son of the late hero Commodore McDonough, was another discipline problem. Percival commended the youngster for his conduct and sense of duty, but when it came to his management of debt, there was nothing good to say about young McDonough. He accumulated debts of $424.89 in Mahón alone. Percival emphatically rejected the prevalent idea that a commander should not concern himself with his officers' debts in foreign ports. Secretary Paulding responded that Percival lacked the authority to direct that McDonough's pay be applied to the discharge of his debts. He suggested that the best remedy would be to prohibit McDonough and other officers similarly inclined from going ashore to contract debts.

Despite his poor health and the fact that the Navy Department had already dispatched Comdr. William K. Latimer to replace him, Percival went out on another patrol. Early in August the *Ohio* and the *Cyane* sailed to the eastern reaches of the Mediterranean Sea. The pair touched at such ports as Smyrna and Athens and cruised in the Gulf of Salonica. Levantine and Greek pirates were their principal interest; however, they found piracy to be on the wane.

Percival's favorite midshipman remained a concern. While at Athens, Midshipmen McRae and Wise got into a row during which McRae cursed and damned Wise. When the matter was brought to Percival's attention, he reprimanded McRae for unofficerlike and ungentlemanly conduct and suspended him. "Blamed me for even noticing such a little brat," wrote Wise. "Afterwards in private conversation he only wished I had knocked him down."[41]

At about the same time, Mad Jack barely averted disaster in the gulf. The ship came within ten yards of grounding on the rocks. "Old Jack is indeed a gallant old sailor & navigator I should say—but he is too venturesome," Wise observed. "He will toss this ship yet if he does not mind his age and then there'll be a Commander less in the Service."[42]

On the way back to Mahón, Wise heard Percival talking to himself in his cabin. "I'm going home, eh! be a millenium [sic], I 'spose. Damn fool to come out. Damn old fool Jack. Never come to Sea again."[43]

Both vessels returned to the headquarters station late in September, and Percival expressed weariness in one of his last reports to Hull. Young Downes had another complaint, and Mad Jack forwarded it according to regulations. Downes, victimized by innocent roughhousing with the other midshipmen, had sworn at his tormentors. Percival lamented the rowdyism. If his circumstances were different, he would prefer charges, Percival noted, but in this case, a note of disapprobation from Hull would probably suffice.

Although Mad Jack wondered whether some of his midshipmen would ever make good sailors, he was unequivocal in his good opinion of a young Swede who shipped aboard the *Cyane*. The foreigner boarded at Marseilles expressing a desire to become familiar with U.S. discipline and seamanship. He picked the right ship. Punctual, energetic, and intelligent, he stood out from most of the young Americans, and Percival never missed an opportunity to encourage his enthusiasm. Before the young Swede left the ship to return home, Percival offered him financial and other assistance if needed. The young man graciously declined the offer, and the two parted.

Almost a decade later, the former *Cyane* commander received an affectionate letter from a naval base in Sweden. The letter, from the Swede who had served on the *Cyane*, expressed deep gratitude for Percival's kindness and paternal care. The man considered his old skipper "my guardian angel, to who, next to God, I am indebted for the happy turn in my destiny, since that time when I young and imprudent, without experience or friends, had thrown myself . . . into the world among strangers."[44] The man had withheld his family background from Percival because he thought it unseemly to take advantage of it and wanted to make his own way. Before he shipped on the *Cyane,* he had completed the Swedish Royal College for the Navy. Percival's good reputation among sailors prompted him to seek a berth on the *Cyane.* His name was not Alexson, the name he used on the American ship. He was Axel Adlersparre, the son of a Swedish admiral. Young Adlersparre returned to the Swedish navy and rose in that service. As a token of his esteem, he sent a portrait of the Swedish author Frederika Bremer. Percival cherished the painting.

Commander Latimer, Percival's replacement, arrived at Marseilles on 5 August while the squadron was far to the east and decided it would be best to remain there and await instructions. He notified Hull of his whereabouts and indicated his desire for the *Cyane* to proceed to the French port. Several days later, he wrote a warm letter to Percival in which he communicated his hope that Mad Jack had recovered his health and mentioned that Mrs. Percival was quite well. He added that if Percival would pick him up at Marseilles, he would carry Percival to any port that would facilitate his embarkation for the United States.

In the end, Percival did not come for him and Latimer had to make his own way to Mahón by backtracking through Barcelona. French troops bound for Algiers had taken over all the steamers at Marseilles. As a result, the *Cyane* did not change hands until the middle of October. The observant Wise chronicled the big event. All hands were called, and Mad Jack came out of the cabin attired in memorable shoes made out of boot legs. He took out a yellow handkerchief, "blew his horn, hopped up on the wardroom combing and said: 'I render unto God the things that are God's and unto Latimer the things that are Latimer's. Gentlemen, step in the cabin and I'll give you some wine.' . . . 'Pipe down,' says the new skipper, and so ended the dynasty."[45]

Percival's *Cyane* tour contributed a great deal to his legacy. He is most often remembered as a patriotic old salt, but his role in advancing naval education before an academy existed should not be overlooked. None of his peers demanded more of their young officers than he did. Percival himself attended school for just nine months, the standard for his period. Indeed, Abraham Lincoln's schooling did not exceed a year. Despite his limited formal instruction, Percival appreciated the value of education. He mastered the technicalities of his profession, was fluent in Spanish, and spoke passable French.

The Civil War–era navy included numerous former Percival students. John L. Worden, the New York farm boy Percival favored and trained on the *Cyane*, rose to the rank of admiral and is remembered as the hero of the *Monitor*. Gustavus V. Fox from the *Cyane* served as assistant secretary of the navy. Reed Werden was a fleet captain in charge of the East Coast Blockading Squadron. George Balch, Charles Caldwell, and John Downes Jr., all onetime *Cyane* midshipmen, also advanced in the navy. Balch made it to rear admiral. Elsewhere, Axel Adlersparre became a commander in the Swedish navy. From the *Dolphin*, Hiram Paulding rose to become a rear admiral and commandant of the New York yard during the Civil War. Charles H. Davis, also of the *Dolphin*, became a rear admiral and served as the flag officer on the Mississippi River during the war. There are more, but the foregoing names are sufficient to illustrate Percival's lasting influence on the U.S. Navy.

Percival did not get back to New York until 24 January 1840. When he arrived, he notified the secretary and asked for a short leave to restore his health. The department placed him on leave effective the twenty-eighth. But he also received a sharp inquiry from the secretary asking why, on his arrival at New York, Percival had failed to report to the station commandant according to the usual etiquette. Percival replied right away, explaining that an attack of inflammation of the brain had confined him indoors for five days. Poor weather delayed him another four days. In fact, he elected to have a fellow officer accompany him to Boston because he was making the trip even though he was sick enough to be hospitalized. He assured the secretary that he prided himself on his observance of regulations. Secretary Paulding accepted Percival's explanation and sincerely regretted his continued indisposition. The navy assigned him to the Boston Navy Yard for pay purposes. On 28 April 1840, although his health was not entirely restored, Percival wrote to the secretary explaining that his reluctance to be idle and his need to be fully employed induced him to report himself ready for any duty.

While he was in Washington on 24 May, Percival sent a note to the secretary passing on a request from the *Cyane*'s crew to end their cruise at Boston, just as he had done for the *Erie*'s crew three years earlier.

Much of the crew came from Massachusetts, he noted. All the apprentices hailed from the Boston area. More important, he explained, if they were paid off in a distant port, land sharks would strip them of their money before they ever made it home. The *Cyane* would need to go into dry dock upon her return, he pointed out, and that would be less expensive in Boston than in New York, Philadelphia, or Portsmouth. The secretary liked Percival's recommendation.

Before he left Washington, Percival submitted a report on possible piracy in the Tenerife area. In it, he recommended that the *Cyane* leave the squadron at Mahón two to three months early for a cruise to Madeira, Tenerife, Cape Verde, Monrovia, and the Azores. This would place the *Cyane* off the U.S. coast during the mild season of spring. Again, he suggested a benefit. The men would be employed in active sea service instead of sitting more or less idle at Mahón.

As well as thinking of his old crew, Percival continued his interest in his friend Hull on the *Ohio*. Hull was having trouble with his lieutenants, who were upset about their quarters. Mrs. Hull and her sister, Miss Jeannette Hart, were on board, thereby aggravating the overcrowding common on the warships of that era. As an experiment, the navy commissioners had assigned the lieutenants to the orlop deck, the lowest deck in a man-of-war. This arrangement would both provide snug quarters for the officers and keep the gun decks clear and ready for action. The quarters proved a little too snug.

Hull felt he did not have the authority to alter the setup, which the orlop occupants considered unhealthy and suffocating. The griping mounted until Hull finally ordered three of the lieutenants—S. W. Godon, J. S. Missroon, and G. J. Prendergast—home. Secretary Paulding promptly sent them back to the *Ohio*. On learning of the secretary's unusual action, Percival sent a few words of comfort to Commodore Hull from Boston on 5 July. Paulding's failure to support Hull's action told greatly on the senior officer. He returned to the United States a year later and, in declining health, went on leave. Some believe the *Ohio* dispute hastened his death, which came in Philadelphia on 13 February 1843.

The new year found Mad Jack Percival melancholy and troubled. In January 1841 his mother passed away as she approached her ninety-eighth year. At her funeral in West Barnstable, he stood uncovered, tears in his eyes, and thanked his neighbors and kinsfolk for their kindness to her.

In May 1841, with time on his hands, he renewed his effort to have his relative rank situation corrected. He wrote to the new secretary, George Badger, explaining the origin of the problem. He added that when he was promoted to master commandant in 1831, the incorrect relative ranking of the lieutenants promoted put several men ahead of him who should have been below him in the relative rankings in the new grade. He was now number 2 on the master commandants' list. Except for the original error, he would be a captain.

Percival's communication was more than a letter. It was a detailed legal brief. The department looked into the matter, but a note in his file argued against him. If the navy made a correction or change, it would be disruptive. Badger was unequivocal. "I regret very much if either by design or oversight, a lower rank was assigned you in 1814 than you were justly entitled." But with twenty-seven years having passed, he told Percival, his application could not "for a moment be entertained."[46]

Four months later the issue became moot. And this may have been the object of Percival's belated plea to Badger. President John Tyler signed commissions promoting thirteen commanders to the lofty grade of captain effective 8 September 1841. Percival headed the list. In the margin of his captain's commission is the notation, "Registered No. One. The lowest number of the same date takes rank."[47] Captain was the highest grade attainable in the U.S. Navy prior to the Civil War. The redheaded boy from Cape Cod had reached the top. No other man who entered the navy as a sailing master did as much. In fact, 150 years would pass before another Cape Codder reached the upper echelon of the service.

Nonetheless, as the months passed, Mad Jack found himself with time on his hands. There were not enough captains' duty assignments to go around. His age and history of poor health worked against him. He was a witness in a court-martial in Norfolk, and he sat on a general court-martial in Boston. He made requests for a command in the home squadron, but to no avail. And late in 1842 he suffered a major personal setback when William Wyman's Phoenix Bank of Charlestown failed. Mad Jack lost most if not all of his savings, some fifteen thousand dollars. Hull, who lost about three hundred dollars, wrote to a friend in the department: "Percival writes that Wyman is the damnedest rascal on earth. It is indeed a hard case for him."[48]

But a few things did go his way in 1842. Late in the year, his old enemies from Hawaii, Alfred Edwards and Leonard Sistair, revived their crusade against him and sent Secretary Abel Upshur the old material on their charges. The secretary asked Percival to explain. He did so with some warmth. Upshur followed the rule set by Badger the year before. He refused to reexamine the case. "I am not influenced by the renewal of accusations," he responded to Edwards and Sistair. "It is settled."[49]

~10~

AROUND THE WORLD
IN THE CONSTITUTION

Without an active command as 1843 began, Percival asked Secretary Upshur to give him a frigate in the East Indies. The secretary acknowledged the letter but did not act on the request. Percival's next meaningful work was in May. Knowing that Mad Jack took a fatherly interest in his midshipmen, Acting Secretary A. Smith assigned him to sit on the board for the examination of midshipmen. The board convened at the Naval Asylum in Philadelphia. When it finished deliberating, Percival sent a short note to a fellow officer anxious to find out how his boy had fared before the examination board. The youngster had just made it. Mad Jack's message was to the point but sensitive.

> Dear X—
> Your son has passed. Do you recollect our taking the *Columbus* out of dock? *She just grazed.*
> Yours truly,
> J Percival[1]

A month later, still in Philadelphia, Percival asked Smith if he could sail the *Franklin* to Boston. The old ship of the line, currently lying at

New York, had been built in Philadelphia in 1815 and now needed repairs. Smith consented and directed him to bring her north to the Charlestown dry dock. Even this fairly routine job landed Percival in the middle of controversy. New York interests, angry about the lost business, complained loudly about the move. In response, the secretary of the navy offered a lengthy formal report that vindicated his decision. *Niles' Weekly Register,* hating to see him condescend so, editorialized, "The secretary will have his hands full if he takes that tack."[2] Meanwhile, with the *Franklin* towed by a pair of steamboats, Percival had an easy time of it. He brought his charge rigged with jury masts, schooner fashion, into Boston in two days. She remained under his supervision until October.

Shortly after he got back to Boston, Percival asked the new acting secretary, David Henshaw, for an active ship. Henshaw responded that he contemplated assigning Percival to command a frigate in the near future. Weeks passed. The department detailed Percival along with his friends John Downes and Joseph Smith to conduct a close examination of the gun carriages of the *Potomac.* Then, on 13 October 1843, Secretary Henshaw gave Percival the most memorable command of his career: the frigate *Constitution.*

Six frigates were built under the 1797 building program. Of the group, the *Congress, Chesapeake,* and *President* were gone. The *Congress* had been broken up at Norfolk seven years earlier, and the British captured the *Chesapeake* and the *President* during the War of 1812. Only the *Constellation, Constitution,* and *United States* were with the navy in 1843. In 1854 the navy so thoroughly rebuilt the *Constellation* from the keel up that the original ship ceased to exist. When the Union forces abandoned the Norfolk yard in 1861, they scuttled the *United States.* In 1843 it looked as if time was about to run out for the illustrious *Constitution* as well.

She was moored at Norfolk and serving as a receiving ship, no more than a floating barracks. In 1830 Oliver Wendell Holmes Sr. had rallied the country to the cause of the legendary warship. His stirring poem "Old Ironsides" hastened repairs costing some $158,000 and saved the ship from being broken up. A decade later the navy once again deemed the grand old ship unseaworthy. Naval constructor Foster Rhodes estimated that it would cost $70,000 to make her ready for sea duty this time because her timbers needed renovation.

Henshaw faced a dilemma. His budget did not contain funds to cover the recommended repairs, but he could not let the nation's favorite ship rot. The secretary, who was from Massachusetts, was familiar with Percival's penchant for frugality and his reputation for excellence in seamanship. This was the man to assess the *Constitution*. He sent Mad Jack to Norfolk to look over the situation and report back to him.

The object was to determine if the *Constitution* could be made ready for extended service in the Pacific at a cost substantially below Rhodes's estimate. Percival made a diligent survey of the ship and traveled to Washington to report that he could get the job done for ten thousand dollars. A lively debate erupted. Critics did not believe anyone could do the work for so little. The *Norfolk Herald* claimed the ship would never complete a voyage without more costly repairs. *Niles'* cautioned that Old Ironsides ought to be in perfect trim before she went to sea. There could be no risk of losing her. Despite the show of concern for the ship, however, reputations and jobs were the underlying issues at stake.

Percival's longtime friend Commo. Lewis Warrington, the chief of the navy's Bureau of Construction and Repair, approved the plan. On 6 November, Henshaw concurred and directed Percival to "proceed without delay."[3] But if he could not meet his estimate, Henshaw warned, Percival must return to Boston with his men and take command of the frigate *Potomac*.

The criticism continued as Percival set to work overhauling Old Ironsides. Henshaw remained steadfast and supportive of the practical estimate. He told Percival, "You could not but expect that those would growl who lost the job and their reputation at the same time."[4] Warrington likewise was encouraging. He told Percival, "I hear it said, you will not do enough to her, that she won't bear service, & that she will drown all hands." But he was not the least bit apprehensive. "My answer is, a man must be a fool, to go to sea in his own coffin." "I know of no better way of repairing a ship," he continued, "than under the eye of him who is to command her."[5]

By the middle of January 1844 laborers working under Percival's direction had recaulked and recoppered the *Constitution*'s bottom; replaced timbers in the decks and sides; and repaired the masts, rigging, and rudder. Mad Jack wrote to the secretary "unhesitatingly" pronouncing the *Constitution* thoroughly ready for "a two or even a three year cruise." He was ready to stake "his life and reputation" on his opinion.[6]

Warrington traveled to Norfolk and inspected the repair work. A critical test measured seawater intake in the well. On her last trip, the *Con-*

stitution had taken on a foot of water every hour. Now, leakage did not exceed an acceptable two inches in twenty-four hours. Warrington, "a gentleman whose opinion [was] looked upon as worthy of confidence," reported favorably on the ship's readiness. Benjamin F. Stevens of Boston, the captain's clerk as of November, said that with Warrington's assessment, "the fears of the people of Norfolk for the safety of the ship were set at rest."[7]

The department issued orders to have the *Constitution* ready for sea by the first of April. The recruiting ship *Pennsylvania* provided stores and men. Henry G. Thomas, the ship's carpenter, wrote in his journal, a rich source of information on the *Constitution*'s round-the-world cruise, "Despite the crew's general dislike, we have also purchased 80 ship's scrapers for hull work, 100 hickory brooms and 66 corn brooms for deck work." He also mentioned that two of his men returned late from town that day. They had been gathering items such as washstands and sofas for Percival and the other officers. The watch did not report them since "their scavenging had become an art to them and a boon to the ship."[8]

Mad Jack had trouble completing his crew in Norfolk. He asked John Y. Mason, the new secretary of the navy, for permission to proceed to New York, where available seamen were plentiful. Commonly one to support his requests with a benefit to the department, Percival added that the trip would serve as a trial of the ship's fitness. Mason approved the move.

Before he left, Percival reviewed the rules and regulations with the crew. "Most of the crew and especially the midshipmen held him in great reverence and not so much because of his age which was four times greater than theirs," Thomas recorded in his journal, "but rather because he had become something of a tradition of the old navy days."[9] On 11 April the *Constitution* dropped from the navy yard and headed for Hampton Roads. Six days later she cleared Cape Henry, discharged the pilot, and stood to the north.

The trip to New York was miserable. Gales and headwinds extended the trip to ten days. Percival told the secretary he wished critics of naval pay could have experienced the painful realities of the passage. By the time they reached shore, they would have shed their notions about the romance of life at sea. Stevens, who experienced violent seasickness, the prince of all ailments, wondered what prompted him "to come to sea when land was plenty in New England."[10] He recovered and went on to write the most thorough of the firsthand accounts of the ensuing voyage. At least seven other members of the crew, mainly midshipmen, maintained journals of varying quality.

Percival used the next month to recruit the full 447-man complement. He wound up with 252 Americans and 195 foreigners in the crew, and ten passengers. There were Canadians, Englishmen, Irishmen, Scots, Frenchmen, Germans, Dutchmen, Russians, Norwegians, Swedes, Danes, Portuguese, Italians, Chinese, and a smattering of other nationalities.

The layover in New York turned out to be an enjoyable respite. Percival's wife, Maria, and their adopted daughter, Maria Weeks, spent several days on board. With them in mind, he asked the department to send three-fifths of his pay to his home in Dorchester while he was away. Crowds of New Yorkers visited the famous frigate. Midn. Dominick Lynch, then only thirteen, recorded, "With the band playing, and young people dancing, our days passed pleasantly."[11] Thomas and Stevens accompanied some officers, including Percival, into the city to attend the theater. The *Constitution* was ready to sail by the end of May. Percival asked Mason to assign a schooner to accompany him on the upcoming extended voyage, but the cost was prohibitive. As things turned out, Percival would miss the assistance of a smaller attendant.

The *Constitution*'s initial assignment was to transport Henry A. Wise, the first U.S. ambassador to Brazil, to his post in Rio. Ambassador Henry Alexander Wise should not be confused with Henry Augustus Wise, Percival's smart-aleck midshipman on the *Erie* and the *Cyane*. They were related; in fact, Ambassador Wise acted as the young officer's guardian. The ambassador had served as a congressman from Virginia as well as governor of the state prior to his appointment, but he is better known today as the Confederate brigadier general who surrendered the infantry of the Army of Northern Virginia to Maj. Gen. Joshua L. Chamberlain at Appomattox.

Percival's orders further directed him to leave Brazil for the eastern coast of Africa and proceed into the China seas, making his way back to the United States as he judged best. He was to protect American maritime interests along the way, survey uncharted waters, check for coal sources in Borneo, and, in general, show the flag.

On 29 May 1844 the *Constitution* left New York on her only circumnavigation of the globe. The steamer *Hercules* towed the venerable warship down to Sandy Hook. The next day, Thomas recorded in his journal, the crew cast off the tow "and made sail to royals and flying jib."[12] "We are now on our way across the broad Atlantic," wrote Stevens.[13] Lynch took a last look at the New York highlands.

The *Constitution* sailed east-southeast for the Azores. Percival planned to slip down the western coast of Africa through Madeira and the Canaries, past Cape Verde, and thence southwest to Rio. Although this course was longer than a direct route southeast to the eastern tip of Brazil around Recife, the favorable winds made it the preferred path. On the second day at sea, in calm weather, Percival permitted men to leave their stations in order to air their quarters. Thomas thought this was a considerate act. On Sunday morning, 2 June, the captain held worship services. Mad Jack first read from his family Bible, then shifted to more immediate—and secular—concerns and read the Articles of War to the assembled crew. After all, this was a warship.

War was possible at any time on two accounts. The boundary of the Oregon Territory continued to be the subject of a lengthy dispute with Great Britain, and the United States and Mexico differed over the ownership of Texas. Either dispute might flare up suddenly into open hostilities. On Sunday afternoon Percival had the marines practice boarding while the gunners engaged in target practice. From time to time, he varied the course to simulate battle maneuvers.

Initial landfall was the island of Flores, which was spotted on the twelfth. Percival moved on to Faial from there, arriving on 17 June and remaining for four days. The locals gave a ball in town, and the Americans reciprocated with a dance on board the *Constitution* before the ship moved on to Madeira. Along the way, the *Constitution* fell in with the Boston-bound American brig *Lycoming*. On receiving word that a number of men on the brig were sick, the navy surgeon crossed over to administer to them. Percival dug into his private stock of chickens and potatoes and sent a quantity to the sick men.

The *Constitution* came to anchor in the Bay of Funchal, Madeira, on 24 June. The traditional salutes were fired and returned gun for gun. During the five days in port, Lynch noted, "the Officers were entertained by the Elite of the place, visiting all points of interest, and enjoying every hour."[14]

On the afternoon of 1 July the ship anchored in the harbor of Santa Cruz de Tenerife. Three days later Thomas wrote, "we celebrated the Fourth of July in the officer's quarters and there was much frivolity all around."[15] Old Ironsides fired a twenty-one-gun salute at noon. The local fort returned the courtesy. After dark, the crew launched rockets and illuminated blue lights. The next day, according to the carpenter, many men were under the weather. Percival took time to show Stevens the prison where he had been held as a young ship captain in 1805.

The ship departed Tenerife on the fifth, accompanied by the French corvette *Berceau*, also bound for Rio. The officers of the two ships had exchanged visits before sailing. A few days out, Captain Percival agreed to demonstrate his firepower, and "for an hour or so it sounded like the days of the old war," Thomas noted.[16]

On 13 July the frigate spoke the British transport ship *Larpin*, Captain Lovewell commanding, homeward bound from Calcutta. The two traded information and compared chronometers, and the navy gave the merchantman a supply of chickens and potatoes. Lovewell was greatly impressed by the Americans' generosity. Just a few days before, a British frigate had refused to offer comparable aid. An officer of the *Larpin* assured them "that 'We had shown them more civility than even their own national ship,'" Stevens noted. "A great compliment coming from an Englishman."[17]

On 22 July events tested Percival's seamanship. While the ship was moving along at a fair eight knots, a seaman named James Corbett fell into the water. Thomas quickly cut away a life buoy and tossed it to Corbett. "Captain Percival acted very quickly while Corbett was in the sea," wrote Thomas, "having hoved the main topsail in a record time and lowered the cutter to retrieve him"—to the regret of some.[18] In fact, Corbett was considered a troublemaker, and he probably did not slip at all, but was pushed by one of his shipmates. Earlier, Percival had punished Corbett with a dozen lashes of the cat for being drunk and disorderly at Funchal.

One of the most pleasant and memorable events of the voyage began the next night. The incident, in fact, provided years of fodder for wardroom storytellers. Old Ironsides arrived at the equator, to the great excitement of the crew. They anticipated a visit by His Oceanic Majesty King Neptune and shaving of the "green 'uns"—those who had never crossed the line. The ceremony was, Lt. John B. Dale noted, "an old custom fast becoming obsolete."[19] The spirited celebration that followed hastened the trend.

The night before the *Constitution* reached the line, someone hailed the ship. The crew hauled up the courses and laid aback the topsails. A creature half man and half fish came over the bow and sought permission to inspect the ship. Captain Percival and the king were old acquaintances, and the skipper granted approval. The parties worked out the particulars over brandy in Ambassador Wise's cabin.

The next morning, the twenty-fourth, Neptune again hailed the ship. Over the bow this time came a "very old Sea-dog, with long white sea weed hair & beard." His train included barbers, latherers, and constables. The king ordered his scribe to take down the names of those who had never before been in his dominions and thus owed tribute. "Then," added Lynch, "he entered the Cabin for some of the stuff that he liked."[20] All aboard were treated to wine or whisky. "I am sorry to say that whisky had the preference," recalled the ship's clerk.[21]

Ambassador and Mrs. Wise received clearance after the ambassador made a stump speech claiming the privilege of free transit through neutral territories. Lieutenant Dale said that Wise offered to "substitute all his children, his Secretary and his servants for the ordeal."[22] But the Wises' diplomatic immunity had less to do with that exchange than with their willingness to "buy themselves off with a bottle of whisky," wrote Stevens.[23] The "*spirited* promises" did the trick.[24]

Joseph Curtis, the lieutenant of the ship's marines, became the first initiate. A latherer used a mop to coat the marine's face with lampblack and tar. A barber employed a hoop-iron a foot long to scrape it off. Handlers flipped the officer backward into a tarpaulin filled with water for a rowdy baptism. Two bears scrubbed him clean, and the engine hose washed him down. Dale observed that the lieutenant took his initiation like a man.

The handling varied according to the person's popularity, or lack of it. "For a few of the younger men," Thomas recalled, "the ritual seemed to be a bit more thorough."[25] Even the Wises' baby was passed through the christening step. Many tried to escape the ordeal by running aloft. Once caught by the constables, they were lowered down by a bowline and accorded rougher treatment for their efforts.

Dale described the overall spectacle and the handling of one "polliwog," as some called the uninitiated. When one of the Wise boys was slow to submit to initiation, a drummer boy grabbed him by the shoulders while another youth took up his heels. Both were dressed as imps. They dragged their prisoner to the dreaded platform. "The spirit of fun was now rife," reported Dale. "Shouts of laughter resounded from all parts of the ship. Little bye plays were going on, very ludicrous in themselves and especially on an occasion where every-body was disposed to laugh."[26]

After two hours of frolic, Neptune queried: "No more?"

"Yes, Sir," responded his chief of staff, "there is still on the ship one who cannot be found."

"Let the ship be searched," ordered Neptune, "and I command you Captain Percival, as an old seaman, to give me all the assistance in your power to find the missing man who is skulking!"[27]

The missing man turned out to be Wise's secretary of legation, Mr. Sargent. Constables found him hiding in his room. He resisted their attempts to pull him out and blustered that if bullied, he would seek Percival's court-martial. For this, Sargent received the extra treatment. When the scrubbers tossed him backward into the water, he got hold of sixty-five-year-old Percival and dragged him in, too. Mad Jack gave Sargent a good ducking for his trouble.

The festivities came to a close as follows:

> The boatswain piped belay. However it closed by a scene not soon forgotten. The Capt. among others had mounted upon the boats amidships to see the fun, when some of the midshipmen got hold of the hose, pointing at some particular person: in the *melee* which occurred our veteran Captain received a full charge from the force pump and there was such a scramble to get off the boats that some came off coatless or tail[l]ess, and all looking like drowned rats. The Capt. laughed as heartily as any of them with his yellow nankens clinging close to his legs, and the grey-head drenched with water.[28]

When the ceremonies ended after more than two hours, Percival generously entertained Neptune. Afterward, escorted by the captain and Mr. and Mrs. Wise, with the ship's band playing, the king marched forward. He turned and granted the ship free pratique to all waters and left over the bow for unknown parts. Midn. William Buckner thought Wise and his family enjoyed the fun as much as anyone, if not more.

The celebrants dunked some 150 people in the royal pool. Those so initiated earned the right to be known as "shellbacks." Sargent, however, did not appreciate the honor. He made such a fuss to Washington about his "disgraceful treatment" that the Navy Department stopped the practice, according to Lynch, "and it was many years before the old play was again enacted."[29]

When relatively new, the *Constitution* had achieved top speeds of twelve and one-half to thirteen and one-half knots. Thus, it seems noteworthy that Mad Jack drove her for fourteen knots as he approached Cape Frio, Brazil. For several days lookouts spotted a strange sail following the ship, and Percival accepted the implied challenge of a race.

Along the way, on 1 August, Percival met his old ship, the *Erie,* homeward bound from the Pacific and most recently from Rio de Janeiro, and learned that Commo. Alexander Dallas of the Pacific squadron was ill. The men of the *Constitution* put letters on board the *Erie,* and the two ships parted.

In the meantime, the stranger had gained on the American frigate. "We showed our ensign," wrote Stevens, "and she hoisted a French flag. By taking a glass into the mizzentop, she was found to be the corvette *Berceau.*"[30] The Frenchman had parted with the *Constitution* on 10 July, taking a different route past the Cape Verde Islands, but the race had continued. On the morning of 2 August the *Berceau* was two miles ahead, becalmed at the mouth of the harbor to Rio. Mad Jack took advantage of an offshore breeze and hove ahead. "But, alas," lamented Stevens, "about nine the wind left us, and we had the mortification of seeing the Berceau shoot ahead."[31] The American ship anchored at 3:00 P.M., just behind the Frenchman.

Percival quickly took a liking to the *Constitution.* Based on what he had learned about her, he subsequently recommended placing her fore and main masts three-quarters of their diameter farther aft and dispensing with all ballast. His evaluation of the ship: "Under all circumstances no ship of her class better; rolls deep and easy; but at anchor, in a seaway, is hard on her cables."[32] One day she covered 240 miles, although a favoring current accounted for 42 of the miles.

The ship remained at Rio for more than a month. Beyond the usual entertainments and visits to interesting places, the crew devoted much time to gathering stores and overhauling the ship for the extended trip in front of them. At this point, Percival made a remarkable alteration in the *Constitution*'s appearance. He put Thomas's eighty scrapers to work and changed the color of the black hull to white (some accounts describe it as lead colored or lead gray) and the white gun stripe to red.

The change, which in fact conflicted with an 1842 navy regulation, caused quite a stir. The Brazilians thought it was war paint. As a result of the novel painting scheme, Lynch recalled, "our ship was reported in the newspapers of the day, as being an Arab slave-ship."[33] Beyond technical and geographical data such as courses, winds, places, and the like, Midn. W. P. Buckner mentioned few incidents in his journal covering the thirteen months; but he did note the sudden color change. Stevens saw an immediate benefit: the *Constitution* could not accept visitors while the crew was painting. The clerk did not regret that restriction, having experienced enough of the naval niceties associated with guests.

The radical change might seem curious to some, thought Lynch, but it "showed great forethought on the part of the worthy old Captain, who was a true sailor, and had the interests of his Officers & crew at heart."[34] Stevens recorded the reason for the innovation in his journal. The idea, he noted, originated with Percival, who knew that black paint absorbs the heat from the sun while white refracts sunlight. By changing the ship's color scheme, Percival brought a semblance of comfort to the gun and berth decks. When the thermometer reached 100 degrees, as it did frequently once the *Constitution* reached the tropics, it was almost impossible to touch the black hammock covers, but the white side of the ship remained relatively cool. Moreover, the white paint cut down on maintenance. In a black ship exposed to heat, the pitch will issue from the seams in the bends sooner than it will in a light-colored ship. "Captain Percival deserves the praise of *all concerned in real improvements* for successfully introducing the above plan," noted Stevens.[35]

During the visit to Rio, Percival received word that Commodore Dallas had died. He contemplated the situation for a week and then decided to apply for the vacancy. Mad Jack knew that, at his age, he would not get another chance for sea duty once he returned from his present cruise. Eventually, however, the secretary responded that he had already filled the post.

Before leaving Brazil, Percival got together with Ambassador Wise for a farewell dinner. The two men had developed considerable fondness and respect for each other during the voyage. In later years Wise used his political influence on several occasions to aid Percival in his dealings with the office of the secretary. Wise described Percival as a clear-headed and good-hearted man who put his country first. Percival thought just as highly of Wise and tended to his every need while en route to Rio. He turned over his entire cabin to the Wises before leaving New York and occupied an improvised apartment on the gun deck. "I question," reported Stevens, "whether any minister to a foreign court on a voyage from *home* ever experienced more attention and courtesy."[36] Midn. Lucius Mason noted that the Wise family made many friends on board and seemed like members of the crew.

At sunrise on 8 September, the first lieutenant called all hands, and Old Ironsides weighed anchor and stood to the east. Percival planned to land at Tristan da Cunha in the South Atlantic, a small, dreary, almost inaccessible island, but a southwest gale kept the ship away. The *Constitution* enjoyed pleasant weather until she reached the Cape of Good Hope late on 3 October. She doubled the Cape on the fourth but ran into an intense storm while standing about two miles from the shore. Stevens termed the event a brief squall. Young Midshipman Mason, sent up into the foretop to supervise reefing the foretopsail, held a different perspective. From his vantage point, the storm was a strong gale. Buffeted by the cold wind and pelted by rain and hail, he developed second thoughts about a life at sea. Mason's apprehension increased when "Captain Percival informed us that the guns should be hoved overboard if she was in danger of sinking to ease her."[37]

When the storm died down, the watch determined the ship to be past Danger Point and on the Agulhas Bank—the beginning of the Indian Ocean. Percival set a course to the northeast and the southwestern tip of the great island of Madagascar. Old Ironsides anchored at the entrance to Saint Augustine's Bay late on 16 October. The next morning, canoes arrived from shore carrying, among others, the local leader, who was known as Prince Green. The royal personage had attired himself in a deteriorated coat, tight white pants, and an old navy cap with a faded gold band. His purser, John Green, was "dressed in the most original manner possible," Stevens noted. An "old tattered navy waistcoat, one epaulet, a sailor's hat, and pieces of cotton composed his wardrobe. To crown the whole," continued the ship's clerk, "he had an American eagle (brass) fastened onto his vest behind." The man had only one eye "and on the whole was the most original looking officer" Stevens had ever seen.[38] Most of Prince Green's entourage carried letters of recommendation from various whaling ships. One letter signed by "Sam Slick" informed those who read it that the bearer was an untrustworthy rascal.

The Madagascans, unable to read English, believed the letters described their honesty.

The place favorably impressed Midshipman Lynch. At the cost of a string of glass beads he was able to fill a boat with fresh fruit. But Stevens was not as pleased. "The people are beggars and robbers," he noted, "and I was eased of my 'kerchief in a very short time." Their bamboo huts, he added, "appear to resemble pigsties more than the habitations of human beings." He concluded: "We shall not regret our departure from this sink of knavery."[39]

The *Constitution* quit Saint Augustine on 20 October and crossed westward to the African coast and Mozambique. The ever-apprehensive Mason described a perilous approach. A fatigued crew and a freshened wind combined to make a critical tack almost impossible. If missed, the ship would have gone ashore, "but oh, not the Constitution," he wrote. "Her guardian angel had not left her to peril on the burning rocks and sand of Mozambique, for go about she did, and the brave action was smartly done."[40]

Mason was greatly impressed with the seamanship involved. He continued:

> It was a beautiful sight. Captain Percival has what most Captains do not, that is the implicit confidence in his abilities to run or manage a ship. He works a ship with the same confidence, and with no more fear of making a mistake, than a skilled musician fears making a mistake in a piece of music. My only wish is that more commanders felt the way that our Captain Percival felt towards the proper handling of a ship. To watch him is to watch a fine surgeon at work, and he takes his work as seriously as a physician as well.[41]

Mozambique, in Lynch's view, was just another filthy, squalid place. Percival remained there only two days, long enough to visit the governor general, His Excellency Brig. Gen. R. L. d'Abun da Luria. Satisfied that American commerce was not suffering at this port, Mad Jack set a course for Bombetoka Bay and the town of Majunga on the northwestern shore of Madagascar, which the *Constitution* reached on 2 November.

Benjamin Stevens observed that the people at Majunga were far advanced over those in the southern part of the island and paid more attention to their dress. Unfortunately, some of the twenty-nine crewmen allowed ashore paid less attention to their behavior. At sunset on the fourth, Thomas recalled, "some returned, most of whom were very drunk with the effects of rum." But a number did not return at all from the liberty. "It was certain onboard," Thomas said, "that a minor mutiny was about to take place."[42]

Mad Jack told his young aide, Midshipman Lynch, to get the gig ready. He stormed on deck wearing "his fighting coat" and carrying "no sword, but a heavy Mangrove cane, with a large ivory knob." "Get in the boat," he shouted to Lynch. "I will show them how to obey orders." Once on shore, Percival bounded up the beach toward a native hut. Inside, he found the boatswain's mate, the purser's steward, and a seaman, all drunk. Lynch's journal paints a lively picture of the rout that followed.

> "You wont go off eh," said the captain. "I'll see." With that he brought his cane down on the back of the Boatswain's mate, who got away. The Purser's steward . . . in endeavoring to escape, ran between the old gentleman's legs, who made a horse of him, riding on his back, and belaboring him with his cane—Getting outside, the steward managed to escape and ran to the water, into which he went followed by the captain, beating and ducking him.—A picture was drawn of this affair and sent to the President, with this Inscription. "Mad Jack Percival getting *his crew* on board the Constitution in the Bay of Majunga, Island of Madagascar."—This picture went all over the United States on the ship's arrival home in 1846. He was greatly beloved by all his officers and his crew.[43]

The picture described by Lynch was reproduced, and a copy made its way to West Barnstable, but it has since disappeared. Neither the Navy Department, the National Archives, the Library of Congress, nor anyone else, it seems, knows the current whereabouts of the picture or a copy. Most likely, Midshipman Dale, an active artist on the trip, drew the sketch.

American trade dominated the commerce of Majunga; the Pingree firm of Salem even had a resident agent at the place. However, the French, attempting to extend their influence over the island's western coast, had convinced the local authorities to tax American imports. Shortly after he left, Percival wrote to Madagascar's queen, Ranavalon I, advocating the advantages of free trade. He stressed that the United States, unlike the European powers, would never interfere with another nation's government or religion. Nor, he added, was his country interested in colonization or conquest.

After a sail to the northeast, Old Ironsides anchored off the French island settlement of Nosy Be in the Mozambique Channel on 7 November, the first American man-of-war to visit. Stevens thought the island the prettiest place he had seen since Rio. Percival took time there to add to his reputation for eccentricity. One afternoon he directed Lynch to take him ashore in the gig. While casually walking the beach they came upon a large log on the drift line. The captain pondered a bit, then sent Lynch back to the ship to bring the carpenter. Thomas showed up with an ax and cut into the log, and found it to be valuable wood. The carpenter's gang returned to the beach the next day and cut the log into planks. After Thomas returned with the lumber to the ship, Percival directed him make a coffin. "In case of his death before his return home, he was to be brought back in it," reported Lynch.[44]

Percival's action was not really so eccentric. He was becoming increasingly ill as the voyage progressed. Gout in his feet and right hand forced him to use crutches or confined him to his cot. He also suffered bouts of dysentery, like many of the crew. By the time the carpenter finished the coffin early in December, Percival was so sick that he gave up executive command and navigation of the frigate to Lt. Amasa Paine.

Nor was his foresight unique. The revered Lord Nelson, seven years before Trafalgar, made a long box from the mainmast of the French *L'Orient*. His men carried Nelson off the *Victory* in that coffin. Luckily, Percival's health improved, and he put his box to a happier use. He brought the casket home full of silks, teas, curios, and a Chinese long bow purchased during the cruise. After that, in a display of Yankee thrift, he used it as a watering trough in front of his Dorchester home.

After the stopover, Percival moved back toward the African coast and headed for Zanzibar. Along the way, on 18 November, the captain dealt with the disobedience at Majunga. The ship's log notes that he called all hands at 8:20 A.M. to witness the punishment of Seaman Ed Britt. Percival read Articles 170, 171, 172, and 185 from the Articles of War. Britt, though a troublemaker, was popular among the men, and Percival thus decided to read the charges himself, explaining that a threat against the captain is a threat against the ship and cannot be tolerated.

Midn. Patterson Jones reported that Britt received twelve lashes for his insubordination. His journal continues:

The following are the words he made use of, which were read by the Captain at the gang-way. "You are guilty of having made use of the following language, on the afternoon of the day, you returned on board from shore at Majunga." "You were confined for acting like a man and that old jack the son of a bitch struck you, and you would have knocked him down, if you had, had a chance. You continually repeated the language, and said that the Captain could only punish you, and for that you did not care a d—d. You again said that you attempted to strike him while on shore and would have done so if it had been *Jesus Christ.* The time you made use of this language you were apparently, more sober than drunk and appeared anxious to have your words heard by those around you."[45]

Thomas thought the punishment fair, and Britt deserving of it. Before long, all appeared forgotten, and Percival did not raise the issue again.

The ship arrived at Zanzibar on 19 November 1844. The Americans were pleased to find their French friends in the corvette *Berceau* in the harbor. The French paid them a visit, along with the officers of an English sixteen-gun brig and the U.S. vice consul, W. C. Waters. Some months later, the men of the *Constitution* learned that their sometime companion the *Berceau* subsequently wrecked on the rugged coast of Madagascar with all hands lost. Nobody survived, lamented Stevens.

The next day, the sultan of Muscat, who held Zanzibar among his possessions, entertained Percival and a party of his officers. Stevens thought His Highness seemed partial to Americans. Lynch described the entertainment at the palace as a lunch, while Stevens said that he and most of the officers considered it the feast of a lifetime. "Plates were piled upon plates, and the table was literally groaning with the weight."[46]

Before Percival left the island, the sultan presented him with a splendid sword with a curved steel blade, golden hilt and guard, and an ivory clip. It is on display today at the Naval Academy Museum. The legend of Mad Jack Percival is such that the sword is never viewed as an ordinary gift; a tale is necessary. Thus, lore describes the sword as a reward from the sultan to Percival after Mad Jack rescued him from the clutches of a band of pirates just as the bloodthirsty corsairs were about to put him to torture. There is no record of Percival ever telling this story; nor did any of the journalists on the *Constitution* mention such a noteworthy incident or anything comparable. The colorful explanation is simply one of many fictitious yarns associated with Mad Jack.

The American frigate weighed anchor on 27 November and headed for Sumatra. Dysentery broke out on the way. By the middle of December, forty-three men were on the sick list. Stevens believed the sickness stemmed from sleeping on wet decks, eating large amounts of unripe fruit, and similar imprudent acts. The *Constitution* had up to that point been a healthy ship. On 18 December, Stevens asserted that no place anywhere else in the world with the same number of people had been free of death for more than seven months. Unfortunately, he was too optimistic. Two days later, a seaman named Wester went to his reward. Two days after that, an older bandsman named Christian Fischer died as his son, Frederick, tended to him. "We had been for so long a time spared, that we had almost cherished a hope the 'ruthless destroyer' would have passed us by," wrote Stevens.[47]

Percival converted the forward cabin into a hospital. The arrangement was more comfortable and less cramped than the gun deck or the sick bay, Stevens noted. "Captain Percival has shown towards the sick a kindly feeling, and a desire to make their condition as pleasant as possible, which would do any one a credit." This was not always the practice, especially on naval ships with a large sick list, he noted. "Therefore these little acts of kindness . . . and benevolence should receive the praise of all."[48]

The *Constitution* was nearing Sumatra as 1845 dawned. On 2 January the watch sighted a proa, a sailboat characteristic of the region. Percival ordered a white flag of peace run up, but the native craft stayed away. He had a blank cartridge fired, but it, too, failed to bring her to. When gunners fired a 32-pound shot across her bow, however, she lowered all her sails instantly. Percival sent a boat alongside the proa, and the Americans found what seemed to be stolen articles of gold and silver as well as U.S. Navy clothing. The natives protested loudly but did not struggle when Percival ordered them placed under arrest as pirates. Thomas noted, "They all seemed frightened beyond their wits."[49] Percival drew on their local knowledge and required them to pilot his ship into the celebrated port of Quallah Battoo at the western tip of Sumatra, a known haven for pirates and ruffians. As soon as the ship anchored on 4 January, the pirates were taken under guard to the authorities in town.

The initial purpose for the stop was to talk with the rajah about his treatment of American ships. In 1831 local pirates had captured the American merchantman *Friendship* and killed some of her crew. The

USS *Potomac* meted out ample punishment a year later, but American shipping interests remained concerned. Percival summoned the rajah to palaver.

Accompanied by his "tagrag and bobtail," he appeared on board. "Quite a party congregated in the cabin," reported Stevens.[50] Percival, though confined to his berth with the gout, told the natives that if they let American traders alone, "without robbing or murdering them, there never would be a shot fired at them in hostility from under the American flag." On the other hand, he declared, if they plundered American ships and killed their men, the United States would send a ship to "wage an exterminating warfare" around the island. "They therefore might make the selection—to live in peace, or abide the result." The rajah responded that "peace was their object."[51]

In his report to the secretary of the navy, Percival said that most of the natives believed that America had few men-of-war. "I read to them the number of each grade, of which they kept an account," he wrote. "They were very much surprised to find the aggregate more than seventy and that four were at the present time in India." They repeated their desire for "peace and quiet commerce." Percival stressed to the natives "that, if those were their objects, the best way to secure them was by keeping their creases [*sic*] in their scabbards."[52]

By this time the sick list included sixty-four men, most of them down with dysentery. Percival strictly prohibited the procurement or consumption of local fruit. Some of the crew grumbled, but others such as Thomas strongly endorsed the precautionary measure. The safeguard was too late for popular Midn. Lucius Mason of Virginia. His dysentery turned into an inflammation of the brain, and he died on the sixth, much to the sorrow of his messmates. The ship's crew buried Mason with the appropriate ceremony due his rank. The band played a "dead march" as the body was borne to the gangway. The flag had been at half-mast all day. An attendant placed Mason's coat, sword, and cap on his breast. An officer read the service, and crewmembers committed the body to the deep. Stevens recorded: "The awful splash was heard, and the shock went to the heart of every one."[53]

The *Constitution* stopped next at the nearby port of Wylah. Lieutenant Paine put off a Malayan from Quallah Battoo to tell the local chiefs about the purpose of the American naval ship's visit. About 5,250 tons of U.S. shipping carried on trade worth $525,000 off the coast of

Sumatra each year, Percival noted in his report. He thought this amount of trade did not warrant the expense of maintaining a frigate on the station. He recommended instead a pair of sixteen-gun brigs working as a team. He stressed that brigs are generally healthier than frigates or sloops. The brigs should carry "practical and experienced officers, possessing a large share of common sense and a knowledge of commerce," he concluded.[54]

The *Constitution* next moved to the southeast. On 2 February, after a disagreeable passage down the Strait of Malacca, she pulled into Singapore. Calms and opposing currents extended this leg of the voyage. "It was a most agreeable change to once again get into civilization," thought Lynch, "after our long time among the heathen."[55] The American frigate remained at Singapore for more than a month—sufficient time to replenish bread supplies and give the sick a chance to recover. By the middle of the month, 150 men were down with dysentery; thirteen would die. Percival, still plagued with the gout, sought relief on shore at U.S. consul Joseph Balestier's bungalow.

"I would remark, that the greatest courtesy has been extended to me by the officer commanding her majesty's naval forces at this place," Percival wrote in a report to the secretary.[56] Almost as soon as the *Constitution* anchored, Commo. Henry D. Chads of HMS *Cambrian* unselfishly provided medical assistance. This was not the first time Chads had stepped on board Old Ironsides. He was first lieutenant on the *Java* when the *Constitution* took her in 1812. During the engagement the British commander, Capt. Henry Lambert, had been mortally wounded, and Chads had assumed the inglorious task of surrendering the dismasted *Java*. Chads told Percival that during the battle, the *Constitution* "was manoeuvered in a masterly manner, and it made me regret that she was not British." But, he continued, "it was 'Greek met Greek,' for we were of the same blood after all."[57]

In keeping with an 1818 directive, the ship's company celebrated Washington's Birthday with salutes and rockets. "The old ship looked beautifully," noted her clerk, "and her appearance attracted a crowd of spectators on shore."[58] Then the crew made final preparations to return to sea. The ship's log for 6 March describes one preparatory step and a concurrent precaution: "At 9 A.M. opened the Spirit Room to ventilate and placed a sentry over it."[59]

Just before leaving Singapore early in March, the *Constitution* experienced a portentous encounter. "The Commander-in-Chief of the Cochin China Squadron, 3 ships, visited us," ship's carpenter Thomas wrote in his journal.[60] Cochin China is now known as Vietnam. The ships were transporting sugar for sale. Fifth Lt. John Dale thought the vessels looked very dirty, although the commodore looked impressive. He came aboard the *Constitution* with pomp accompanied by a group of attendants and officers. This seems to have been the first meeting of American and what can be termed Vietnamese armed forces. The next meeting between the two navies would not be as friendly.

On 10 March the *Constitution* stood out to sea by way of the China passage. A week later she approached the island of Borneo—the first visit ever by a U.S. warship. Events made this clear. The approaches to Borneo were for the most part unsurveyed and poorly charted. In fact, the ship nearly grounded because of a twenty-mile error on one chart. She came "as close to defeat as ever she would," notes Tyrone Martin in his history of Old Ironsides.[61]

The frigate scraped on a coral reef just south of an area that to this day is called Dangerous Ground. First Lieutenant Paine, who was handling the ship, demonstrated superb skill in avoiding calamity. If the *Constitution* had been damaged, Lynch thought, America would have censured everyone on board. Percival reported to Secretary Bancroft that when the ship touched, it was imperceptible "to at least five eighths of those on board, and was only noticed by those whose anxiety . . . had rendered the senses more acute."[62] Thomas considered the ship's escape from the ticklish situation "certainly good luck, but it is soon learned by sailors that the Captain makes all the difference. So far we have had excellent management."[63]

Stevens did not concern himself with navigational matters. The sick list was foremost in his mind. A decrease to twenty-seven from the high of sixty on the list when the ship reached Singapore pleased the clerk; however, Percival remained on the list, and that was cause for worry. "The only anxiety on my mind is that of the captain's sickness," Stevens wrote. "Should his gout become worse, and he be taken away, I shall lose the best friend I have met with."[64] The fact that the temperature was "hot as hell" did not help matters.[65]

As he contended with his painful malady, Mad Jack twice sent 2d Lt. William Chaplin and men in cutters and the gig ashore to explore.

Although the naturalist in the party, Dr. J. C. Reinhardt, gathered valuable knowledge and many specimens on Borneo, coal was the principal object of Chaplin's expeditions. With the coming of steam navigation, the need for an American coaling station in the region would grow. Chaplin's efforts to establish a source of coal for U.S. ships were unsuccessful. The British had purchased exclusive rights to the coal just days earlier.

The *Constitution* left Borneo on 10 April and moved north across the South China Sea. This leg of the journey was more or less uneventful, but it did bring satisfaction to Midshipman Buckner, who was at last allowed to close his journal. Journal keeping was not a personal choice of the journalist. Regulations required officers to maintain official journals recording courses, winds, ground covered, and the like. Percival enforced the requirement with his midshipmen. Some officers included their observations of local geography and social and religious customs. A few kept more expansive and private journals. Buckner followed the basic approach with his journal and avoided commentary. His book ended on 30 April 1845. Mad Jack reviewed and approved the work, signing: "Very well Mr Buckner J Percival."[66]

By 2 May the higher land of Cochin China was in sight. On 10 May the ship anchored in Touron Bay (now Danang). Percival later reported to the Navy Department that "a circumstance occurred while at this place, which I shall make the subject of a special communication."[67] The "circumstance" required much more than one report. In fact, the incident has received more attention than any other episode in Percival's career.

The visit started routinely enough. As soon as the ship was securely anchored in Touron Bay, the crew began to obtain provisions and water. On the thirteenth, Lieutenant Chaplin went ashore to meet the local officials. He accomplished little. The mandarins appeared suspicious. They wanted to know why the American ship had come, why it did not leave, how long the Americans planned to stay, "and perhaps twenty other questions, one of which was 'What we were going to do at Canton?'" Chaplin answered, "'None of your business.' This answer put an end to further inquiries and they said we could have chickens, fish, water, etc."[68]

The next day several curious mandarins and their bodyguards paid a call on the *Constitution*. Percival received and entertained them in his cabin and then sent them on a general tour of the ship. A few minutes into the tour, their interpreter slipped back to the cabin and left a letter for Captain Percival. With broken Portuguese and hand signs, the man made it clear that if he were discovered, he would be executed.

Percival did not read the letter until after the visitors left the ship. The message was from a French missionary, Bishop Dominique Lefevre, Apostolic Vicar of Western Cochin. Bishop Lefevre reported that local mandarins had pillaged his house and the nearby village and had arrested him and a dozen or so of his followers. Lefevre wanted Percival not only to liberate him, but also to exact a pledge from the king of Cochin China to permit the churchman to remain in the country to proselytize without interference. The Treaty of Nanjing (1842) that concluded the Opium War permitted Christian missionaries in China and its tributaries. Lefevre hoped Percival would "give the Cochin Chinese a lesson. A very proper occasion now presents itself for such a lesson." In a postscript, the bishop stressed the need to hurry: "I am condemned *to death* without delay. Hasten or all is finished."[69]

In two sentences in his journal, the ship's clerk both defined the dilemma and explained much of Percival's thinking at the time. "A Frenchman was at the mercy of barbarians. He was a Christian and humanity called for our assistance."[70] A thrill of excitement ran through the ship. "What caused me the greatest anxiety," Percival later reported to the navy secretary, "was to decide how far I might proceed and not over step the limits." He felt that he had an obligation "towards a subject of a Nation united to us by the bonds of treaty, stipulations, and bygone though not forgotten acts of kindness in the days of our national infancy."[71] Lieutenant Dale saw a need for the "strongest and most instant measures. . . . Humanity was to be our warrant."[72]

Some modern commentators overlook this understandable reason for Percival's response to the situation. There is an inclination to label the "circumstance" the precursor of the modern Vietnam War. Percival is drawn as a villain, facts are misrepresented, and the result is termed a defeat for the United States. People who advance this line make something complex out of something simple. One recent account even calls a routine maintenance step an act of aggression. Peter Kneisel claims in a *Boston Globe Magazine* article that the *Constitution* left New York painted white because it was on a goodwill mission.[73] This is incorrect. As mentioned, the ship's color was changed from black to white for an altogether different reason while at Rio. The author goes on to support the theme that Percival acted in a warlike manner by claiming that when a standoff developed, he had the ship painted black in preparation for battle. This is partially true. On the second day in port, Thomas started the men repainting the ship black, but it was not in preparation for battle. Due to the passage of time and the wear and tear of an ocean voyage, the "pitch had begun to run out of the seams" and a general repainting was in order.[74] The task was not completed until some time after early August when the ship was in the Canton River. A careful consideration of the facts makes it clear that Percival did only as much as he considered necessary to rescue the bishop.

At any rate, a little more than an hour after receiving Lefevre's message Percival and eighty well-armed men, including thirty marines, stormed ashore in four boats. As he made his way to the chief mandarin's quarters, Mad Jack stationed men at intervals to form an unbroken line back to the boats. Armed Chinese outnumbered the Americans three to one. A fort was within pistol range and another was within musket range.

Percival delivered two letters, one for Lefevre and the other to the king of Cochin China, Thieu Tri. Lefevre's letter asked him to inform Percival of his location if he was not immediately released. Percival's letter to the king was concise and straightforward. Since the prisoners were subjects of a nation friendly with the United States, he said, he was bound by duty to demand their immediate release. To make his point, Mad Jack arrested three mandarins and carried them back to the ship as hostages. To remove suspicion, Percival included the messenger as one of the three detainees. Stevens was amazed that the locals did not offer any resistance.

The next day, at Percival's direction, 3d Lt. James Alden captured three junks belonging to the king. The captain moved the *Constitution* closer to the forts and town, thinking that a bold demonstration would gain the release of the bishop. Again, all of these steps were taken without resistance.

Several days passed without event except for the exchange of correspondence. On hearing that a mandarin representing the king at Hue had arrived, Percival and a force went into town. Unable to locate the official, the Americans returned to the ship. Percival released his three hostages in the hope of ending the stalemate. They promised to proceed the forty-five miles to Hue and make every effort to obtain the release of Lefevre.

The next day, the twentieth, the three prize junks took advantage of stormy weather and attempted to escape. The marines fired musket shots over and around them. Eyewitness accounts of the incident vary. Percival and the ship's clerk insisted that no lives were lost and no one was hurt in the skirmish. Lieutenant Dale recorded a rumor that some of the men on one of the junks drowned in the confusion.[75] The *Constitution*'s carpenter, clearly relying on hearsay, said that "several were seen to drown."[76] Despite the uncertainty regarding what actually happened, this action became the focal point of the overall affair and colored its subsequent history. Although the Cochin Chinese steadfastly denied that there were casualties, and no eyewitness account mentions any, a number of people, from President Zachary Taylor to recent writers, have believed otherwise. It is unthinkable, however, that Percival would write a contemporary official report ignoring or covering up casualties. Aside from his integrity, he had no reason to do so.

What is certain is that a vigorous pursuit followed. The Americans recaptured one junk within minutes. The other two escaped upriver with five American boats at their heels and anchored alongside ten well-armed junks. Both of the prize junks were retaken there. The guns of a fort on each bank covered the spot. "The whole shore was lined with soldiers," recalled Thomas. "We now thought that the soldiers and forts would surely open fire upon us."[77] The Americans landed with cutlasses drawn and, with a shout, charged the native soldiers watching them from the beach. The soldiers fled in haste. Having cleared the field, the American boat crews returned the prizes to the *Constitution*. Lieutenant Dale, amazed at the absence of an armed response from the Chinese, thought them "a queer people for belligerents."[78]

On the twenty-first, lookouts on Old Ironsides spotted three armed brigs flying the national flag of Cochin at the entrance to the bay. The following day, Percival led a small force to investigate. As he came alongside one brig, the natives pushed off his gig with spears and oars. Undaunted, Mad Jack, pistol in hand, clambered aboard, seated himself on the quarterdeck, and looked around. The crews rushed forward in alarm. "Everything was in confusion," Stevens noted, even though "the brigs must have had at least 100 men on board and ten guns."[79] When he had satisfied himself that the gunships were not a threat, Percival returned to his ship. The Americans returned to the routine tasks of provisioning and watering the ship. The two sides exchanged more letters, and Percival released the junks. Lefevre did not appear, and his where-abouts remained uncertain. Reluctantly, Percival prepared to leave.

Mad Jack explained his reasons in a letter to Adm. Jean Cecille, the commander of French naval forces in the region: "I could not proceed to hostilities without violating the instructions of my Government, unless an offence had been committed on a citizen of the United States, or an insult offered to its Flag." He thought a single frigate "entirely adequate to take possession of the town of Touron and its fortresses, . . . perhaps without the loss of a man."[80] This letter contradicts a modern theory that Percival felt he was outgunned and in danger, and therefore withdrew in defeat. As if to make the point that he could have acted if he had felt jus-tified in doing so, just before the *Constitution* left on 27 May, Mad Jack conducted gunnery exercises on a small, uninhabited island in the har-bor. Gunners fired half a dozen shots from the starboard Paixhans guns. Two of the shells burst above the target, and the rest fell short in the water. As the *Constitution* stood to the north, a disapproving Lieutenant Dale saw "a sad want of 'sound discretion,' in commencing an affair of this kind, without carrying it through to a successful issue."[81]

A short while later, the French minister to China and Admiral Cecille reported the release of Bishop Lefevre. The French credited the Ameri-cans with preserving the bishop's life. In fact, according to Stevens, King Louis Philippe intended "that the captain, officers and crew of the Con-stitution . . . be rewarded by the government of France for saving the life of the Bishop Lefevre." Political unrest in Paris intervened. The king "took a hurried journey from his capital, and no recognition of their ser-vices was ever received by the American tars." Their compensation went "over the walls of the Tuileries gardens" as Louis Philippe escaped to England.[82] Nevertheless, the French minister, M. Legrene, and Admiral Cecille warmly acknowledged Percival's friendly service. Several months later Mad Jack had the satisfaction of meeting Lefevre at Manila.

Within weeks, the Touron incident, blown far out of proportion, became a national concern. The Navy Department initially disapproved of Percival's actions and demanded a full report. Percival's communica-tions, especially a detailed 6 June report from Macao, seemed to satisfy the officials in Washington. Two years later, however, Joseph Balestier in Singapore wrote a highly exaggerated account of the events in Touron to the secretary of state. In it, he claimed the Cochin Chinese had told him that Percival had destroyed the port of Touron; sunk a number of junks;

and killed a score of men, women, and children. In August 1849 President Taylor apologized to the king of Cochin China for the deaths and injuries described by Balestier. But in his patronizing letter Taylor also cautioned that if the incident was not forgiven and set aside, he would dispatch naval forces to straighten things out and the king would bear the consequences.

In 1850 Secretary of State John Clayton, interested in promoting U.S. trade in the area, commissioned Balestier to make amends for the alleged outrage. The Cochin Chinese denied the incident had happened, however, and would not accept an apology. Rebuffed, Balestier found himself in an embarrassing situation. He had reported an atrocity on people who vowed that it never took place. So he rationalized to the State Department that the Cochin Chinese were scheming. He thought as long as the American apology remained unaccepted, the issue remained an unresolved grievance entitling the Cochin Chinese to seek redress by plundering U.S. shipping. At this point he took an aggressive position and considered a show of force in order. Balestier told officials in Washington that "the appearance of three ships of war . . . would be sufficient to obtain everything that could reasonably be asked of them."[83] The administration dropped the matter.

In recent decades the *Constitution*'s skirmish in Vietnam has received renewed attention. A French writer described the affair as the first armed intervention by a Western nation against present-day Vietnam. Other commentators agree, while just as many consider that judgment an overstatement. Nevertheless, there is some validity to the proposition that the 1845 confrontation should have been instructive to American policymakers in the 1960s and 1970s. The clash of cultures at Touron demonstrated the likely outcome when a major power like the United States relies on superior firepower in a quest for swift results in a confrontation with a resolute nation that has the fortitude to outlast an outside enemy. At neither time did the United States understand its opponent.

Percival may be excused for unilaterally leading an armed force ashore against a sovereign nation because he was operating in terra incognita. Only a few American warships had preceded him to this part of the globe. Westerners, steeped in the doctrines of Carl von Clausewitz, were unfamiliar with the gradualist military strategy of Sun Tzu adopted by the Chinese and their immediate neighbors centuries earlier. In keeping with that strategy, Percival's Cochin adversaries avoided battle with an uncertain outcome, took little risk, and used time instead of power to wear him down.

The *Constitution* arrived off Macao, China, in the Canton River delta on 5 June. She rested there for two weeks and then moved upstream toward Canton, coming to anchor at the outport of Whampoa. There the men received the first mail from home since Brazil. The bag contained an account of a tragedy in America. Newspapers reported a disastrous fire in Pittsburgh. Mad Jack promptly solicited the crew for contributions to a relief fund. In an August letter to his friend Chief Justice Shaw in Boston, he said he was proud of the crew. To a man, they donated. Their contributions totaled $1,729. He added $221 of his own money and purchased a draft on a Boston bank for $1,950. Percival asked Shaw to handle the matter and forward the money to Pittsburgh. Should the draft be not accepted, he wanted Shaw to hand it to William Sturgis and ask him to pay. He pledged his property to Sturgis for remuneration, feeling that his honor required that the sum reach the Pennsylvania city. He enclosed a list of the subscribing crewmembers, which he wanted published in a Pittsburgh newspaper because if a man "does not see his name against the amount he contributed, he will . . . think the money, or part of it at least, had been lost on the way."[84]

Such generosity seems unusual in light of the fact that almost half of the men on the ship were foreigners with, at best, little knowledge of Pittsburgh. Percival was sensitive to the matter and had several officers watch over the solicitation so that no man was pressured and everyone who gave, contributed willingly. The charity of the sailors, who had just weathered a serious outbreak of dysentery, was remarkable. *Nautical Magazine* and *Niles' Weekly Register,* among others, recognized the paradox and praised the men of the *Constitution* for their generosity.

Captain Percival had planned to stay in China for only a month, but the U.S. consul, John Forbes, and a group of American merchants asked him to remain longer. As he explained to the Navy Department in a 21 August letter, piracy and popular unrest offset his strong desire to be on his way. The *Constitution* moved back to her initial Macao anchorage on 27 August. The China layover proved boring and tedious for the crew, but Mad Jack stirred things up before he left.

When he first arrived in June 1845, he found the U.S. Navy storekeeper and the local clerk, William Lewis, in violation of regulations and reported them to the department. When he returned to Macao, Percival went ashore to rest at the house of William Delano. Lewis took the opportunity to demand satisfaction for the perceived wrong Percival had done to him. Lewis repaired to Delano's house, where Percival, who was not well, lay stretched on a couch. When Lewis demanded to see Percival, an aide said that he was engaged. "Heedless of this he [Lewis] thrust himself into the private apartment where I was," Percival later told Secretary Mason, and "seated himself before me in much temper and began in an insulting and rude manner to question me."[85]

Percival asked Lewis to leave, telling him they could talk when he was feeling better. He withdrew to an adjoining apartment, but the clerk followed right at his heels. Fearing an attack, Percival drew a pistol from his vest pocket and wheeled around. He warned Lewis, "If you follow me into this apartment, I will shoot you down." Lewis was thereby "deterred and left the house." Mad Jack felt "this mode of defense" was justified. "At my age . . . I would not with a debilitated frame enter on a rencontre with a robust young man of 30."[86]

The incident appeared to energize the sixty-six-year-old captain. He completed arrangements preparing the ship for sea, and the men finished repainting her. On 1 September, at daylight, the *Constitution* got under way and stood out of Macao Roads headed for Manila. A week out, the *Constitution* found herself becalmed within sight of six unidentified European men-of-war. "A few light cats-paws fanned us along until we were within two miles of them, and then the wind left us," wrote one of the officers.[87] The Americans made out a large line-of-battle ship, a pair of frigates, one brig, and two steamers. Without a breeze, their ensigns could not be distinguished. "As we had been a number of months without hearing from home," observed Stevens, "any guess as to our surroundings was as good as another."[88]

The ship's log indicates that "at 1.30, one of the Steamers stand down to us under steam, beat to quarters and cast loose the guns for action."[89] The Americans did not know whether peace or war prevailed. Clerk Stevens observed, "It would never have done in any event to give up 'Old Ironsides' to any other nation than the one which built her and had fought her."[90]

As the steamer bore down, Percival ran up the Stars and Stripes. The steamer reacted by sending up the Union Jack. In a few minutes, a boat put out from the English ship and a young lieutenant came onboard the

Constitution. As the man approached the quarterdeck, Captain Percival asked if it was peace or war. The lieutenant responded that peace obtained.

"Then the captain of the Yankee ship and the lieutenant of the English steamer shook hands and left for the cabin," wrote Stevens, "where, I think—in fact I know—that they hobnobbed a bit before getting to business."[91] The visitor indicated that he was a member of Rear Adm. Sir Thomas John Cochrane's East India squadron, which consisted of the ships *Agincourt, Vestal, Daedalus, Wolverine, Vixen,* and *Nemesis.*

The British ships were short of bread, water, and other staples, the lieutenant told Percival, and were hoping for help from the Americans. They were ten days out of Manila, and "drifting our lives away. . . . [I]f we are pressed, we have not enough provisions to last ten days longer, while if you help us, we will shower down blessings on your head."[92] Admiral Cochrane hoped that the *Constitution* had recently left port and was loaded with provisions and able to spare some. "Then came the order," wrote Lynch. "Secure the Guns, pipe down, and open the Spirit Room & the Hold."[93]

An unnamed *Constitution* officer described the encounter for *Niles' Weekly Register.*

> We of course complied. No sooner asked than done. No sailor ever stops to count the biscuit in his locker when he sees a hungry customer. Then a lively scene occurred, gratifying, I assure you, to both sides. Our guns had to be secured, and, indeed, we must have presented rather a hostile appearance to Mr. Bull; in fact, one of the officers good humoredly observed, he "thought we were going to blow him out of the water." We turned to with light hearts, and broke out the provisions and sent them on board, while we entertained the officers in very gallant style, in fact doing the clean and genteel thing by them.[94]

Lynch noted that American seamen promptly commenced to send over beef, bread, and provisions of every description, including whisky. The surgeon on the *Agincourt,* Dr. Edward Cree, visited while the crew went about the task. "Captain P. was polite," he later recalled, "drinking brandy and water, and smoking cigars, and spitting all about the cabin, which was in great confusion, with his furniture piled in a heap to clear away the stern guns."[95]

Two hours later, after receiving their provisions and arranging for Percival to draw on the British storehouse at Rio de Janeiro, the Englishmen departed. As they went over the side, one of the British officers remarked: "The good Old Ironsides—always the *first* to *prepare* for her friends or foes; and her gentlemanly officers, the *first* to *treat* them accordingly."[96]

The American frigate was off Corregidor by 11 September and reached Manila one week later. Resident Americans and Europeans hospitably put up the ship's officers in their homes. After a round of balls and parties, the *Constitution* left on 21 September, as Lynch put it, "to continue our trackless way across the Great Deep."[97] Percival headed up through the Grand Bashi Channel and sheered to the northeast to gain the lee of Formosa, where he caught the westerly winds coming off Japan. And the *Constitution* went hurrying off eastward across the Pacific. Along the way she encountered some rough weather. "Our Main Yard carried away in the Strings, and such," during a 4 November gale, recalled Lynch. "Terrible work! Ship rolling with the yard arms thrashing, the Main Rigging endangering the Main Mast. However, with good Seamanship all was secured."[98]

The ship made the island of Oahu on Sunday, 16 November 1845. Remembering his 1826 visit, Percival waited until the next day to salute the fort at Honolulu. Commo. John D. Sloat of the Pacific squadron greeted Percival and his crew with disappointing orders. War with Mexico appeared imminent. Sloat directed Mad Jack to take on provisions to last six months and prepare to proceed to the coast of California and join up with his squadron. The *Constitution*'s officers and crew had been expecting a direct trip back to the United States. "But," lamented Dale, "such is life! especially *Naval* life! Little did we think that the Texas question would so sensibly affect us in the Pacific Ocean!"[99]

As was his practice at other stops, Stevens described Hawaii in some detail. The scenery around Honolulu was grand, but things were much worse for the natives now, he thought, than before the arrival of fanatical Christian missionaries. Obviously, his close association with the missionaries' chief villain, Mad Jack Percival, colored Stevens's view. Yet he was not alone in thinking that. It is noteworthy that in 1852, Mrs. E. M. Wills Parker wrote a scathing denunciation of the Hawaiian missionaries that went well beyond Stevens's criticism. She claimed that thirty years of missionary work on the islands had left the natives poorer and more debased than before. In an 1873 letter to the *New York Tribune,* Mark Twain was equally critical of the manipulations of the missionaries.

One *Constitution* officer made the most of his stay. Local authorities asked Lt. Joseph Curtis to survey the Honolulu area and recommend sites for fortifications to foil hostile intervention. Quite naturally, Curtis stressed the critical strategic value of Pearl Harbor.

Three days before the *Constitution*'s scheduled departure date, a severe storm came out of the southeast. The frigate's anchor parted during the blow, and Percival ordered all hands to get her under way. For the next two days, he kept his ship off and on, standing in to meet the boats carrying out stores, and then returning to the open water to await another load. On 2 December, Thomas wrote in his journal: "We are standing off in Honolulu Bay. At 4:30, we discharged the pilot and filled away."[100] The ship's destination was Monterey, California. Percival did not find the American squadron when he arrived there at the end of the month and year; consequently, he continued down the coast.

He reached Cabo San Lucas, at the end of the Baja Peninsula, on 11 January 1846 and spotted two American commercial ships at anchor. Percival sent his aide Lynch over in the gig to ask if they knew the whereabouts of the U.S. Navy squadron. Since it was suppertime, one of the masters invited the young midshipman to be his dinner guest. In his journal, Lynch wrote: "Broiled beef-steaks, hot biscuits, and other good things were too tempting to a famished Middy, so I stayed but told the Captain, I would get Hail Columbia when I got back to the ship. So he said 'I guess old Mad Jack would like a Beef-steak, take this Quarter of Beef to him with my compliments.'" As soon as the returning aide was within earshot, Percival began to give him the expected lecture. The midshipman cut the denouncement short by exclaiming, "'The Captain killed a Bull and sent a Quarter to his old friend Captain Jack Percival.'—so that fixed me all right. . . . So a Bull got me out of a scrape, and gave me a good supper."[101]

While he was having his dinner, the midshipman learned that Sloat and the squadron were at Mazatlán, the major seaport near the entrance to the Gulf of California. The *Constitution* moved on and joined the force on 15 January. In addition to Sloat's flagship, the *Savannah,* Thomas noted the presence of a dozen other men-of-war of different classes. One was the *Cyane* and another was the *Levant,* both members of the U.S. Navy compliments of the *Constitution,* which had captured them from the British in the War of 1812. In full view of a smaller British squadron, Old Ironsides came to anchor between the pair.

The *Constitution* bided her time on this station for more than three months. The expected hostilities did not commence, and the men grew restless and yearned for home. The only incident of note is a puzzle. Jones's journal entry for 11 April 1846 indicates that the ship's carpenter, Thomas, was court-martialed, suspended for six months effective 20 March 1846, and severely reprimanded. Not one other *Constitution* journalist, including Thomas, recorded the matter. The popular Thomas, according to Jones, was not restored to duty until 31 August. Yet Thomas's journal continues through the suspension period as if the court-martial did not happen. As notable, throughout the entire cruise, Thomas remained loyal to Percival, and the captain retained faith in his ship's carpenter. Most likely, Thomas's offense occurred off the ship. Commodore Sloat had a hand in the incident as well. Jones noted that Sloat ordered a month of the suspension remitted in the event the carpenter's conduct justified such mitigation.

Mad Jack and his ship remained in Mexican waters until the end of April. Unaware that hostilities were just beginning along the Rio Grande, Sloat finally acceded to Percival's request to leave. The *Constitution* exceeded Sloat's needs, and many of the men were nearing the end of their enlistments. Sloat transferred other men in the squadron nearing the end of their terms to Old Ironsides, and the ship got under way for home on 23 April. Three weeks later, on 12 May 1846, Congress declared war with Mexico.

Percival headed south to Valparaiso, Chile, on the way to the Horn. Along the way, Thomas wrote: "We are experiencing the most hot and unpleasant weather, but tis no matter as we are homeward bound. It could be twice as hot."[102] The ship reached the Chilean port on 11 June. "Now commenced a round of gaieties—Balls, Parties, Theatre parties, Bull Fights," reported Lynch.[103] According to Thomas, liberty leave led to much disorderliness in the city. The starboard watch behaved badly. Chilean officials arrested some twenty crewmen for rowdyism and sent them back to the ship. The timing of Percival's response is interesting. He waited until the morning of 4 July to punish the offenders. "As a little memento" of their misbehavior, Lynch reported, "they each received one dozen lashes with the cats for disgracing themselves, the ship, the Flag, and their country, while on shore."[104]

Inclement weather set in and Percival decided to leave, notwithstanding the fact that most of the crew agreed with Lynch's assessment of Valparaiso as one of the best ports they had visited on the cruise. Old Ironsides got under way at 10:00 A.M. The British steamer *Sampson* moved the American frigate ahead, and boats from British and French men-of-war took her in tow. Just before noon, the American ship hoisted the jib and flying jib and cast off the foreign boats.

The *Constitution* "rounded Cape Horn in a most gallant style" on the Fourth of July, reported Percival, in heavy snow squalls out of the southeast.[105] "The Frigate rolled tremendously," noted Dale, and "our 'Independence dinner' underwent marvelous transmutations and chaotic confusions, . . . broken crockery, gravy capsized, and turkeys that took wing even from under the carver's fork."[106]

While the ship made her way up the eastern coast of South America, and with the end of the cruise drawing near, Stevens philosophically summed up the voyage to that point with the observation: "Not one soul was saved from the Berceau, while but twenty-seven of our entire crew passed over the borderland. Strange is the lot of those 'who go down to the sea in ships.'"[107]

Old Ironsides came to anchor at Rio de Janeiro on 29 July. Ambassador Wise hosted Percival and his officers, and the crew loaded provisions and water for a trip of two months. Due to the war with Mexico, six American merchantmen—*Mazopha, Chenongo, Margret Hugg, Tweed, Fabin,* and *Abo*—formed in convoy to tag along with the *Constitution* en route to the States. Percival signaled his charges to get under way on 6 August. Other boats, most of them carrying coffee, joined the convoy until it totaled sixteen ships. As the old frigate plowed for home, the crew remained alert for Mexican privateers but the passage was smooth and uneventful. Once he reached the Delaware breakwater, Percival told the merchantmen they were on their own, and they scattered.

On 18 September the *Constitution* fell in with the U.S. surveying brig *Washington,* which was proceeding under jury-masts. A 7 September gale had thrown the brig on her beam-ends near Smith Island in the Chesapeake. The *Washington* lost her poop deck, boats, and eleven of her twenty-five-man crew, including the skipper. The brig *J. Peterson* lay by the *Washington* for four days and supplied her with spars, a cable, and an anchor. On the fifteenth, a second storm separated the pair and placed the *Washington* at the mercy of the sea until the navy ship came along and took her in tow. Percival towed the crippled brig back to the breakwater and turned her over to the pilot boat *Enoch Turley* out of Philadelphia, then continued on his course for Cape Cod.

On Saturday, 26 September 1846, a Boston newspaper reported: "Our latest news from the frigate Constitution, Captain Percival, is of her being spoken on Monday the 21st, 40 miles south of Cape Henlopen, bound for Boston."[108] In reality, as the newspaper hit the streets a midshipman was making the following entry in the ship's log: "At 4 Chatham light house bore, per compass, W 3/4 N. A number of small fishing vessels in sight."[109] At midnight, Mad Jack saw a familiar sight. He knew where to look for Nauset Light. The three beacons he had positioned a decade earlier "bore, per compass W 1/2 N distant about 5 miles."[110]

The *Constitution* was off Cape Cod Light in Truro at 8:00 A.M. and received a Boston pilot at 3:30 P.M. on 27 September. The log describes the scene as the grand old ship came to anchor off India Wharf: "At Meridian the Citizens hoisted the American Ensign ashore—fired a salute of 28 guns and cheered the ship—manned the rigging and cheered in return."[111] Percival's hometown newspaper, the *Barnstable Patriot,* noted with pride, "The Constitution . . . has circumnavigated the globe."[112] Midn. John Hart wrote, "she is now come home like her aged Commander to lay her old bones up 'for a full due.' . . . I can scarcely bear the idea of leaving her, but I must."[113]

Before the ship was towed over to the Charlestown navy yard, Stevens took the time to conclude another important duty. When the *Constitution* had begun her epic voyage more than two years earlier, Mad Jack put a question to his crew. He believed the ration in the U.S. Navy was overgenerous and asked the crew if they would agree to subsist on a ration reduced by one-quarter. In other words, each mess of a dozen men would draw an allowance for nine. The money saved as a consequence would be turned over to the men during the trip. The prospect of extra spending money was inviting, and the crew unanimously accepted Percival's proposal. Once back in Boston, after the successful conclusion of the experiment, Stevens closed the special account book and stated: "This course served to keep the crew in funds from the beginning to the end of their terms of service, besides establishing the important fact of the extreme liberality of the ration allowed by the government."[114]

On 1 October 1846, Capt. John Percival stepped down from the quarterdeck of the *Constitution* and went on leave. And thus ended the most memorable peacetime chapter in the saga of America's favorite ship. She had been at sea for 495 days and had covered 52,370.5 miles. John Y. Mason, once more serving as navy secretary, told Percival: "The Department takes pleasure in communicating its approval of your movements during your return cruise."[115]

This voyage is noteworthy for two reasons. First, it typifies the U.S. Navy of the period. The symbolic ship of the young republic carried out the service's general mission—advancement and protection of U.S. commerce, exploration, and experimentation. Present generations have a greater appreciation for the second reason. In 1997 the government completed a multi-million-dollar renovation of Old Ironsides. In 1998, with great fanfare, the national shrine celebrated her bicentennial. Percival's success in marshaling and leading a force of ship riggers and workmen at Norfolk in the winter of 1843–44 was a critical point in the ship's history. If he had failed in his ten-thousand-dollar rehabilitation project, the *Constitution* might well have been scrapped. Over two centuries, several saviors have stepped forward to sustain the venerable ship. Although the fact is often overlooked, John Percival was one of them. His critical contribution should not be diminished or underrated.

~❧ II ❧~

ON PROBATION

*A*fter leaving the *Constitution* at the Charlestown yard, Mad Jack withdrew to his home in the Dorchester section of Boston. His residence was located on Meeting House Hill, at the corner of that road and the present Percival Street (named in his honor). He considered the location advantageous because it was close to the yard and because it was situated on the way to his beloved Cape Cod. But Percival's leave was not a restful period. Before October passed, Secretary Mason sent him copies of complaints filed by Lieutenant Chaplin and Surgeon D. D. McLeod alleging wrongdoing on the round-the-world cruise. Percival replied that he was ill and asked for a few days to respond.

Chaplin's complaint alleged that Percival had used improper and threatening language. In addition, the lieutenant complained that his captain carried arms upon his person and was not reluctant to produce them when agitated. McLeod's charges were old ones. Percival had addressed them while in Hawaii in a November 1845 letter to the department. In brief, McLeod grumbled about the length of the cruise and, especially, the visits to unhealthy ports such as Canton and Manila.

Percival sent a detailed eight-page reply to the secretary at the end of October. He referred to his private diary, "which has been kept of every minute event from the date of my orders . . . to the day of my return from a long and as I supposed successful cruise." He commented first on Chaplin's complaints. Lieutenant Chaplin penned his complaint on 30 August 1845, the day before the ship departed China. Percival informed the secretary that he had gone over his diary and examined the papers of his officers but could not find "the slightest trace of any occurence [sic] on which the allegations" of Chaplin could be grounded. Percival explained his resort to a pistol when William Lewis at Macao accosted him. Otherwise, he said, he never carried a weapon except for "wearing a dress sword on suitable occasions." As for a threat, Percival did recall an "indistinct impression" of "one occasion when in familiar conversation . . . upon the suggestion of a hypothetical case—as for instant an assault on myself, or an attempt to usurp my authority as Commander of the frigate—I stated that I should shoot the person without hesitation."[1]

As for McLeod, he and a few others, according to Percival, were disappointed that the cruise was not a short, pleasant voyage to the Mediterranean. The surgeon had included the particulars of his complaint in his routine report for the quarter ending 30 September 1845, and Percival had provided some explanations when he forwarded the report in November 1845. At the time, Percival said McLeod "is entitled to much credit for the ability he has displayed with his pen in highly colouring descriptions, and I wish I could accord him an equal amount for the rectitude of his heart and intentions."[2]

Percival maintained that McLeod's facts were inaccurate or biased. His descriptions of some of the ports of call, Percival wrote, "relate to places better and more faithfully described a hundred years since." In particular he disagreed with the surgeon's "overwrought description of Canton river."[3] Despite McLeod's insistence that tropical ports were unhealthy for the crew, Percival said he saw no need to run the ship in higher latitudes.

McLeod also alleged that the *Constitution* had encountered British navy ships fleeing Manila because of an outbreak of cholera in the city but had proceeded into port anyway. Percival retorted that this was not the case. He described meeting the captain of HMS *Vixen* outside Manila and being told that the health situation there was satisfactory. Two men from the *Vixen* died in port, true, but the British captain explained that those men went on a drunken spree on shore, ate fruit with abandon, and slept in the street. Other than that, the British squadron enjoyed good health. There was another explanation for the British fleet's rapid exodus from Manila: it was the "custom of Admiral Cochrane, who is a rigid disciplinarian of the old school, to get under way at signal notice, without consulting with his officers to ascertain whether they are or are not ready."[4] On the day in question, the *Vixen* had not been ready.

Percival also described encountering an American ship outward bound from Manila. "I boarded her *myself* and the Captain, an intelligent man (brother to Judge Story) expressed great surprise when I enquired of him in relation to the cholera." Story "had heard nothing of the kind."[5]

In his initial November 1845 response to McLeod's accusations, Percival told the secretary that he got no pleasure from refuting the charges. He answered them because "my reputation is my only inheritance, for which I have long toiled unaided, and am anxious to guard it from misrepresentations which invite censure by their pictorial and highly coloured delineations."[6]

It seemed that the *Constitution*'s cruise would never end for Percival. One small detail after another required his attention. The matter of payment for the ship's naturalist was particularly annoying. Before the *Constitution* left port, President John Tyler had suggested that a naturalist should be part of the crew. On 13 March 1844 Secretary Henshaw authorized the position at the same salary as a chaplain's. A Mr. Chandler was retained as the ship's naturalist, but he elected to leave the ship when it got to Rio in 1844. Dr. J. C. Reinhardt replaced him on the spot and remained aboard until the ship returned to Brazil in 1846. On 28 July 1846, Percival forwarded Reinhardt's report to the department along with a letter that commended the naturalist and listed the contents of eleven boxes containing geological and plant specimens, seeds, and birds gathered by Reinhardt for scientific purposes. Secretary Mason accepted the boxes in October 1846 and directed the navy agent at Boston to ship them to Washington.

Now, incomprehensibly, President James Polk's Treasury Department disallowed the twelve hundred dollars the *Constitution*'s purser had paid to Reinhardt and ruled that Percival was liable for it. The accounting officer of the Navy Department recovered the amount by making deductions from Percival's pay and allowances. The inequity was obvious, but Percival had to expend considerable energy to correct the error. He had a private bill for relief introduced in the last session of the 29th Congress, but it was not enacted. In October 1847 Percival wrote to Secretary Mason about the matter. He wanted to know how the department planned to proceed in the next Congress and if there was any action he could take to help push the appropriation. "Having acted under the *authority* of the President given in writing by the then acting Secretary of the Navy," he said, "I wish to place myself in a right position not only in a pecuniary but in every other point of view."[7]

Six months later, in March 1848, Percival asked for permission to repair to Washington to give his attention to the reintroduced bill. "The flagrant injustice of my being held individually liable for the pay of an officer in the public service to the creation of which I was *utterly impotent*" demanded personal intervention.[8] A month earlier, Congressman White of the Naval Affairs Committee had reported the bill and had it committed. The House passed the measure without debate on 7 April. Finally, on 1 February 1849, the full Congress gave the bill its approval and the president signed the measure into law. The legislation directed the navy accounting officer to credit Percival with the amount charged against him for Reinhardt's pay.

In 1847, at the conclusion of the three-month leave that followed the return of the *Constitution,* Percival's official status became "awaiting orders." He knew he would never again go to sea, and there is no evidence that he sought to return to the quarterdeck. He was sixty-eight years old and not in the best of health. Ague, fevers, dysentery, tonsillitis, and a liver ailment had all taken a toll on his health over the years. The double hernia incurred two decades earlier on the *Dolphin* still bothered him. His most debilitating affliction was gout. In addition to considerable discomfort, the disease forced him to use crutches from time to time.

Rather than a sea command, Percival sought an appointment to head the Boston Navy Yard. In November 1847 he asked to be assigned to the post whenever incumbent Foxhall Parker's term ended. A little more than a year later, he learned that the department expected to replace Parker and renewed his application. In one of his March 1849 letters to the secretary he requested the assignment "not *as a favor* . . . but as an act of sheer justice."[9] In another letter, he said he had not asked political friends to lobby or influential men to speak in his behalf because it would be indelicate to do so.

The choice assignment went to his longtime friend John Downes. Percival's career was at an end. The navy carried him on the roster as awaiting orders for a decade after the *Constitution* command. But the orders never came. On 13 September 1855, the department placed him on the reserve list. He took his last official act on the nineteenth when he wrote to Secretary James Dobbin acknowledging receipt of the official notice. Altogether, Percival served forty-six years in the U.S. Navy. His active service amounted to thirty-seven years, and his sea service totaled seventeen years and five months.

As the Boston appointment slipped away, the *Constitution* voyage came back to haunt him yet again. In June 1849 Secretary Preston sent him a dispatch from the U.S. consul in Singapore to the secretary of state. "You will be pleased to furnish this Department," wrote Preston in the cover letter, "as early as practicable, with an explanation of the transaction therein referred to, which occurred in Cochin China, while you were at that place."[10] The dispatch was the highly exaggerated report of Joseph Balestier on the Touron incident.

Percival, his dander up, sent a lengthy reply on 14 June. Balestier's dispatch was two years old, he noted. Percival had been home for a year and had been in Washington just a few weeks earlier, "yet I have never 'till now heard that any such despatch existed." Moreover, the communication concerned an event that had taken place four years ago. Soon after the incident, Percival noted, he had addressed the subject in a "special communication" to the department, and his conduct had been "approved by two successive Secretaries."[11]

Percival described how shortly after the incident he contacted his friend William Sturgis, "who had been much in that quarter of the world and was intimately acquainted with the character of the people." Sturgis met with Secretary Bancroft and gave him a full explanation of Percival's actions. According to Sturgis, "Mr. Bancroft expressed himself entirely satisfied." Furthermore, Percival said, when Secretary Mason, full reports in hand, detached him from the *Constitution,* he "expressed to me in most flattering terms his gratification of the manner in which I had performed my cruise, and he has subsequently given me assurances to the same effect."[12]

Percival's letter thereafter covered much of the same ground treated in his original report to the department from the Canton River. He added some comments about Balestier. While the *Constitution* was at

Singapore, he said, Balestier had described the Cochin Chinese as "nothing less than barbarians." This assessment was a factor prompting him to act as he did. Percival blasted Balestier for believing the mandarins who told him about the alleged attack, particularly for not checking to see if the forts they claimed had been destroyed were still standing. Being a consul, Percival declared, Balestier was certainly "not ignorant of the fact that the Cochin Chinese are proverbial for lying." In looking back, he concluded, he could "see nothing" in the case to regret; "nothing that I would alter." This response finally ended the Touron affair for Percival, and the navy closed the book on the *Constitution*'s round-the-world cruise.[13]

During what amounted to his retirement years, Percival favored a number of his friends with souvenirs such as precious metal cups made from prize money or naval epaulets. Charles H. Bursley of West Barnstable received one along with the laconic expression, "Farewell." Mad Jack did not overlook William Sturgis, another distinguished Barnstable mariner. The inscription on his cup read: "To W. Sturgis, Esq., as a feeble tribute of gratitude for his many Acts of friendship to me when I was friendless and in want, J Percival, Capt. U.S.N."[14]

A similar token was sent to Ambassador Wise, who had resumed his law practice in Accomac County, Virginia. Upon receiving the gift, Wise wrote a warm note of thanks. Mad Jack answered it, still full of the old fire. He had heard in Washington, he wrote, that Mrs. Wise was displeased with the voyage from New York to Brazil on the *Constitution*. He knew who was behind the insinuation that he, Percival, was the worst man on the high seas since Red Rover, he told Wise. His detractor had a malignant heart. He bemoaned the fact that "a fair share of patriotism & bravery, with a full share of zeal and integrity in the execution of my duty as a Navy Officer" was an insufficient counter to "sectional and political prejudice."[15]

Percival visited his native Barnstable frequently during his later years and maintained an active interest in community affairs. He enjoyed calling on his acquaintances in the several villages. In October 1855 he attended the annual dinner of the Barnstable County Agricultural Society. The event once again presented to view Percival's long-standing interest in young people. Aware of this side of the old naval officer, the toastmaster asked Mad Jack to respond to what might seem an unlikely toast: "The children of Cape Cod." In doing so, Percival spoke at length about his "early experience, and enlisted the undivided attention of the large company."[16]

Oftentimes, especially during the spring and fall, his Cape trips were cut short by attacks of the gout. A servant named Isaac Chapman attended him constantly. When an attack came, it was Chapman's responsibility to hustle his charge onto the first train for Boston. Mad Jack could be anything but amiable on such occasions.

At the end of each month, Percival crossed over to Charlestown to draw his pay. This was a great excuse to get together with some of his old messmates and protégés. By the winter of 1856 he seemed to have some doubt about his ability to continue. He began a letter to John P. Healy, a Boston lawyer and close friend, with the thought, "I apprehend this season will close my journey through this transitory life."[17] Consequently, he wanted to make the proper arrangements for his wife, who, he feared, was not a good judge of people and would spend money unwisely. In the event that her financial affairs were in poor order one year after his death, Mad Jack wanted Healy to sell his "cottage and grounds, furniture, paintings, plate of every description, and invest the proceeds in some permanent and secure institution, or on bond, and mortgage on real estate." After taking out his own fee, the attorney was to put "one 24th part" of the revenue in "a sinking fund in case of accidents, sickness, disease, etc. etc." Above all else, he wanted Healy to "advise her[;] she will *follow* your counsels." Dejectedly, Percival closed: "Excuse this Dear Healy, I am laboring under a severe attack of the blue devils, therefore drop a tear of kindness on the weakness of the poor old sailor."[18]

In an attempt to remedy the old officer's despondency, Healy gathered up a bundle of his private correspondence with Daniel Webster and sent it to Dorchester for Percival's amusement. When he thanked the lawyer for the "evidence of . . . friendship and good will," Percival assured him he would "cherish it as a token of . . . sympathy for my infirmities."[19]

Percival's thoughts were with Maria more and more as time passed. He cared for her deeply, and his poor health and the sixteen-year difference in their ages made him certain that she would outlive him. When he left the Philippines in the *Constitution,* with the worst of the cruise behind him, he shared his feelings of affection for her with his men. In his journal entry for 30 September 1845 carpenter Thomas reported:

"Today we spliced the main brace because on this day [*sic*] 36 years ago, the Captain got spliced to his better half."[20]

Maria Percival never needed the counsel of Healy—or the advice of Chief Justice Shaw, as her husband also anticipated she might. On 13 September 1857, in her sixty-fourth year, she died of congested lungs at their Dorchester home. She was buried in the West Barnstable cemetery next to Percival's parents. Her epitaph includes the phrase, "Sincerely lamented by her husband and friends." That Percival took the loss to heart is evident in a note to Shaw written two months after Maria Percival's passing: "My mind is broken and intellects shattered, yet there is I trust sufficient glimmering of light left to appreciate and express my gratitude for your innumerable acts of kindness."[21]

A year and a half later, Percival again found himself preparing for the great adventure, although he retained some of his former spirit. Over the years, Percival had put together a creditable estate, and the community knew it. Some of his friends hoped he would contribute money to various worthy causes in Barnstable. Charles Bursley recommended that Percival donate some funds to the village school. Percival had another idea. He mailed his friend a check for one hundred dollars and asked him to use the money to build a stone wall on the north side of the village cemetery "commencing at Heman Bursley's tomb and proceeding westward as far as the amount will pay; leaving the rest to be finished and paid for by the selectmen." He hoped Bursley could get the job "done before *I die*." He promised that the school would get "ample funds at my death and more."[22]

Mr. Bursley completed the task, and the result is visible today. The stone retaining wall running west from the Bursley tomb past the Percival family plot is an outstanding example of craftsmanship. The point where the hundred dollars ran out is obvious, and the continuation done under the town's selectmen is inferior.

The overlooked Bursley letter deserves further comment because it refutes one of the most popular local tales about Mad Jack. The yarn, told since the 1930s, has Percival asking Bursley to construct the wall but without first sending him the hundred-dollar check. When Bursley completed the project, the officer reportedly told his friend not to submit a bill. Instead, Percival supposedly told Bursley that he "would do better for him later." Bursley thought that the "later" implied that he would receive a cash amount from Percival's will. But under its terms, Mad

Jack left only a portrait of himself for Bursley. The bequest, it is said, did not meet Bursley's expectations of being "done better for," so he hung the painting face to the wall, where it allegedly remained for many years.[23]

The tale, although a Cape favorite, is clearly a fabrication. The letter shows that Bursley received at least one hundred dollars for the job, just about what the project would have cost in those days. More to the point, Percival did not bequeath a portrait to anyone except William S. Rogers of Boston. However, the Bursley family has possessed a Percival portrait for generations. Allyn P. Bursley of Richmond, Virginia, restored the painting some years ago. The portrait passed on to Wade D. Rankin, a Bursley descendant residing in Mandeville, Louisiana. During the Barnstable Tercentenary in 1939, a local historian commissioned a copy and eventually donated it to the Peabody Museum in Salem. Allyn Bursley believed the original painting dates to about 1841, and that Percival presented it to either his great-great-grandfather Heman or his great-grandfather Charles. Allyn never heard the face-to-the-wall story from his father, John, or anyone within the family circle. The only other Mad Jack tall tale with a more persistent life is the discredited account suggesting that he served under Nelson on the *Victory* at Trafalgar.

During the last years of his life Percival was almost, but not quite, dominated by women. Three lived in his Dorchester home, including his niece Sarah Barnes Percival, daughter of his brother Isaac, whom he had taken in a number of years earlier when Isaac died. Another niece, Martha Crocker, also lived in his home. The third woman was Mrs. E. A. C. Brown, a Dorchester widow. Many years later, Sarah remembered that her uncle "was a lovely man to live with, very kind, but when he was in command, that was a different story."[24] Maria Weeks Percival, the daughter of Maria Pinkerton Percival's sister, was out of his house by this time. Maria Weeks came to live with the Percivals before her teens and was effectively adopted by the couple. The Percivals did not have children of their own. In 1854 Maria Weeks married Edward Gassett, a local merchant.

In August 1861 Percival drew up his final will. His acquaintances knew that he possessed a noble liberality, and this trait prompted a certain amount of speculation. Maj. Sylvanus Phinney, founder of the *Barnstable Patriot* newspaper, got wind of the fact that Mad Jack had made provisions for the Barnstable County Agricultural Society, the group behind the annual cattle show and fair. Early in 1862 a gale raised havoc with the Agricultural Hall on the fairgrounds. In view of Percival's deep interest in the fair and in agriculture in general, Phinney decided to hit him up for an advance to pay for the necessary extensive repairs to the building. Mad Jack responded to the plea in what Major Phinney described as a "characteristic letter":

> Mr. Phinney,
> *Dear Sir:*
> I herewith return your subscription list, drawn up for the purpose of obtaining aid "to promote the best interests of the Barnstable Co. Agricultural Society," and return it without my name.
>
> I think your remark, when you handed it to me, was, that street rumors had advised you of my having made some provision for the wants of this Society in my *last will and testament,* and that as it was much in want of a new Hall, the said provision would be *very acceptable now*!
>
> Let me assure my anxious friends, that as it may be for the promotion of *my* best interests to remain here on probation as long as possible, and as my old enemy, the gout, has not been able to storm Old Jack's Castle, I don't mean that the anxiety of my *friends* shall induce a surrender, and hoping that they will wait as patiently as is consistent with the circumstances for my *last* will, I remain, in pretty hale bodily condition,
> Yours truly,
> J. Percival[25]

The agricultural society remained patient and in due time received its reward. Percival's will left four hundred dollars to the organization, the income thereof to fund premiums for agricultural entries. Major Phinney's *Patriot* would observe, "This will place the financial affairs of the Society in excellent and even prosperous condition. We hope that the other means of the Society will pay for the improvements about the Hall, and that this may be held as a *reserve* fund."[26] The bequest paid for awards of silverware known as "Percival Premiums." First-place prizewinners in a number of categories ranging from apples to heifers received the premiums. When the fair ceased to operate for some years, the Cape Cod Horticultural Society got hold of the income and used it for premiums awarded at its shows.

Wills generally are not of interest to anyone except the beneficiaries. Percival's will is worth reviewing, however, because it says a great deal about the man and the kinds of things that were important to him. After settlement of his debts, the cash balance in his estate amounted to just over seventeen thousand dollars. In addition, he had a fund with the Massachusetts Hospital Life Insurance Company. He directed the Hospital Life fund to be permitted to accumulate until it amounted to ten thousand dollars, at which time his adopted daughter, Maria Gassett, could draw out the interest.

Since the seventeen thousand dollars added up to 95 percent of his intended monetary bequests, the executor reduced all awards by 5 percent. In any event, Percival earmarked one hundred dollars for the almshouse in West Barnstable "so as to render it more comfortable and convenient to its inmates."[27] He gave the West Parish of Barnstable two thousand dollars "to be invested as a permanent fund, and the interest and income thereof to be appropriated always towards paying an adequate compensation to the teachers of the common schools" of the village.[28] The money was put in the hands of Stephen Smith of Boston at 6 percent interest. For years, teachers in the West Barnstable grammar school received an annual bonus of fifty to a hundred dollars from the fund. In the late 1950s the town consolidated the West Barnstable school with the Barnstable village school. The local school ceased to exist, and the account became dormant. In 1962 the West Parish Congregational Church in West Barnstable succeeded in getting the fund transferred to support its Sunday school. Percival's interest in children was also evident in his bequests of two hundred dollars to the school connected with the Warren Street Chapel and to the Children's Friend Society, both of Boston.

Mad Jack never lost the abiding interest in the welfare of the common seaman that had characterized his career. With that still uppermost in his mind, he left one thousand dollars to Massachusetts General Hospital to "be invested as a permanent fund, and the interest and income thereof to be appropriated for a free bed or free beds—and, as this is the gift of a poor old sailor, preference shall always be given to mariners."[29] This fund continues as an asset of Massachusetts General. Percival demonstrated the same interest in a fifty-dollar bequest to Mrs. Sarah Noyes, the widow of Abraham Noyes, yeoman on the *Constitution*.

Percival made a cautionary stipulation in the provision leaving five hundred dollars to Mrs. Clarissa Gifford. He wanted the money to go for "her sole and separate use, free from the interference or control of her husband." Mrs. Brown of his household received five thousand dollars "for the comfort her constant cheerfulness, her intellectual and amiable qualities, have afforded an old man at the fag end of his life."[30]

There were a number of other bequests with a story behind them. Some included characteristic commentary. Percival left Boston attorney William S. Rogers a gold ring as a token of appreciation for his assistance in "the cause of truth and justice, when I was assailed and persecuted by a combination of persons, whose chief characteristics were hypocrisy in religion and giddiness from their elevation to places in the Navy, which, though not of a high grade, were above their merit."[31]

At about the time he was preparing his will, Percival submitted to an interview that became a primary source of information about his life. In the summer of 1861 Percival was still relatively vigorous and retained his nationalistic fervor. Benjamin Stevens, his loyal clerk on the *Constitution,* sat down with him and put together a two-part biographical sketch that appeared in the *Boston Saturday Evening Gazette.* Stevens concluded his piece with the following observation:

> He is now nearly eighty-three years of age, and although time has somewhat impaired the accuracy of his memory, yet his scorn for administrative imbecility, and the milk and water of executive protraction, has outlived the modifying influence of years; and the impatient wish that he sometimes expresses to touch with his own hand the helm of the ship of State, shows that the marvelous energies of the youth are not wholly wasted in the octogenarian.

The *Gazette* article also relates an engaging conversation from this time, just at the beginning of the Civil War. A friend asked him what he would do if he were still in the service. Mad Jack straightened up and replied: "I would first concoct a scheme by which to catch Jeff Davis, whether on land or sea, and placing a fathom of hemp around his neck, I would *very politely* wish him a safe passage, and run him up to the yard arm, trusting to my country to do him justice." Stevens concluded: "One cannot help feeling that a chosen few like him might effectually crush, with the iron heel of an unrelenting will, the rattlesnake of any treason which ever poisoned a country with its virus."[32]

On Wednesday morning, 17 September 1862, "Old Jack's Castle" was finally stormed. He died peacefully at his home in Dorchester at the age of eighty-four. The immediate cause of death was given as cholera morbus. On Friday, well-attended funeral services were conducted at Reverend Hall's church on Meeting House Hill, Dorchester. The Reverend Doctor Samuel Lothrop came from Boston to lead the prayers. Percival's body was then moved to West Barnstable, where the native son briefly rested in state at the Congregational meetinghouse. Percival's passing saddened the townsfolk, but they were unable to subdue their pride. Dressed in the full uniform of a U.S. Navy captain, Mad Jack Percival was an impressive sight in his splendid rosewood casket. For the rest of his life John Bursley remembered being lifted up as a youngster to view the venerable officer. The captain's distinctive epaulets thrilled him. Many recalled a silver plate affixed to the coffin with the inscription: "Captain John Percival, U.S.N., died September 17th 1862, aged 84 years, 5 months, 14 days."[33]

The burial took place in the local cemetery "in presence of a large number of the citizens of the village," reported the *Patriot*. In its obituary, the town's newspaper said: "He was generous, kind hearted, and a good navigator, always ready to do battle for his country and its flag. . . . Thus has another old hero passed from this world."[34]

Percival's estate placed a marble marker on his grave. The headstone included an engraved chronology of his life showing the dates of his birth, navy promotions, and death. By 1962 the etching was almost illegible, victim of the effects of one hundred years of open north winds. In 1964 the Barnstable Board of Selectmen replaced the twin gravestones of John and Maria Percival with new granite markers bearing the original inscriptions.

It is hardly surprising that distinguished authors such as Hawthorne, Melville, and Michener were attracted to John Percival. He was an exciting and interesting person with a solid record of achievement. He served in three navies (two briefly and reluctantly) and four wars. His naval career began on England's favorite warship, the *Victory*, and ended on America's favorite warship, the *Constitution*.

Yet Percival was much more than a colorful salt of the old school who attracted yarns and tall tales. He was a pioneer, and in more than one way. Obviously, he was a pathfinder. Percival routinely sailed in uncharted waters, and he captained the first U.S. naval vessel into numerous distant ports, from the Mulgrave and Sandwich Islands to places such as Nosy Be and Borneo.

His origins and career path were an inspiration for post–War of 1812 midshipmen, and his climb to the top remains instructive today. He came from a family without influence and initially entered the navy as a master's mate. Nonetheless, he applied himself, plunged into his duties, and earned the reputation of one of the finest sailors of the sailing navy. In rising to the top of the officer corps, he set a demanding standard of seamanship worthy of emulation then and now.

Perhaps because of his early days in the merchant service, Percival fully appreciated the important connection between the navy and commerce. He understood that commerce sustained the navy, and as much as any officer of his period, he exerted himself to support and aid American merchants and seamen he found abroad. His cruises in the *Erie* and the *Cyane* demonstrate the point. This object became and remains a primary component of the navy's mission.

There are measurable highlights in Percival's career. Congress commended him for meritorious action in the War of 1812. His 1825 pursuit in the Pacific of the *Globe* mutineers is an epic maritime adventure. And his 1844 rescue of Old Ironsides would have made him a national hero even if he had done nothing else notable in his career. But his most profound contribution to the development of the U.S. Navy is less tangible.

Percival was ahead of his time in the way he handled men under his command. His flashy nickname misleads some people to conclude that he was a martinet. Certainly, he was a disciplinarian. Though stern and fair, however, he was not rigid. The miscreants on the *Dolphin* received swift and deserved punishment, while he interceded with the secretary of the navy in behalf of two contrite deserters off the *Potomac*. He read his family Bible to his crews before he got into the Articles of War.

In a time when some military and naval leaders still considered their charges little more than criminals and cannon fodder, Mad Jack Percival exerted himself to ensure the health and welfare of his crews. On more than one voyage, he turned his cabin over to sick sailors. Early in the *Cyane* cruise, he let his middies go ashore while he stood watch. When the *Porpoise* received a six-hundred-dollar reward for saving an American merchantman, Percival excluded the officers from sharing and gave the entire amount over to the enlisted men. His conscientious and diligent administration of an 1837 trust for several injured sailors epitomized his conduct as an officer. Repainting the *Constitution* a cooling white before entering the oppressive Indian Ocean demonstrated that he could be innovative when it came to the well-being and comfort of his crew.

In the absence of a naval academy, Percival embraced his role in the shipboard training and education of young men for the officer corps. He doted over his midshipmen but kept them hard at their duties and studies. Percival's serious approach to the matter is best demonstrated by comparing his dedication to the task with the relaxed methods employed by Commo. Isaac Hull when the two sailed together in the Mediterranean. Moreover, he could spot and nurture talent. A number of midshipmen tutored by Percival went on to distinguish themselves in the Civil War. His advocacy of naval education may be the most important part of his legacy. And his benevolent but firm style of leadership remains worth emulating in any organizational setting.

Not many years before he died, Percival did as good a job as anyone in recapitulating his life. One of the engraved silver cups he gave away as tokens of friendship during his later years featured a brief summary of much of his career. It is a fitting close to the story of John "Mad Jack" Percival.

> *This Cup, with the Donor, has made three cruises to the*
> *Pacific, one to the Mediterranean, one to the Brazils,*
> *two to the West Indies, and once around the world, a*
> *distance of about 150,000 miles. Has been 37 years*
> *in service and has never refused duty.*[35]

~❧ Notes ❧~

ABBREVIATIONS USED IN THE NOTES

CMD   Letters Received by the Secretary of the Navy from Commanders, 1801–86, National Archives, Microfilm Publication M147

CPT   Letters Received by the Secretary of the Navy from Captains, 1805–61, 1866–85, National Archives, Microfilm Publication M125

NA   National Archives, Washington, D.C.

RG   Record Group (National Archives)

SNL   Letters Sent by the Secretary of the Navy to Officers, 1798–1868, National Archives, Microfilm Publication M149

PREFACE

1. Henry C. Kittredge, *Cape Cod: Its People and Their History*, 53.

CHAPTER 1. AN EARLY TRIUMPH

1. Reprinted in *Niles' Weekly Register*, 26 December 1812 [henceforth *Niles'*].

2. William Corbbett, *The Pride of Britannia Humbled; or The Queen of the Ocean Unqueened by the American Cock Boats*, 22.

3. Edgar S. Maclay, *A History of American Privateers*, 469.

4. Ibid.

5. Ibid.

6. *Niles'*, 10 July 1813.

7. Ibid.

8. *Boston Saturday Evening Gazette*, 24 August 1861.

9. *Niles'*, 10 July 1813.

10. R. S. Guernsey, *New York City and Vicinity during the War of 1812–15*, n.p.

11. Alton H. Blackington, "Mad Jack," 41.

12. Commo. Jacob Lewis to Secretary William Jones, 6 July 1813, in Letters Received by the Secretary of the Navy from Captains, 1805–61, 1866–85, National Archives, Microfilm Publication M125 [henceforth CPT].

13. Mary J. Stafford, "A Commander of the *Constitution*," 385.

14. Benton P. Crocker, "Percivals of Cape Cod and Some Descendants," 8.

15. Barnstable [Mass.] Town Records, 3:320.

16. Frederick Freeman, *The History of Cape Cod*, 1:742.

17. Discourse of John Gorham Palfrey, printed in S. B. Phinney, *The Cape Cod Centennial Celebration at Barnstable*, 39.

18. Dudley Pope, *Decision at Trafalgar*, 93.

19. J. R. Hutchinson, *The Press-Gang Afloat and Ashore*, 171.

20. Ibid., 110.

21. Personal communication, M. Godfrey, Public Records Office, London, England, to James H. Ellis, 3 January 1962.

22. Personal communication, Vivian S. Heath, Admiralty, to James H. Ellis, 27 July 1961.

23. Hutchinson, *The Press-Gang Afloat and Ashore*, 29.

24. Stafford, "A Commander of the *Constitution*," 386.

25. Secretary Benjamin Stoddert to Captain Thomas Baker, 25 June 1799, in U.S. Department of the Navy, *Naval Documents Related to the Quasi-War between the United States and France*, 403.

26. Stoddert to Baker, 13 July 1799, in ibid., 497.

27. Charles J. Peterson, *The American Navy*, 27.

28. A New England Farmer, *Mr. Madison's War*, n.p.

29. *Boston Weekly Messenger*, 6 May 1814.

CHAPTER 2. THE WAR OF 1812

1. Deck Log, Gunboat *No. 6*, 3 November 1813, National Archives, Washington, D.C., Record Group [henceforth NA, RG] 24.

2. Ibid., 29 November 1813.

3. William James, *The Naval History of Great Britain*, 160.

4. Journal of the U.S. Sloop *Peacock*, L. Warrington, Esq., 29 April 1814, NA, RG 24.

5. James, *The Naval History of Great Britain*, 160.

6. Journal of the U.S. Sloop *Peacock*, 29 April 1814.

7. *Niles'*, 21 May 1814.

8. Ibid.

9. *Boston Weekly Messenger*, 20 May 1814; *Connecticut Courant*, 17 May 1814.

10. *Niles'*, 21 May 1814.

11. James, *The Naval History of Great Britain*, 160–61.

12. James R. Soley, *The Boys of 1812*, 270.

13. Ralph D. Paine, *The Fight for a Free Sea*, n.p.

14. Allan Westcott, "Captain 'Mad Jack' Percival," 315.

15. Donald G. Trayser, *Barnstable: Three Centuries of a Cape Cod Town*, 201.

16. Capt. Lewis Warrington to Secretary William Jones, 30 October 1814, in *Niles'*, 12 November 1814.

17. Ibid.

18. *Niles'*, 27 October 1814.

19. Ibid., 15 October 1814.

20. Ibid., 27 October 1814.

21. Ibid., 29 October 1814.

22. *Naval Chronicle*, 32:244.

23. Percival Papers, Massachusetts Historical Society, Boston [henceforth Percival Papers].

24. *Niles'*, 27 August 1814.

25. James Fenimore Cooper, *History of the Navy of the United States of America*, 243.

26. Warrington to Secretary Benjamin Crowninshield, in *Niles'*, 18 November 1815.

27. Ibid.

28. Ibid.

29. Ibid.

30. Ibid.

31. Barnstable [Mass.] Town Records, 5:15, 17.

CHAPTER 3. BICKERING AT BOSTON

1. Benjamin F. Stevens, *Isaac Hull and American Frigate* Constitution, 17.

2. Ibid., 18.

3. Nathaniel Hawthorne, *American Note-Books*, 91.

4. Journal of Lt. Charles Gauntt, aboard the USS *Macedonian*, 1818–19, ii, National Archives, Microfilm Publication M875 [henceforth Gauntt Journal]. Most of the journals cited in this book do not have numbered pages. Gauntt's is an exception. Otherwise, from time to time, an entry is identified as an entry of a particular day.

5. Deck Log, *Macedonian*, No. 3, 21 September 1818, NA, RG 24.

6. Gauntt Journal, 1.

7. *Norfolk Herald*, 12 October 1818.

8. *Niles'*, 17 October 1818.

9. Deck Log, *Macedonian*, No. 3, 27 September 1818.

10. Gauntt Journal, 4.

11. *Boston Saturday Evening Gazette*, 24 August 1861.

12. See Herman Melville, *White-Jacket*, 101–11, for a similar deed by the fictitious Lieutenant Mad Jack, probably inspired by Percival's *Macedonian* feat.

13. Gauntt Journal, 3.

14. Ibid., 5.
15. Journal of Charles J. Deblois, Captain's Clerk aboard the USS *Macedonian*, 1818–19, n.p., n.d., National Archives, Microfilm Publication M876 [henceforth Deblois Journal].
16. Gauntt Journal, 36.
17. Deblois Journal, n.d.
18. Ibid., 12 March 1819.
19. Ibid., 5 April 1819.
20. Ibid., 25 April 1819.
21. Ibid., 15 April 1819.
22. Ibid.
23. Ibid., n.d.
24. Ibid., 13 May 1819.
25. Ibid.
26. Ibid., 30 May 1819.
27. Ibid.
28. *Niles'*, 25 March 1820.
29. *Boston Daily Advertiser*, 23 April 1820, reprinted in *Niles'*, 6 May 1820.
30. *Trial of Lieutenant Joel Abbot*, 80.
31. Linda M. Maloney, *The Captain from Connecticut: The Life and Naval Times of Isaac Hull*, 300.
32. See ibid., 292–363.
33. *Trial of Lieutenant Joel Abbot*, 89.
34. Maloney, *The Captain from Connecticut*, 336–37.
35. *Minutes of the Proceedings of the Court of Enquiry into the Official Conduct of Captain Isaac Hull*, 243–44.

Chapter 4. Tracking Mutineers

1. Secretary Samuel Southard to Lt. John Percival, 6 December 1823, in Letters Sent by Secretary of the Navy to Officers, 1798–1868, National Archives, Microfilm Publication M149 [henceforth SNL].
2. Herman Melville, *White-Jacket*, 151–57; Melville, *Moby-Dick*, 228.
3. James M. Hoppin, *Life of Andrew Hull Foote*, 28.
4. Edwin P. Hoyt, *The Mutiny on the* Globe, 73.
5. William Lay and Cyrus Hussey, *A Narrative of the Mutiny on Board the Whaleship* Globe, 15–16.
6. Ibid., 21.
7. Commo. Isaac Hull to Percival, 14 August 1825, in *House Reports*, 22d Cong., 2d sess., no. 86, 3–5.
8. Hiram Paulding, *Journal of a Cruise of the United States Schooner* Dolphin, 82–84.

9. Ibid., 93.
10. Ibid., 96.
11. Ibid.
12. Charles H. Davis Jr., *Life of Charles Henry Davis*, 17.
13. Paulding, *Journal of a Cruise of the Schooner* Dolphin, 103.
14. Hoyt, *The Mutiny on the* Globe, 188.
15. Paulding, *Journal of a Cruise of the Schooner* Dolphin, 125.
16. Rebecca Paulding Meade, *Life of Hiram Paulding*, 17.
17. Paulding, *Journal of a Cruise of the Schooner* Dolphin, 133.
18. Lay and Hussey, *Mutiny on the* Globe, 65.
19. Ibid., 46.
20. Ibid., 66–67.
21. Percival to Congressman John Anderson, 17 January 1833, in *House Reports*, 22d Cong., 2d sess., no. 86, 6.
22. Lay and Hussey, *Mutiny on the* Globe, 67–68.
23. Percival to Secretary Levi Woodbury, 28 October 1832, in *House Reports*, 22d Cong., 2d sess., no. 86, 6–7.
24. Lay and Hussey, *Mutiny on the* Globe, 71.
25. Deck Log, *Dolphin*, 15 January 1826, NA, RG 24.

Chapter 5. Trouble in Paradise

1. Deck Log, *Dolphin*, 15 January 1826.
2. Hiram Bingham, *A Residence of Twenty-one Years in the Sandwich Islands*, 283.
3. Deck Log, *Dolphin*, 16 January 1826.
4. Paulding, *Journal of a Cruise of the Schooner* Dolphin, 198.
5. Statement of John Morris of the *Dolphin*, in Percival Papers.
6. Statement of A. Thurston et al., General Meeting of the Sandwich Island Mission, 3 October 1826, in Percival Papers.
7. Percival, "Defence of Capt. John Percival, U.S.N., June 12, 1828, before a Court of Inquiry Held at the Navy yard in Charlestown, Mass. to Investigate Charges of Misconduct at the Sandwich Islands in 1826," n.p., Boston Public Library, Boston, Mass. [henceforth "Defence"].
8. *Facts respecting the Conduct of Lieut. John Percival Commander of the United States' Schooner* Dolphin *at the Sandwich Islands in the Year 1826* [henceforth *Facts*], 15–17.
9. Alfred P. Edwards to Secretary Samuel Southard, 3 February 1827, in *Facts*, 7–13.
10. *Missionary Herald*, July 1827.
11. Paulding, *Journal of a Cruise of the Schooner* Dolphin, 225.
12. "Defence," n.p.
13. Statement of Dr. Abraham Blatchley, in Percival Papers.

14. Bingham, *Twenty-one Years in the Sandwich Islands,* 283.
15. "Defence," n.p.
16. Rev. William Richards to Southard, 1 March 1826, in *Facts,* 1–6.
17. Bingham, *Twenty-one Years in the Sandwich Islands,* 288.
18. *Facts,* 6–7.
19. "Defence," n.p.
20. Linda McKee, "'Mad Jack' and the Missionaries," 35.
21. "Defence," n.p.
22. McKee, "'Mad Jack' and the Missionaries," 36.
23. Edwards to Southard, 3 February 1827, in *Facts,* 7–13.
24. "Defence," n.p.
25. Edwards to Southard, 3 February 1827, in *Facts,* 7–13.
26. "Defence," n.p.
27. Ibid.
28. McKee, "'Mad Jack' and the Missionaries," 87.
29. Richards to Southard, 1 March 1826, in *Facts,* 1–6.
30. Statement of Peter Cornelius of the *Dolphin,* in Percival Papers.
31. Deck Log, *Dolphin,* 11 May 1826.

CHAPTER 6. THE TRIALS

1. Paulding, *Journal of a Cruise of the Schooner* Dolphin, 236.
2. Hull to Percival, 1 September 1826, in Maloney, *The Captain from Connecticut,* 404.
3. *Niles',* 28 April 1827.
4. Ibid., 30 December 1826.
5. *Facts,* 17–18.
6. "Defence," n.p.
7. James C. Swain to Southard, 29 September 1828, in Percival Papers.
8. "Defence," n.p.
9. Southard to Percival, 20 January 1829, in SNL.

CHAPTER 7. CAUGHT IN ANOTHER CONTROVERSY

1. Trayser, *Barnstable: Three Centuries of a Cape Cod Town,* 203.
2. *Boston Saturday Evening Gazette,* 31 August 1861.
3. Percival to Commo. Jesse Elliott, 10 February 1832, in Letters Received by the Secretary of the Navy from Commanders, 1801–86, National Archives, Microfilm Publication M147 [henceforth CMD].
4. Percival to Elliott, 8 February 1832, in CMD.
5. Percival to Secretary Levi Woodbury, 10 February 1832, in CMD.
6. An oft-cited biographical series in the *Boston Saturday Evening Gazette,* 24 and 31 August 1861, suggests that Mad Jack and Old Hickory were cast from

the same mold. The article laments that "we had no longer any of the Percival or Jackson school left in our Navy or Army." The "striking similarity" between the two was notable. "Both were self-made, self-confident, and self-reliant."

7. Ira N. Hollis, "The Frigate *Constitution*," 601.

8. Russell Jarvis, *Biographical Notice of Com. Jesse D. Elliott*, 315.

9. *Boston Evening Mercantile Journal*, 24 March 1834.

10. Ibid., 28 March 1834.

11. Ibid., 24 March 1834.

12. Jarvis, *Biographical Notice of Com. Jesse D. Elliott*, 322.

13. Ibid.

14. Percival to Woodbury, 24 June 1834, in CMD.

15. Percival to Woodbury, 25 June 1834, in CMD.

16. Ibid.

17. Woodbury to Percival, 28 June 1834, in SNL.

CHAPTER 8. THE VERY PATTERN OF OLD INTEGRITY

1. Percival to owners of the Brig *Mexican*, 4 February 1835, in CMD.

2. Percival to Secretary Mahlon Dickerson, 14 May 1835, in CMD.

3. Ibid., 28 June 1835.

4. Ibid., 1 July 1835.

5. Ibid., 7 October 1835.

6. Ibid., n.d. March 1836.

7. David F. Long, *"Mad Jack": The Biography of Captain John Percival, USN, 1779–1862*, 118–19.

8. Ibid., 118.

9. Ibid., xix.

10. Ibid., 117.

11. Howell ledger, in Percival Papers.

12. Percival to Charles Chauncey, 18 April 1837, in Percival Papers.

13. Trust Agreement, 6 January 1837, in Percival Papers.

14. Mary Roache to Percival, 24 April 1837, in Percival Papers.

15. Percival to Roache, 26 April 1837, in Percival Papers.

16. Long, *"Mad Jack"*, 117.

17. Percival to Thomas Murdock, 10 August 1840, in Percival Papers.

18. Percival to Dickerson, 9 November 1836, in CMD.

19. Percival to Dickerson, 23 November 1836, in CMD.

20. Ibid.

21. Percival to Dickerson, 28 August 1837, in CMD.

22. Hawthorne, *American Note-Books*, 91.

23. Ibid.

24. Ibid., 91–92.
25. Melville, *White-Jacket,* 36.
26. Harry Gringo, *Tales for the Marines,* 25–26.

Chapter 9. The Old, Gouty Devil

1. Percival to Congressman William Parmenter, 11 January 1838, in CMD.
2. Percival to Dickerson, 25 March 1838, in CMD.
3. Percival to Dickerson, 5 May 1838, in CMD.
4. Percival to Dickerson, 6 May 1838, in CMD.
5. Private Journal of Henry A. Wise, U.S.N. on USS *Cyane,* n.p., n.d., in NA, RG 45 [henceforth Wise Journal].
6. Percival to Secretary James K. Paulding, 24 July 1838, in CMD.
7. D. B. Conrad, "Some Yarns Spun by an Officer of the Old Navy," 326–36.
8. Wise Journal, 6 September 1838.
9. Percival to Commo. Isaac Chauncey, 19 September 1838, in Hull Papers, Boston Athenaeum, Boston, Mass.
10. Wise Journal, 18 September 1838.
11. Ibid., 22 September 1838.
12. Ibid., 14 October 1838.
13. Ibid., 19 October 1838.
14. Ibid., 21 October 1838.
15. Ibid., 8 November 1838.
16. Prof. James Major to Percival, 22 November 1838, in Gardner W. Allen, ed., *Papers of Isaac Hull,* 170.
17. Wise Journal, 29 November 1838.
18. Ibid., 17 January 1839.
19. Ibid.
20. Ibid., 21 January 1839.
21. Paulding to Percival, 28 February 1839, in SNL.
22. Percival to Hull, 1 February 1839, in Allen, *Papers of Isaac Hull,* 152–54.
23. Percival to Lt. John Simpson, 24 February 1839, in ibid., 270–71.
24. Wise Journal, 25 February 1839.
25. Allen, *Papers of Isaac Hull,* 273.
26. Percival to Hull, 26 March 1839, in ibid., 177.
27. Percival to Hull, 26 March 1839 (second letter), in ibid., 178.
28. Wise Journal, 5 March 1839.
29. Percival to Paulding, 2 March 1839, in CMD.
30. Percival to U.S. Consul John L. Payson, 23 April 1839, in John Percival Letter Book, 1838–1839, U.S. Naval Academy Museum, Annapolis.
31. Wise Journal, 15 April 1839.
32. Ibid., 17 April 1839.

33. Ibid., 18 May 1839.

34. Ibid., 20 May 1839.

35. Percival to Hull, 25 May 1839, in Hull Papers.

36. Acting Midn. Edward Allen to Hull, 25 May 1839, in ibid.

37. Percival to Hull, 5 June 1839, in ibid.

38. Wise Journal, 15 June 1839.

39. Ibid., 21 June 1839.

40. Conrad, "Some Yarns Spun by an Officer of the Old Navy," 336.

41. Wise Journal, 9 August 1839.

42. Ibid., 12 August 1839.

43. Ibid.

44. *Boston Saturday Evening Gazette*, 24 and 31 August 1861.

45. Maloney, *The Captain from Connecticut*, 460.

46. Secretary George E. Badger to Percival, 18 May 1841, in SNL.

47. Commission, in Percival Papers.

48. Maloney, *The Captain from Connecticut*, 479.

49. Secretary Abel P. Upshur to Percival, 1 December 1842, in SNL.

CHAPTER 10. AROUND THE WORLD IN THE *CONSTITUTION*

1. William Harwar Parker, *Recollections of a Naval Officer*, 137.

2. *Niles'*, 5 August 1843.

3. Secretary David Henshaw to Percival, 6 November 1843, in SNL.

4. Henshaw to Percival, 21 December 1843, in SNL.

5. Warrington to Percival, 26 December 1843, in Long, *"Mad Jack,"* 135.

6. Percival to Henshaw, 16 January 1844, in CPT.

7. Benjamin F. Stevens, *A Cruise on the* Constitution, 2.

8. Thomas, *Around the World in Old Ironsides*, 4.

9. Ibid.

10. Stevens, *A Cruise on the* Constitution, 3.

11. Journal of D. H. Lynch relating to the Cruise of the *Constitution* around the World, n.p., NA, RG 45 [henceforth Lynch Journal].

12. Thomas, *Around the World in Old Ironsides*, 10.

13. Stevens, *A Cruise on the* Constitution, 4.

14. Lynch Journal, n.p.

15. Thomas, *Around the World in Old Ironsides*, 17.

16. Ibid., 19.

17. Stevens, *A Cruise on the* Constitution, 13.

18. Thomas, *Around the World in Old Ironsides*, 19.

19. Journal of J. B. Dale, U.S. Frigate *Constitution*, 1844–1846, n.p., New England Historic Genealogical Society, Boston, Mass. [henceforth Dale Journal].

20. Lynch Journal, n.p.

21. Stevens, *A Cruise on the* Constitution, 13.

22. Dale Journal, n.p.

23. Stevens, *A Cruise on the* Constitution, 13.

24. Dale Journal, n.p.

25. Thomas, *Around the World in Old Ironsides,* 21.

26. Dale Journal, n.p.

27. Lynch Journal, n.p.

28. Dale Journal, n.p.

29. Lynch Journal, n.p.

30. Stevens, *A Cruise on the* Constitution, 14.

31. Ibid.

32. George F. Emmons, *The Navy of the United States, from the Commencement, 1775 to 1853,* 90.

33. Lynch Journal, n.p.

34. Ibid.

35. Stevens, *A Cruise on the* Constitution, 43.

36. Ibid., 20.

37. Letter Book of Midn. Lucius M. Mason, reprinted in Thomas, *Around the World in Old Ironsides,* 38.

38. Stevens, *A Cruise on the* Constitution, 26.

39. Ibid., 26–27.

40. Mason, in Thomas, *Around the World in Old Ironsides,* 46.

41. Mason, reprinted in Long, "*Mad Jack,*" 153.

42. Thomas, *Around the World in Old Ironsides,* 50–51.

43. Lynch Journal, n.p.

44. Ibid., n.p.

45. Journal of a Cruise in the U.S. Frigate *Constitution* . . . M. Patterson Jones, U.S.N., 18 November 1844, NA, RG 45.

46. Stevens, *A Cruise on the* Constitution, 36.

47. Ibid., 43.

48. Ibid., 44.

49. Thomas, *Around the World in Old Ironsides,* 64.

50. Stevens, *A Cruise on the* Constitution, 45.

51. Percival to Secretary John Y. Mason, 7 February 1845, in CPT.

52. Ibid.

53. Stevens, *A Cruise on the* Constitution, 46.

54. Percival to Mason, 7 February 1845, in CPT.

55. Lynch Journal, n.p.

56. Percival to Mason, 7 February 1845, in CPT.

57. Edmund J. Carpenter, "Old Ironsides," 279.

58. Stevens, *A Cruise on the* Constitution, 50.

59. Deck Log, *Constitution*, No. 14, 6 March 1845, NA, RG 24.

60. Thomas, *Around the World in Old Ironsides,* 72.

61. Tyrone G. Martin, *A Most Fortunate Ship,* 235.

62. Percival to Secretary George Bancroft, 9 June 1845, in CPT.

63. Thomas, *Around the World in Old Ironsides,* 82.

64. Stevens, *A Cruise on the* Constitution, 50.

65. Thomas, *Around the World in Old Ironsides,* 82.

66. Journal of the U.S. Ship *Constitution* . . . , Midshipman W. P. Buckner, 30 April 1845, NA, RG 45.

67. Percival to Bancroft, 9 June 1845, in CPT.

68. Stevens, *A Cruise on the* Constitution, 54.

69. Bishop Dominique Lefevre to Percival, 10 May 1845, in CPT.

70. Stevens, *A Cruise on the* Constitution, 55.

71. Percival to Bancroft, 21 June 1845, in CPT.

72. Dale Journal, n.p.

73. See Peter Kneisel, "Searching for the Lost Grave," *Boston Globe Magazine,* 29 October 2000, 16–24.

74. Thomas, *Around the World in Old Ironsides,* 91.

75. Dale Journal, n.p.

76. Thomas, *Around the World in Old Ironsides,* 89.

77. Ibid., 90.

78. Dale Journal, n.p.

79. Stevens, *A Cruise on the* Constitution, 57.

80. Percival to Adm. Jean Cecille, 6 June 1845, in CPT.

81. Dale Journal, n.p.

82. Stevens, *A Cruise on the* Constitution, 58.

83. Robert H. Miller, *The United States and Vietnam,* 48.

84. Percival to Lemuel Shaw, 13 August 1845, in Percival Papers.

85. Percival to Mason, 30 October 1846, in CPT.

86. Ibid.

87. *Niles',* 2 May 1846.

88. Stevens, *A Cruise on the* Constitution, 61.

89. Deck Log, *Constitution*, No. 14, 8 September 1845.

90. Stevens, *A Cruise on the* Constitution, 61.

91. Ibid.

92. Ibid., 61–62.

93. Lynch Journal, n.p.

94. *Niles',* 2 May 1846.

95. Edward H. Cree, *Naval Surgeon: The Voyages of Dr. Edward H. Cree,* 172.

96. *Niles',* 2 May 1846.

97. Lynch Journal, n.p.

98. Ibid.

99. Dale Journal, n.p.

100. Thomas, *Around the World in Old Ironsides,* 116.

101. Lynch Journal, n.p.

102. Thomas, *Around the World in Old Ironsides,* 120.

103. Lynch Journal, n.p.

104. Ibid., n.p.

105. Percival to Mason, 27 September 1846, in CPT.

106. Dale Journal, n.p.

107. Stevens, *A Cruise on the* Constitution, 66.

108. *Boston Post,* 26 September 1846.

109. Deck Log, *Constitution,* No. 15, 27 September 1846, NA, RG 24.

110. Ibid.

111. Ibid., 28 September 1846.

112. *Barnstable Patriot,* 7 October 1846.

113. Martin, *A Most Fortunate Ship,* 244.

114. Stevens, *A Cruise on the* Constitution, 67.

115. Mason to Percival, 17 October 1846.

CHAPTER 11. ON PROBATION

1. Percival to Mason, 30 October 1846, in CPT.

2. Percival to Bancroft, 16 November 1845, in CPT.

3. Ibid.

4. Ibid.

5. Ibid.

6. Ibid.

7. Percival to Mason, 29 October 1847, in CPT.

8. Percival to Mason, 6 March 1848, in CPT.

9. Percival to Mason, 6 March 1849, in CPT.

10. Preston to Percival, 5 June 1849, in SNL.

11. Percival to Preston, 14 June 1849, in CPT.

12. Ibid.

13. Ibid.

14. *Barnstable Patriot,* 26 June 1883.

15. Percival to Ambassador Henry A. Wise, 2 August 1848, in Percival Papers.

16. *Barnstable Patriot,* 16 October 1855.

17. Percival to John P. Healy, 20 December 1856, in Percival Papers.

18. Ibid.

19. Percival to Healy, 25 December 1856, in Percival Papers.

20. Thomas, *Around the World in Old Ironsides,* 112.

21. Percival to Shaw, 20 November 1857, in Percival Papers.

22. Percival to Charles Bursley, 25 May 1859, letter in author's possession.

23. Trayser, *Barnstable: Three Centuries of a Cape Cod Town,* 204.

24. Notes of Alton H. Blackington, 7 July 1947, Beverly Farms, Mass.

25. *Barnstable Patriot,* 7 October 1862.

26. Ibid.

27. *Barnstable Patriot,* 20 October 1863.

28. Ibid.

29. Ibid.

30. John Percival Will, 26 August 1861, Norfolk Registry of Probate, Dedham, Mass.

31. Ibid.

32. *Boston Saturday Evening Gazette,* 31 August 1861.

33. *Barnstable Patriot,* 23 September 1862.

34. Ibid.

35. Westcott, "Captain 'Mad Jack' Percival," 319.

~❧ *Bibliography* ✑~

UNPUBLISHED SOURCES

Barnstable (Massachusetts) Town Records, vols. 2–5

Blackington, Alton H. Notes, 7 July 1947, Beverly Farms, Massachusetts

Boston Public Library

"Defence of Capt. John Percival, U.S.N., June 12, 1828, before a Court of Inquiry Held at the Navy Yard in Charlestown, Mass., to Investigate Charges of Misconduct at the Sandwich Islands in 1826"

Massachusetts Historical Society

John Percival: commissions for lieutenant, master commandant, and captain; and miscellaneous letters and notes

John Percival Papers: Letters and Papers relating to Edwards and the Different Trials Brought by Him and his Coadjutors in Villainy; the accts of Thos Murdock, James Thompson, Joshua Howell, and Charles W. White, settled, & signed & sealed, thank God—J. Percival Trustee

National Archives, Washington, D.C.

Journal of Charles J. Deblois, captain's clerk aboard the USS *Macedonian,* 1818–19, Microfilm Publication M876

Journal of Lt. Charles Gauntt aboard the USS *Macedonian,* 1818–21, Microfilm Publication M875

Letters, Miscellaneous, Received by the Secretary of the Navy, 1800–84, Microfilm Publication M124

Letters, Miscellaneous, Sent by the Secretary of the Navy, 1798–1886, Microfilm Publication M209

Letters Received by the Secretary of the Navy from Captains, 1805–61, 1866–85, Microfilm Publication M125

Letters Received by the Secretary of the Navy from Commanders, 1801–86, Microfilm Publication M147

Letters Received by the Secretary of the Navy from Officers below the Rank of Commander, 1802–84, Microfilm Publication M148

Letters Sent by the Secretary of the Navy to Officers, 1798–1868, Microfilm Publication M149

Record Group 24:

Deck Log, *Constitution*, 23 June 1842–16 February 1843 (No. 13); 26 March 1844–30 November 1845 (No. 14); and 1 December 1845–5 October 1846 (No. 15)

Deck Log, *Cyane*, 26 May 1828–10 October 1844

Deck Log, *Dolphin*, 22 April 1824–19 January 1827

Deck Log, *Erie*, 24 June 1834–17 December 1835

Deck Log, Gunboat *No. 6*, 23 August 1813–3 November 1815

Deck Log, *Macedonian*, 19 September 1818–19 March 1819 (No. 3)

Deck Log, *Peacock*, 28 November 1815–19 January 1818

Deck Log, *Porpoise*, 30 March 1821–20 September 1822

Deck Log, *United States*, 19 November 1823–30 April 1827

Journal of L. Warrington, Esq., U.S. Sloop *Peacock*, 15 April–30 August 1814

Record Group 45:

"History of the Boston Navy Yard, 1797–1874," by Commo. George Henry Preble

Journal of Midn. W. P. Buckner, USS *Constitution*, Capt. John Percival, 25 July 1844

Journal of M. Patterson Jones, U.S. Frigate *Constitution*, Capt. John Percival Commanding

Journal of D. H. Lynch relating to the Cruise of the *Constitution* around the World, 1844–46

Journal of Midn. Colville Terrett, U.S. Frigate *Constitution*, 1845–46

Journal [private] of Henry A. Wise, USS *Cyane*, 1838–39

Records of General Courts-Martial and Courts of Inquiry, 1799–1867, Microfilm Publication M273

New England Historic Genealogical Society, Boston, Massachusetts

Journal of J. B. Dale, U.S. Frigate *Constitution*, 1844–46

Percival, John. Will, 26 August 1861. Registry of Probate, Dedham, Massachusetts

Sturgis Library, Barnstable, Massachusetts

"Percivals of Cape Cod and Some Descendants," by Benton P. Crocker, Foxboro, Mass., 1938

United States Circuit Court for the Southern District of New York

Minutes and Records, 2 July 1827–8 November 1828

United States Department of the Navy
  Abstracts of Service Records, John Percival
  Court-Martial Records, vol. 23, no. 531
United States Naval Academy Museum, Annapolis, Maryland
  Journal of John Downes, U.S. Sloop of War *Cyane*, 1838–39
  Journal of John Percival, U.S. Frigate *Macedonian*, to the South Pacific
    Ocean, 1819
  Journal of John Percival, U.S. Recg. Ship *Columbus*, John Percival Esq.
    Commd., 1833–34
  Journal of R. Werden, U.S. Sloop of War *Cyane*, 1838–39
  Letter Book of John Percival, 1838–39

NEWSPAPERS

Barnstable (Mass.) Patriot, 10 and 24 August 1831; 7 October 1846; 16 October
  1855; 23 September 1862; 7 and 14 October 1862; 20 October 1863; 26 June
  1883; 23 June 1988
Boston Cultivator, 3 October 1846
Boston Daily Evening Transcript, 14 September 1857
Boston Evening Mercantile Journal, 24, 25, 27, and 28 March 1834
Boston Evening Transcript, 20 May 1911; 23 December 1912
Boston Morning Post, 22 March 1834; 4 July 1834
Boston Post, 26 and 28 September 1846; 20 September 1862
Boston Saturday Evening Gazette, 24 and 31 August 1861
Boston Weekly Messenger, 6 and 20 May 1814
Connecticut Courant, Hartford, 17 May 1814
Missionary Herald, Boston, vols. 22–24, 29
Nantucket Inquirer, 28 October 1826
Naval Chronicle, London, vols. 31–34
Niles' Weekly Register, Baltimore, 1811–49, vols. 3–71
Norfolk Herald, 12 October 1818
Washington Post, 6 December 1931
Yarmouth (Mass.) Register, December 1931–January 1932

PUBLISHED SOURCES

Abbot, Willis J. *The Naval History of the United States.* New York: Peter Fenelon
  Collier, 1886.
A Biography of Captain John Percival, U.S.N. New York: National Americana
  Society, 1927.
Adams, Charles F., ed. *The Works of John Adams.* Boston: Little, Brown, 1856.

Alden, Carroll S., and Allan Westcott. *The United States Navy: A History*. New York: J. B. Lippincott, 1943.

Allen, Gardner W. *Massachusetts Privateers of the American Revolution*. Boston: Massachusetts Historical Society, 1927.

————. *Our Naval War with France*. Boston: Houghton Mifflin, 1909.

————. *Our Navy and the West Indian Pirates*. Salem: Essex Institute, 1929.

————, ed. *Papers of Isaac Hull*. Boston: Athenaeum, 1929.

Amory, Thomas C. *The Life of Admiral Sir Isaac Coffin Baronet*. Boston: Apples, Upham, and Company, 1886.

Anonymous. *Service Afloat: Comprising the Personal Narrative of a British Naval Officer during the Late War*. Philadelphia: Edward C. Mielke, 1833.

Barber, Joseph, Jr. *Hawaii: Restless Rampart*. Indianapolis: Bobbs-Merrill, 1941.

Barnes, James. *Naval Actions of the War of 1812*. New York: Harper and Brothers, 1896.

Beirne, Francis F. *The War of 1812*. New York: E. P. Dutton, 1949.

Bingham, Hiram. *A Residence of Twenty-one Years in the Sandwich Islands*. Hartford: Hezekiah Huntington, 1848.

Biographical Directory of the American Congress, 1774–1949. Washington, D.C.: Government Printing Office, 1950.

Blackington, Alton H. "Mad Jack." *Yankee* 25 (July 1961): 40–43, 74–76.

Bowen, Abel. *The Naval Monument*. Boston: George Clark, 1830.

Brackenridge, Henry M. *History of the Late War between the United States and Great Britain*. Baltimore: Cushing and Jewett, 1817.

Bradlee, Francis B. C. *Piracy in the West Indies and Its Suppression*. Salem: Essex Institute, 1923.

Bradley, Harold W. *The American Frontier in Hawaii*. Stanford: Stanford University Press, 1942.

Brannan, John, ed. *Letters of the Military and Naval Officers of the United States during the War with Great Britain in the Years 1812, 13, 14 & 15*. Washington, D.C.: Way and Gideon, 1823.

Brooks, George S., ed. *James Durand, an Able Seaman of 1812*. New Haven: Yale University Press, 1926.

Bryant, Samuel W. *The Sea and the States*. New York: Thomas Y. Crowell, 1947.

Callahan, Edward W., ed. *List of Officers of the Navy of the United States and of the Marine Corps from 1775 to 1900*. New York: L. R. Hamersly, 1901.

Callan, John F., and A. W. Russell, comps. *Laws of the United States relating to the Navy and Marine Corps*. Baltimore: John Murphy, 1859.

Carpenter, Edmund J. *America in Hawaii*. Boston: Small, Maynard, 1899.

————. "Old Ironsides." *New England Magazine* 17 (November 1897): 263–82.

Chapelle, Howard I. *The History of the American Sailing Navy.* New York: W. W. Norton, 1949.

————. *The History of American Sailing Ships.* New York: W. W. Norton, 1935.

Chase, Frederic H. *Lemuel Shaw.* Boston: Houghton Mifflin, 1918.

Chidsey, Donald B. *The Battle of New Orleans.* New York: Crown, 1961.

Clark, E. S., Jr. "Discussions." *U.S. Naval Institute Proceedings* 61 (June 1935): 854–56.

Coggeshall, George. *History of the American Privateers and Letters-of-Marque.* New York: privately printed, 1856.

The Commissioned Sea Officers of the Royal Navy 1660–1815. Vol. 1. London: The Admiralty, 1954.

Comstock, William. *The Life of Samuel Comstock, the Terrible Whaleman.* Boston: James Fisher, 1840.

Conrad, D. B. "Some Yarns Spun by an Officer of the Old Navy." *United Service,* n.s., 8 (October 1892): 326–36.

Cooper, James Fenimore. *History of the Navy of the United States of America.* New York: G. P. Putnam, 1856.

Corbbett, William. *The Pride of Britannia Humbled; or The Queen of the Ocean Unqueened by the American Cock Boats.* Cincinnati: Williams and Mason, 1817.

Cranwell, John P., and William B. Crane. *Men of Marque.* New York: W. W. Norton, 1940.

Cree, Edward H. *Naval Surgeon: The Voyages of Dr. Edward H. Cree, Royal Navy.* New York: E. P. Dutton, 1981.

Cutler, Carl C. *Greyhounds of the Sea.* New York: Halcyon House, 1930.

"Daniel Webster on Cape Cod and Its People." *New England Magazine* 17 (November 1897): 323–26.

Davis, Charles H. Jr. *Life of Charles Henry Davis.* Boston: Houghton Mifflin, 1899.

Day, A. Grove, and Ralph S. Kuykendall. *Hawaii: A History.* New York: Prentice-Hall, 1948.

deKay, James Tertius. *Chronicles of the Frigate* Macedonian, *1809–1922.* New York: W. W. Norton, 1995.

DeWeerd, H. A., ed. *The War of 1812.* Washington, D.C., Infantry Journal Press, 1944.

Deyo, Simeon L., ed. *History of Barnstable County, Massachusetts.* New York: H. W. Blake, 1890.

Dibble, Sheldon. *History and General Views of the Sandwich Islands' Mission.* New York, Taylor and Dodd, 1839.

Dudley, William S., ed. *The Naval War of 1812: A Documentary History.* Vols. 1 and 2. Washington, D.C.: U.S. Government Printing Office, 1985, 1992.

Du Pont, Henry A. *Rear-Admiral Samuel Francis Du Pont, United States Navy.* New York: National Americana Society, 1926.

Emmons, George F. *The Navy of the United States, from the Commencement, 1775 to 1853.* Washington, D.C.: Gideon, 1853.

Facts respecting the Conduct of Lieut. John Percival Commander of the United States' Schooner Dolphin *at the Sandwich Islands in the Year 1826.* Washington, D.C., n.p., 1828.

Fischer, Frederick C. *Experienced and Conquered.* Ed. Annabelle F. Fischer. Westminster, Md.: Peach Originals, 1996.

Forester, C. S. *The Age of Fighting Sail.* New York: Doubleday, 1956.

Foster, F. Apthorp, ed. *The New England Historical and Genealogical Register.* Vol. 63. Boston: New England Historical and Genealogical Society, 1909.

Freeman, Frederick. *The History of Cape Cod.* Vols 1 and 2. Boston: W. H. Piper, 1869.

Frost, John. *The Book of the Navy.* New York: D. Appleton, 1845.

Gardner, Will. *The Coffin Saga.* Cambridge: Riverside Press, 1949.

Gessler, Clifford. *Tropic Landfall.* New York: Doubleday, Doran, 1942.

Grant, Bruce. *Isaac Hull, Captain of Old Ironsides.* Chicago: Pellegrini and Cudahy, 1947.

Gringo, Harry [Henry A. Wise]. *Tales for the Marines.* Boston: Phillips, Sampson, 1855.

Guernsey, R. S. *New York City and Vicinity during the War of 1812–15.* New York: Charles L. Woodward, 1889.

Gulick, Rev. Orramel H., and Mrs. Gulick. *The Pilgrims of Hawaii.* New York: Fleming H. Revell, 1918.

Harper, Robert G. *Observations on the Dispute between the United States and France.* London: Philanthropic Press, 1797.

Harris, C. E. *Hyannis Sea Captains.* Yarmouth Port, Mass.: Register Press, 1939.

Hart, Albert B., ed. *Commonwealth History of Massachusetts.* New York: States History Company, 1929.

Harvey, Peter. *Reminiscences and Anecdotes of Daniel Webster.* Boston: Little, Brown, 1877.

Hawes, Charles B. *Whaling.* New York: Doubleday, Page, 1924.

Hawthorne, Nathaniel. *The American Note-Books.* Boston: Houghton Mifflin, 1896.

Hill, Frederic S. *Twenty-six Historic Ships.* New York: G. P. Putnam's Sons, 1903.

Hollis, Ira N. *The Frigate* Constitution. Boston: Houghton Mifflin, 1931.

———. "The Frigate *Constitution*." *Atlantic Monthly* 80 (November 1897): 590–604.

Hopkins, Manley. *Hawaii: The Past, Present, and Future of Its Island-Kingdom.* New York: D. Appleton, 1869.

Hoppin, James M. *Life of Andrew Hull Foote.* New York: Harper and Brothers, 1874.

Horgan, Thomas P. *Old Ironsides: The Story of USS* Constitution. Boston: Burdette, 1963.

Hoyt, Edwin P. *The Mutiny on the* Globe. New York: Random House, 1975.

Hutchinson, J. R. *The Press-Gang Afloat and Ashore.* New York: E. P. Dutton, 1914.

Ingersoll, Charles J. *History of the Second War between the United States of America and Great Britain.* Philadelphia: Lippincott, Grambo, 1852.

James, Marquis. *The Life of Andrew Jackson.* Indianapolis: Bobbs-Merrill, 1938.

James, William. *The Naval History of Great Britain.* London: Richard Bentley and Son, 1886.

Jarves, James J. *History of the Hawaiian Islands.* Honolulu: Henry M. Whitney, 1872.

———. *History of the Hawaiian or Sandwich Islands.* Boston: Tappan and Dennet, 1843.

Jarvis, Russell. *Biographical Notice of Com. Jesse D. Elliott.* Philadelphia: printed by the author, 1835.

Johnson, Allen, and Dumas Malone, eds. *Dictionary of American Biography.* New York: Charles Scribner's Sons, 1928–37.

Johnson, Robert Erwin. *Thence round Cape Horn.* Annapolis: U.S. Naval Institute, 1963.

Jones, Charles C., and J. R. F. Tattnall. *The Life of Commodore Tattnall.* Savannah: n.p., 1878.

Keegan, John. *A History of Warfare.* New York: Alfred A. Knopf, 1994.

Kelley, J. D. Jerrold, and Fred S. Cozzens. *Our Navy: Its Growth and Achievements.* Hartford: American Publishing Company, 1897.

Kittredge, Henry C. *Cape Cod: Its People and Their History.* Boston: Houghton Mifflin, 1930.

———. *Shipmasters of Cape Cod.* Boston: Houghton Mifflin, 1935.

Kneisel, Peter. "Searching for the Lost Grave." *Boston Globe Magazine,* 29 October 2000, 16–24.

Knipe, Emilie B., and Alden A. Knipe. *The Story of Old Ironsides.* New York: Dodd, Mead, 1928.

Knox, Dudley W. *A History of the United States Navy*. New York: G. P. Putnam's Sons, 1936.

Kuykendall, Ralph S. *A History of Hawaii*. New York: Macmillan, 1926.

Lay, William, and Cyrus M. Hussey. *A Narrative of the Mutiny on Board the Whaleship* Globe *of Nantucket*. New London: printed by the authors, 1828.

Leech, Samuel. *Thirty Years from Home; or A Voice from the Main Deck*. Boston: Tappan, Whittemore and Mason, 1843.

Long, David F. *"Mad Jack": The Biography of Captain John Percival, USN, 1779–1862*. Westport, Conn.: Greenwood Press, 1993.

Loomis, Albertine. *Grapes of Canaan*. New York: Dodd, Mead, 1951.

Lossing, Benson J. *The Pictorial Field-Book of the War of 1812*. New York: Harper and Brothers, 1869.

Low, Charles Rathbone. *Her Majesty's Navy*. London: J. S. Virtue, n.d.

Maclay, Edgar S. *A History of American Privateers*. New York: D. Appleton, 1899.

Mahan, Alfred T. *Sea Power in Its Relations to the War of 1812*. Boston: Little, Brown, 1905.

Maloney, Linda M. *The Captain from Connecticut: The Life and Naval Times of Isaac Hull*. Boston: Northeastern University Press, 1986.

Marsh, William S. *The History of the War between the United States and Great Britain*. Hartford: B. and J. Russell, 1815.

Martin, Tyrone G. "A Loved and Respected Machine." *Naval History* 11 (July–August 1997): 26–56.

———. *A Most Fortunate Ship: A Narrative History of "Old Ironsides."* Chester, Conn.: Globe Pequot Press, 1980.

Mason, Lucius M. Letter Book. Excerpted in *Around the World in Old Ironsides: The Voyage of USS* Constitution, *1844–1846*, by Henry George Thomas, ed. Alan B. Flanders; and David F. Long, *"Mad Jack": The Biography of Captain John Percival, USN, 1779–1862*.

McKee, Christopher. *A Gentlemanly and Honorable Profession: The Creation of the U.S. Naval Officer Corps, 1794–1815*. Annapolis: Naval Institute Press, 1991.

McKee, Linda. "'Mad Jack' and the Missionaries." *American Heritage* 22 (April 1971): 30–37, 85–87.

Meade, Rebecca Paulding. *Life of Hiram Paulding*. New York: Baker and Taylor, 1910.

Meade, R. W. "Admiral Hiram Paulding." *Harper's New Monthly Magazine* 58 (February 1879): 358–64.

Mechlin and Winder, comps. *A General Register of the Navy and Marine Corps of the United States.* Washington: C. Alexander, 1848.

Melville, Herman. *Moby-Dick.* Boston: L. C. Page, 1892.

———. *White-Jacket.* Boston: L. C. Page, 1892.

Michener, James A. *Hawaii.* New York: Random House, 1959.

Miller, Robert H. *The United States and Vietnam, 1787–1941.* Washington, D.C.: National Defense University Press, 1990.

Minutes of the Proceedings of the Court of Enquiry into the Official Conduct of Captain Isaac Hull. Washington, D.C.: Davis and Force, 1822.

Morison, Samuel Eliot. *The Maritime History of Massachusetts.* Boston: Houghton Mifflin, 1921.

———. *The Oxford History of the American People.* New York: Oxford University Press, 1965.

Murray, John, ed. *Voyage of H.M.S.* Blonde *to the Sandwich Islands in the Years 1824–1825.* London: Thomas Davison, 1826.

The National Cyclopedia of American Biography. New York: James T. White, 1929.

The Naval Temple. Boston: Barber Badger, 1816.

Neeser, Robert W. *Ships' Names of the United States Navy.* New York: Moffat, Yard, 1921.

A New England Farmer. *Mr. Madison's War.* Boston: Russell and Cutler, 1812.

O'Brien, Maurice N., and Ralph De Sola, eds. *A Maritime History of New York.* New York: Doubleday, Doran, 1941.

Orcutt, William D. *Good Old Dorchester.* Cambridge, Mass.: Cambridge University Press, 1893.

Paine, Ralph D. *The Fight for a Free Sea.* New Haven: Yale University Press, 1921.

Parker, E. M. Wills. *The Sandwich Islands as They Are, Not as They Should Be.* San Francisco: Burgess, Gilbert and Still, 1852.

Parker, William Harwar. *Recollections of a Naval Officer.* Annapolis: Naval Institute Press, 1985.

Paulding, Hiram. *Journal of a Cruise of the United States Schooner* Dolphin. New York: G. and C. and H. Carvill, 1831.

Paullin, Charles O. *Diplomatic Negotiations of American Naval Officers.* Baltimore: Johns Hopkins University Press, 1912.

Perkins, Samuel. *A History of the Political and Military Events of the Late War between the United States and Great Britain.* New Haven: S. Converse, 1825.

Perry, E. G. *A Trip around Cape Cod.* Boston: Charles S. Binner, 1898.

Peterson, Charles J. *The American Navy.* Philadelphia: James B. Smith, 1858.

Phelps, Thomas S. "A Reminiscence of the Old Navy." *United Service* 7 (August 1882): 147–54.

———. "Reminiscences of the Old Navy." *United Service* 7 (November 1882): 480–505.

Phinney, S. B. *The Cape Cod Centennial Celebration at Barnstable.* Barnstable, Mass.: Patriot Office, 1840.

Pope, Dudley. *Decision at Trafalgar.* New York: J. B. Lippincott, 1960.

Pratt, Fletcher. *The Navy: A History.* New York: Doubleday, Doran, 1938.

Rives, F., J. Rives, and George H. Bailey. *The Congressional Globe.* Washington, D.C.: Office of the Congressional Globe, 1849.

Roberts, W. A., and Lowell Brentano. *The Book of the Navy.* New York: Doubleday, 1944.

Roosevelt, Theodore. *The Naval War of 1812.* New York: G. P. Putnam's Sons, 1897.

Roscoe, Theodore, and Fred Freeman. *Picture History of the U.S. Navy.* New York: Charles Scribner's Sons, 1956.

Sabin, Edwin L. *Pirate Waters.* Philadelphia: J. B. Lippincott, 1941.

Shay, Edith, and Frank Shay. *Sand in Their Shoes.* Boston: Houghton Mifflin, 1951.

Sketches of the War between the United States and the British Isles. Rutland: Fay and Davidson, 1815.

Smith, Bradford. *Yankees in Paradise.* Philadelphia: J. B. Lippincott, 1956.

Snider, C. H. J. *The Glorious "Shannon's" Old Blue Duster and Other Faded Flags of Fadeless Fame.* Toronto: McClelland and Stewart, 1923.

Snow, Edward Rowe. *A Pilgrim Returns to Cape Cod.* Boston: Yankee Publishing Company, 1946.

Snow, Elliot, and H. Allen Gosnell. *On the Decks of "Old Ironsides."* New York: Macmillan, 1932.

Soley, James R. *The Boys of 1812.* Boston: Estes and Lauriat, 1887.

Spears, John R. *A History of the United States Navy.* New York: Charles Scribner's Sons, 1908.

——— "'Old Ironsides' as Sailors Saw Her." *Chautauquan* 31 (July 1900): 377–82.

Stackpole, Edouard A. *Mutiny at Midnight.* New York: Morrow, 1939.

———. *The Sea-Hunters.* Philadelphia: J. B. Lippincott, 1953.

Stafford, Mary J. "A Commander of the *Constitution.*" *Army and Navy Life* 9 (October 1906): 385–88.

Stephen, Leslie, and Sidney Lee, eds. *The Dictionary of National Biography.* Vol. 4. London: Oxford University Press, 1937.

Stevens, Benjamin F. *A Cruise on the* Constitution. New York, 1904. Reprinted from *United Service Magazine.*

————. *Isaac Hull and American Frigate* Constitution. n.p.: Bostonian Society, 1890.

Swift, Charles F. *Cape Cod.* Yarmouth, Mass.: Register Publishing Company, 1897.

————. *Genealogical Notes of Barnstable Families.* Barnstable, Mass.: F. B. & F. P. Goss, 1888.

Taylor, Albert P. "The American Navy in Hawaii." *U.S. Naval Institute Proceedings* 53 (1927): 907–24.

Thomas, Henry George. *Around the World in Old Ironsides: The Voyage of USS* Constitution, *1844–1846.* Ed. Alan B. Flanders. Lively, Va.: Brandylane Publishers, 1993.

Thoreau, Henry D. *Cape Cod.* New York: W. W. Norton, 1951.

Thygeson, Rev. H. E. *Articles of Faith and Covenant of the Congregational Church, West Barnstable, Mass., with Brief Historical Sketch, Regulations, and Catalogue of Members.* Hyannis, Mass.: F. B. and F. P. Goss, 1892.

Trayser, Donald G., ed. *Barnstable: Three Centuries of a Cape Cod Town.* Hyannis, Mass.: F. B. and F. P. Goss, 1939.

————, ed. *Report of the Proceedings of the Tercentenary Anniversary of the Town of Barnstable, Massachusetts.* Hyannis, Mass.: F. B. and F. P. Goss, 1940.

Trial of Lieutenant Joel Abbot. Boston: Russell and Gardner, 1822.

Trulock, Alice Rains. *In the Hands of Providence: Joshua L. Chamberlain and the American Civil War.* Chapel Hill: University of North Carolina Press, 1992.

United States Bureau of the Census. *Heads of Families at the First Census of the United States Taken in the Year 1790—Massachusetts.* Washington, D.C.: Government Printing Office, 1908.

United States Congress. House of Representatives. *House Reports.* 18th Congress, 2d Session, No. 92.

————. *House Reports.* 22d Congress, 2d Session. No. 86.

————. *House Reports.* 27th Congress, 2d Session. No. 811.

————. *House Reports.* 28th Congress, 2d Session. No. 92.

————. *House Reports.* 30th Congress, 2d Session. No. 41.

United States Department of the Navy. *Naval Documents Related to the Quasi-War between the United States and France.* Washington, D.C.: Government Printing Office, 1936.

Warner, Oliver. *Victory: The Life of Lord Nelson.* Boston: Little, Brown, 1958.

Westcott, Allan, ed. *American Sea Power since 1775.* New York: J. B. Lippincott, 1947.

————. "Captain 'Mad Jack' Percival." *U.S. Naval Institute Proceedings* 61 (March 1935): 313–19.

Whipple, A. B. C. *Yankee Whalers in the South Seas.* New York: Doubleday, 1954.

Whitehill, Walter Muir, ed. *New England Blockaded in 1814—The Journal of Henry Edward Napier.* Salem: Peabody Museum, 1939.

Wilson, James G., and John Fiske, eds. *Appleton's Cyclopedia of American Biography.* New York: D. Appleton, 1888.

⤳ *Further Reading* ⤶

While John Percival gained something of a legendary status in his own time and continues to be mentioned in numerous books and articles, *"Mad Jack": The Biography of Captain John Percival, USN, 1779–1862*, by David F. Long, is the only full-length biography of the man published prior to this one. The National Americana Society's *A Biography of Captain John Percival, U.S.N.*, limited in depth and scope, is little more than a monograph.

Unfortunately, Long's work contains a fatal flaw. His wholly erroneous conclusion that Percival stole money entrusted to him for the relief of several injured sailors is so egregious that it overshadows the author's solid research and writing. Long made the error on his own. But because his book is essentially the only biography of Percival, the mistake is magnified. An unknowing reader is likely to believe Long's false charge of consummate greed and dishonesty and view Percival accordingly. This perception clearly influenced Long's own approach to his subject. To term his book a hostile biography is not an overstatement. Hostile criticism can serve a worthwhile function, but Long allowed his bias to get the better of his judgment.

As just one example, without any need to do so Long discredits Percival's claim, made in the *Boston Saturday Evening Gazette*, that when the British impressed him in February 1797, he was sent to the *Victory*, the flagship of Adm. Sir John Jervis. Long says this cannot be true because Jervis commanded the *Lively* at the time, and Nelson had the *Victory*. Students of naval history will notice the error at once. Nelson moved his broad pennant from the *Minerve* back to the *Captain*, Capt. Ralph W. Miller commanding, a day before the 14 February 1797 Battle of Cape Saint Vincent and gained lasting fame for saving the day in this ship.

Nelson did not get to the *Victory* until May 1803. As for Jervis, he did indeed have the great ship of the line *Victory* as his flagship at this time. Capt. Robert Calder served as the *Victory's* captain. The *Lively*, a thirty-two-gun frigate and an unlikely flagship, was under Capt. Lord Garlies during the period in question. Isolated mistakes are not the issue here, however; the errors in Long's work are bothersome because they color the reader's interpretations and conclusions, almost always to Percival's disfavor.

Biographical pieces on Percival do exist. Allan Westcott's "Captain 'Mad Jack' Percival," published in the March 1935 issue of *U.S. Naval Institute Proceedings,* and Donald G. Trayser's brief in *Barnstable: Three Centuries of a Cape Cod Town* are among the more notable.

Few published sources relate details of John Percival's early life. However, Trayser's *Barnstable* includes an excellent description of the West Barnstable community that so greatly influenced Percival the youngster. An understanding of this village in the late eighteenth century contributes to an understanding of Mad Jack Percival.

Impressment also played a key role in Percival's life. J. R. Hutchinson's *The Press-Gang Afloat and Ashore* remains a fine single source on this controversial practice.

The Quasi-War with France at the beginning of the nineteenth century is a neglected chapter in U.S. history. The best book on the subject may be Gardner W. Allen's *Our Naval War with France.* The leading research resource is the Navy Department's *Naval Documents Related to the Quasi-War between the United States and France.*

By contrast, there is a great deal of reading material on the War of 1812, the event in which Percival first gained national attention. Every U.S. naval history devotes space to the topic. Theodore Roosevelt's *The Naval War of 1812,* first published in 1882 but available in current reprint, is exceptional. Roosevelt himself recommends the earlier general works by James Fenimore Cooper, George F. Emmons, and William James. William S. Dudley's recent two-volume work, *The Naval War of 1812: A Documentary History,* is a superb collection of official documents related to the conflict. Walter Muir Whitehill's *New England Blockaded in 1814—The Journal of Henry Edward Napier* is an overlooked book. As much as any other publication, this entertaining journal describes how completely the Royal Navy dominated the American coastline during the last year of the war. This dominance gives perspective to the wartime success of the U.S. sloop-of-war *Peacock,* the ship on which Percival served as sailing master and lieutenant. Edgar S. Maclay's classic *A History of American Privateers* includes an account of Percival's daring capture of the *Eagle* in 1813. Maclay's book, important to an appreciation of the conflict, details a slighted side of the war at sea. During the hostilities, 517 American privateers went to sea, compared with only twenty-two American men-of-war. The privateers, as he points out, made a significant contribution to the U.S. war effort.

In its infancy the U.S. Navy was plagued by factionalism and internal competition. Some of this can be traced to national politics and sectionalism, and some was due to too many officers competing for too few billets of stature. In this setting, in 1817, Percival began a lasting friendship with one of the great men of the navy, Capt. Isaac Hull. He served under Hull at Boston and in the Pacific and Mediterranean. Each man had a high regard for the other's professional competence. Right away Percival became identified as a Hull man. During Hull's unhappy tenure as commandant of the Boston Navy Yard, a period marked by infighting, trials, and inquiries, Percival stood fast at his side. Consequently, the unequaled biography by Linda M. Maloney entitled *The Captain from Connecticut: The Life and Naval Times of Isaac Hull* sheds considerable light on Percival. He is mentioned numerous times, from the Baker's pump deal to the cruise in the *Cyane.* As important, the book is an authoritative description of navy life during that period. Another book of considerable worth is the *Papers of Isaac Hull,* edited by Gardner W. Allen. A significant amount of correspondence between Hull and Percival appears therein.

Percival's remarkable pursuit of the *Globe* mutineers is described in several books. Hiram Paulding's *Journal of a Cruise of the United States Schooner* Dolphin is one of two primary sources. First published in 1831, it is readily available as a 1970 reprint. *A Narrative of the Mutiny on Board the Whaleship* Globe *of Nantucket,* by two members of that ship's crew, William Lay and Cyrus Hussey, is the second primary source. Both Edwin P. Hoyt's *The Mutiny on the* Globe and Edouard A. Stackpole's *Mutiny at Midnight* draw on Paulding and Lay and Hussey. Two recent books—Gregory Gibson's *Demon of the Waters: The True Story of the Mutiny on the* Globe and Thomas F. Heffernan's *Mutiny on the* Globe: *The Fatal Voyage of Samuel Comstock*—are detailed accounts of the event including Percival's key role.

Paulding is also a reliable source on the *Dolphin*'s memorable 1826 visit to Hawaii. A balanced version of the controversy can be found in Linda McKee's article "'Mad Jack' and the Missionaries" published in *American Heritage* in April 1971. Most published accounts of what went on in Hawaii are brief, secondhand, and rely on the missionaries' writings. There is considerable original material in the National Archives, the Boston Public Library, and the Massachusetts Historical Society, among other places. Any serious attempt to get to the bottom of things must rely on these contemporary documents. The society's holdings are available on microfilm.

Beyond the foregoing, little has been published specifically about Percival during the period beginning with his service on the *Macedonian* (1816) up to his assignment to the *Constitution* (1843). There is a wealth of material in private journals and archived documents, but only with his memorable command of Old Ironsides do the published choices for further reading become plentiful.

Benjamin F. Stevens's *A Cruise on the* Constitution is the leading firsthand account. Stevens served as the captain's clerk during the 1844–46 round-the-world cruise, remained friendly with Percival, and became a success in Boston. Two other members of the crew kept journals that have made it into print. Annabelle F. Fischer edited musician Frederick C. Fischer's *Experienced and Conquered,* and Alan B. Flanders edited carpenter Henry George Thomas's *Around the World in Old Ironsides.* The latter book includes fifteen detailed maps charting the course of the voyage that cannot be improved upon. At least five other men maintained journals that remain unpublished. Many histories wholly or partly about the frigate *Constitution* mention Percival and the cruise, Tyrone G. Martin's *A Most Fortunate Ship* being the best of these. Martin devotes one of his nineteen chapters to Percival's epic voyage. And as might be expected, Martin's book serves as an authoritative and readable history of the U.S. Navy during the age of sail.

~❧ Index ❧~

❦ *About the Author* ❦

James H. Ellis, a Cape Codder and descendant of the first settlers of that maritime region of Massachusetts, is a management consultant. Educated at Michigan State University, he served in the U.S. Air Force during the Korean War. He spent a career in government, managing in the Massachusetts State Police and the U.S. Departments of Justice, Interior, Treasury, and Labor.

The Naval Institute Press is the book-publishing arm of the U.S. Naval Institute, a private, nonprofit, membership society for sea service professionals and others who share an interest in naval and maritime affairs. Established in 1873 at the U.S. Naval Academy in Annapolis, Maryland, where its offices remain today, the Naval Institute has members worldwide.

Members of the Naval Institute support the education programs of the society and receive the influential monthly magazine *Proceedings* and discounts on fine nautical prints and on ship and aircraft photos. They also have access to the transcripts of the Institute's Oral History Program and get discounted admission to any of the Institute-sponsored seminars offered around the country.

The Naval Institute also publishes *Naval History* magazine. This colorful bimonthly is filled with entertaining and thought-provoking articles, first-person reminiscences, and dramatic art and photography. Members receive a discount on *Naval History* subscriptions.

The Naval Institute's book-publishing program, begun in 1898 with basic guides to naval practices, has broadened its scope to include books of more general interest. Now the Naval Institute Press publishes about one hundred titles each year, ranging from how-to books on boating and navigation to battle histories, biographies, ship and aircraft guides, and novels. Institute members receive significant discounts on the Press's more than eight hundred books in print.

Full-time students are eligible for special half-price membership rates. Life memberships are also available.

For a free catalog describing Naval Institute Press books currently available, and for further information about subscribing to *Naval History* magazine or about joining the U.S. Naval Institute, please write to:

Membership Department

U.S. Naval Institute

291 Wood Road

Annapolis, MD 21402-5034

Telephone: (800) 233-8764

Fax: (410) 269-7940

Web address: www.navalinstitute.org